O FATHER MINE

A TRUE STORY

ERIN KELAART

O Father Mine—A True Story
Published by Erin Kelaart
Sydney NSW
Australia
ofathermine@yahoo.com.au
www.erinkelaart.com

Copyright © 2006, Erin Kelaart

All rights reserved. No part of this publication may be reproduced, stored in a retrieval system, or transmitted, in any form or by any means, without the prior written permission of the author, nor be otherwise circulated in any form of binding or cover other than that in which it was published and without a similar condition being imposed on the subsequent purchaser.

National Library of Australia
Cataloguing-in-Publication Entry

Kelaart, Erin.
    O Father Mine.
    ISBN 0 646.45908 2.
    1. Kelaart, Erin. 2. Women - Australia - Biography. 3. Fathers and daughters - Sri Lanka - Biography. 4. Sri Lanka - History - 1948- . I. Title.

920.720994

Front cover photograph: 'Maussekelle' Sri Lanka, by Udaya Amaradasa, webmaster, www.lankatown.com
Cover design: Kylie Prats and Andrew Mihaleff
Internal design: Best Legenz
Project management: Best Legenz www.bestlegenz.com.au

NB. For Sri Lankan readers:
    The suburb Merinda in this story is Dehiwela

To my beautiful Mother
Anne Victoria Kelaart

The 'Troubles' are over, Angel,
for you and for me.

BACKGROUND

In the little teardrop-shaped island of Ceylon (Sri Lanka), during the 1950's, age-old cultural beliefs steeped in ritual sorcery are very much alive under the veneer of an urbanised and colonised population. The island's indigenous beliefs barely touch the idyllic lives of Ben and Anita Roberts, until a former neighbour perpetrates a powerful occult charm upon Anita's husband, to lure him away from his wife.

Tragedy follows, and Anita's and her children's lives are shattered by the terror that descends upon their home.

Reviews:

A powerfully moving account of a woman's life journey, told against the backdrop of profound shifts in Sri Lankan society. 'O Father Mine' will not only strike a chord with many readers because of its understanding of the human psyche, but it will stir you with its passion and the portrayal of the devastating effects of the charm/hex phenomenon, little appreciated in secularised Australia of the Third Millennium.

It is here that the author and her family, perhaps paradoxically, eventually find a measure of healing and peace. It has been a privilege to read such a great story.

Josephine M. Wilson, Author and Editor, Sydney.

'O Father Mine' will astonish and educate readers to the terrifying realities of the supernatural realm, so little understood by the Western world. Erin Kelaart has written a masterpiece, poignantly portraying the devastation of innocent lives beyond what seems humanly bearable. At the heart of her story is the tragic loss of a father's love, brought about by a deadly occult charm.

I have been privileged to know the author and her family for many years, and I have seen the ultimate grace and peace their strong faith in

God has brought them. It was this that helped carry 'Anita' and 'Rina Roberts' on their journey from hell to redemption.
Rev. Dr. Gary Mulquiney, Sydney.

A word from the Author:
I read somewhere that man has three fundamental instincts that fuel his achievements: to have something to love, something to believe in and something to do. These have all propelled me to write 'O Father Mine.'

Primarily, I have written it to honour my mother, Anne Victoria Kelaart. She is 'Anita Rose Roberts'. The dream to tell her story has been in my heart for over twenty-five years.

This then is a true story ... the story of my family. It was easier for me to write about the 'Roberts' rather than the 'Kelaarts'. That licence allowed me to distance myself, marginally, from the emotional burden of writing such a chronicle.

However, the people you encounter in these pages are real, and their tragedies and triumphs are true. Some significant names and places have been changed to preserve the identity of folk still living, and a few pieces of dialogue have been creatively reconstructed around salient points that are factual. This was essential in order to provide a literary vehicle for the telling of these events.

Erin Kelaart
March 2006
Sydney, Australia

ACKNOWLEDGEMENTS

My first and most heartfelt thanks go to Joy Atkin. Her creative guidance encouraged me to take those dark lumps of carbon from my soul and transform them into living lights. Thank you, Joy!

To Dr Mark Treddenick for teaching me to 'Write the Real' — my gratitude. I sat in your class for many weeks, Mark, glued to every word you spoke. You were truly inspirational.

I am indebted to my old school friend, Sherrine de Silva (Herft) and her son, Denham. They read through every gruelling chapter of the first rough draft and told me it was a story worth telling. Denham likened it to 'Angela's Ashes.' High praise indeed! I was deeply touched, my friends, and your support meant more to me than you knew.

Helen Elward's unceasing dedication to perfection through the design phase of the book pulled me through some bad moments of panic and stress. Thank you for being so gracious, Helen. Above all you understood just what this story meant to me — my very life.

My sweet niece, Beverlee Hamilton, read a few chapters of 'O Father Mine' just before it was published. These were her heartening words to me, 'What an interesting, intriguing, mesmerising story! I cannot wait to read this book.' Bev, your love and affirmation cheered me considerably during the last, long, and tedious lap of polishing my manuscript.

Most importantly, I thank my God, Who carried Rina Roberts through an incredible journey.

To my family:

Joan ... I want you to know that you're my hero; you're everything I wish I could be. I still admire you and I always will.

Erma ... we've been through the hardest times together as children. We are still one blood and I love you. Nothing will change that.

Noble ... your childlike nature delights me. Thank you for the endless supplies of sustenance you brought to my door, when I was locked away, week after week, knee deep in pages, writing this book.

Ray ... my faithful and caring brother, for all that you've done for me — in Mum's simple words — you've been a good son.

Darling Amy, your unfailing words of faith, hope and encouragement were precious sunbeams during lightless days. You are my special treasure.

GENESIS

*He was the centre of my childhood days.
His personality was vivid as the lightning
that streaked the skies, illuminating my heart.
His enveloping love was like rain,
drenching the earth of our lives
and encircling our home like a reservoir.
Mum drank from it, we frolicked in it,
even the servants were happy,
simply because his presence heralded fun,
laughter, music, and above all,
LOVE.
His patriarchal care shouted like the thunder,
unafraid in its assurance.
But he also had a gentle, delightful core.
I was safe, and he was strong
until …*

Part One
Anita's Story

PROLOGUE
1957

Rina Roberts sat solemnly beside the open casket, her tear-rimmed eyes fixed on her baby sister. *She's dead! And it's my fault. My fault!* The words kept repeating inside her eleven-year-old head. *Cecily is dead, and it's my fault.*

The unbearable flood of guilt increases the burden of her memories. Cecily wailing in her cot while Rina plays the piano, the servant calling from the kitchen and Emma rushing to her and urging, 'Rina, it's your turn to feed the baby.'

'No! I did it last time, it's your turn now,' Rina would insist, clinging to the piano stool as her sister tries to force her off the seat.

Their mother had instructed her two eldest children to take turns feeding Cecily whenever they were at home, to ease the workload on the servant Roslyn, who would prepare the infant's milk and call for the girls.

But Rina didn't like feeding the baby. She was afraid when she saw her little nostrils panting to breathe, and heard the choking sounds she sometimes made. Her mother's warning would ring in her ears, 'Make sure you pull the bottle out of Cecily's mouth if she's choking.' It was this that scared Rina. She hated seeing the baby splutter and struggle to breathe.

Eventually, Roslyn would rush to the cot, hush Cecily's wails and place a bottle of milk in her hungry mouth.

And now she's dead. Perhaps if she hadn't cried so much she might have lived. Perhaps if I'd fed her when I should have she wouldn't have died ...

It's my fault. Rina was too terrified to tell anyone that her baby sister had died due to her neglect.

Her throat ached with unexpressed grief. This was a now familiar pain. Since the start of the terrible fights between her parents two years ago, Rina's throat often ached as she struggled to hold her emotions in check. She couldn't bear distressing her mother with her own tears.

Sounds of muffled sobs and shuffling feet disturbed the silence as mourners walked past Rina to view the open casket. Some wiped a tear as they glanced down at little Cecily. Dressed in her white christening robe she simply looked as if she were asleep.

Rina heard Aslin, their old servant, asking people to make way for the convent nuns who had just arrived.

Anita Roberts wailed as Mother De Sales strode towards her with outstretched arms. The nun's eyes were filled with sympathy as she gathered the grieving mother in her arms and sat beside her.

Anita poured out a torrent of laments.

Rocking her gently, the nun intoned, 'Oh Anita dear, we must sing the Magnificat! Remember you have an angel up in heaven now.'

But Anita Roberts couldn't be comforted. Though Mother De Sales knew many of her agonies, Anita never revealed to the nun that her husband had valiantly tried to have Cecily aborted. She told no one. She knew he had parted with large sums of money to one of the many unscrupulous apothecaries in Ceylon who mixed costly brews for parents wanting to get rid of unborn children.

Ben Roberts would bring home the murderous concoction every few weeks and force his wife to drink it, standing over her till she drained the dregs of each bottle.

In the fifth month of her pregnancy when she felt the baby kick, Anita said to her husband, 'I don't care what you do to me, Ben, I am not drinking this anymore.'

Cecily Anne Roberts refused to die in her mother's womb.

For the few months that her seventh child had lived, Anita tried to come to terms with the news the doctors had given her, a few weeks after the infant's birth — she was born with cyanotic heart disease; commonly referred to as a "blue baby." Anita was convinced that the bitter potions she had drunk from the hand of her husband had contributed to her daughter's condition.

Cecily was frequently admitted to the Children's Hospital in Colombo, the well-known "Lady Ridgeway." But the day she was discharged from her last stay at the hospital had been especially crushing for her mother.

The cardiac specialist had wanted to see Anita so she took a day off work. Her baby's maid accompanied her, and because of the August school holidays she decided to take Emma and Rina along.

Entering the grounds of the hospital, Anita instructed the servant to stay with the girls near the taxi rank.

Dr Saul, Ceylon's foremost Cardiac Specialist, explained patiently and gently to Anita, with drawings and gestures, the trouble with Cecily's heart. He answered all her questions, and she had many, before he dropped his bombshell.

'I'm sorry, Mrs Roberts, but the only hope for your baby is surgery. If you're willing to take the risk we can perform an operation. It's been done successfully in India, but not in Ceylon … It'll be a first for us here. Without this operation your daughter's life is totally unpredictable. She may live to be sixteen or eighteen, or she may die in a week.'

Anita was dumbfounded. 'You mean you have to cut open her little chest?'

'Yes, Mrs Roberts. There's no other way.'

'But if no-one's done it here how will you know what to do?' She felt a trembling in her body.

'A few of our surgeons have been to India to learn the procedure,' explained the doctor, 'and I'm confident we can operate successfully.'

Anita sat still for several moments, masking the turmoil within. Then weighing her words carefully, she spoke. 'I'm sorry, doctor. I can't allow it. I can't let Cecily become a guinea pig.' Her eyes showed the agony of her decision. 'She's so little,' she whispered, brokenly.

Dr Saul rose from his chair and came around to where Anita sat. Perching himself on the edge of his desk, he told her gently, 'We can't do anything more for her, my dear. Take her home now.'

The doctor placed a hand on Anita's shoulder as she stood up unsteadily. He accompanied her to the corridor outside his rooms and halted briefly. 'If you change your mind, Mrs Roberts, give me a call.'

He walked briskly away.

Anita headed for a nearby seat, feeling shattered.

Had she made the right decision, she wondered. Could they really perform a successful operation on Cecily's little heart? How long would she live if they didn't operate?

Her mind darted like a cornered animal looking for a way of escape. Perhaps she could take her to India. That was a futile hope she realized immediately. Her husband would never give her the money for the trip. Ben didn't want this child. He hadn't even looked at her or picked her up from the day she was born. He never visited her during any of her stays at the hospital. He simply pretended she didn't exist.

Somehow Anita found the courage that had held her together for the past two years. Walking the familiar route to Ward Nine, she came to the cot where Cecily lay.

One of the nurses approached, seeking to console. 'Cecily is a brave little girl, Mrs Roberts. She's fighting to live.'

Anita could only nod. Her body shook with silent weeping as she gazed down at her sleeping infant.

The nurse put an arm around Anita and led her to a chair. 'Have a seat, Mrs Roberts, I'll fetch Matron. She wanted to see you.'

The usually brisk and bustling Matron spoke in hushed tones, offering encouragement and empathizing with Anita over her decision. The nursing staff gathered around to say goodbye.

The weight in Anita's heart was crushing as she walked out of the hospital with Cecily in her arms.

Emma and Rina ran towards their mother. Together with Roslyn they had been waiting on a bench, close to the cabs as instructed. They looked anxiously at Anita's face.

She was silent.

No one spoke.

Anita took a brief cab ride with her daughters and Roslyn to the nearby church, the famous and beloved All Saints.

They formed an odd little procession walking up the aisle. Veering to the right of the sanctuary, Anita approached the large and ornately adorned shrine of the Blessed Virgin. Wrapping Cecily in a blanket, she gently placed her on the floor, knelt down beside her and recited: "Our Father Who art in Heaven …" and several "Hail Marys."

She paused for a moment, reclining on her haunches. Her eyes were tightly shut and her forehead creased as she contemplated the words

PART ONE PROLOGUE

she was about to utter — the prayer that had been forming in her mind since the doctor had given her the awful news. Taking a deep breath, she heaved a mournful sigh before kneeling up straight to make a strange and brave petition: 'Dear Lord, don't give me the terrible heartache of taking Cecily from me when she's sixteen or eighteen,' she pleaded, repeating the doctor's awful indictment. 'If she is to die, let her die as an infant.'

That was last Wednesday, Anita remembered, as she stared at the little white casket.

Rina was also remembering and reliving the previous morning.

She and Emma had been in the front bedroom, standing beside their mother's bed. It was Monday and Anita had gone to work, but the night before she had sent for their Aunt Aileen, who came early in the morning. She was now seated on the bed, her eyes small through crying. Aslin, their beloved old servant and Roslyn were also in the room. Everyone was quiet, watching Cecily lying in the middle of her mother's bed.

At the sound of a car stopping outside, Rina and Emma rushed to the front door, surprised to see Anita running up the pathway to the house. She had left for work only two hours before. The girls joined their mother as she hurried into the front room. Their father was not at home.

Aunt Aileen sent for the parish priest.

He came. He prayed. He went.

Rina returned to her vigil not knowing that her baby sister was dying; not knowing that her own life was about to be changed forever.

Cecily was now lying on her mother's lap, her whole body contorted as she struggled to breathe.

After a while her feet stopped moving. Her fragile arms hung loosely by her side and her tiny fists opened and closed several times, before they too gave out and lay defenseless and still.

Death claimed her slowly.

Her breathing became laboured. She kept turning her head feebly from side to side and her tiny chest rose up and down ... She appeared to be dreaming; her mouth turned down as if she was about to cry and two tears rolled down her cheeks, and then suddenly she smiled an angelic smile.

A few seconds later her head tilted, and she peacefully surrendered her limp little body to her mother's embrace.

Everything in the room stopped.

There wasn't a sound or a movement from Cecily. To Rina it felt as if everyone had stopped breathing.

Aunt Aileen was the first to speak. 'Lay her down, Anita. She's gone to Jesus now.'

Obediently Anita put the baby down. She looked around the room and her eyes, wild with panic, rested briefly on each face. 'My baby's gone! My baby's gone!' The words were torn from her with anguished sobs.

At that very moment Ben Roberts entered the house with a friend. They all heard his voice at the front door.

Rina watched in horror as her mother ran towards him, laid her hands on his chest and sobbed, 'Ben! Ben! Cecily is dead!'

Rina was paralyzed with fear. Her heart beat loud against her ribs. *Mummy's crazy, he'll kill her.* 'Come back! Come back, Mummy darling.' The words died in her throat.

Her father grabbed her mother's hands and cruelly tore them off his shirt. He thrust her away, pushing her hard across the living room floor. Anita staggered backwards, desperately trying to steady herself.

Rina looked at her father's face ... it was wicked and grim. She felt she was looking at the devil himself.

Her mother ran to her bedroom and reached the wall where the large framed picture of Jesus was hanging; the glass had long been shattered. She beat her fists on the picture. 'My God! My God! My baby is dead!'

Aslin rushed to gather Anita in her arms and almost carried her to a chair in the living room. Anita sat down clinging to Aslin's waist as the servant leaned over and held her close. Together, they wept.

Emma and Rina embraced each other and cried. They had just witnessed their father's hatred and their mother's bleeding sorrow.

After a while Rina walked back into the room where death had just entered. She watched her Aunt and the servant Roslyn attending to little Cecily.

'Poor darling,' said Aunt Aileen, glancing up at Rina. 'She was so weak she couldn't even close her eyes.'

Where are you Cecily darling? Did you see what Daddy did to Mummy?

Rina came out of her reverie when the man in black stepped forward to close the satin-lined casket.

Her mother's loud laments grew louder, 'Cecily darling, Mummy did all she could to save you.'

Rina was distracted by the sound of a man weeping. She looked up and was astonished to see her father at the back of the packed room, hiding behind her cousin Mary. He was sobbing too.

Why is he crying, Rina wondered? *He never cared about Cecily. He doesn't care about Mummy or any of us. Why is he crying?* The troublesome question wouldn't leave her mind.

The little white casket and several floral tributes were carried out and placed inside the hearse. Within a few minutes the black motorcar was driven slowly up the street. It turned right onto the Galle Road and headed towards the Mount Lavinia cemetery.

A small procession of cars followed.

After a short graveside service, Cecily Anne Roberts, the youngest of Anita's children was buried, on a grey Tuesday evening in August 1957.

A storm was gathering in from the nearby ocean. Its threatening clouds spread across the darkening sky as Anita stepped into the hired funeral car with her three eldest daughters. Her three smaller children were left at home with the servants.

Drifts of dying leaves were swirling in the wind as the car moved slowly towards the exit gates, its tyres crunching along the gravel lanes of the cemetery.

Rina turned to look at the sudden shaft of sunlight that burst through the heavy clouds. It seemed to follow the car. The girl who loved sunbeams whispered to her sister, 'Look Emma … a sunbeam!'

Emma was quiet.

Soon the car was speeding back to Merinda.

'Are we going home now, Mummy?' Emma asked her mother.

'Yes, darling, we're going home.'

Home!

The thought arrested Anita's deadened mind. She looked around at the sad little faces of her daughters. The past haunted her like shadowy ghosts.

Unbidden memories encroached.

Was it ever possible that her home in Merinda was once filled with love, and the sounds of children's laughter, singing and music?
Was she mad?
Did that life ever exist?
Or was it all a dream?

CHAPTER ONE

1954 – July

Anita Roberts was perched on a stool in her bedroom, coaxing her daughter's hair into its usual cascade of layered curls. She turned the child around to face her.

'Mummy, you look very pretty,' sang the eight-year-old, in her clear, lilting voice.

'You're beautiful too, darling,' said her mother, expertly twisting the last strand of hair into place.

Among her four daughters only Rina had curly hair like her father, and Anita enjoyed transforming the child's tangles into bouncing curls that sprang to the touch. She had already prettied up her three other girls for the evening ahead.

Glancing out through the open window, her eyes rested on the warm glow of twilight spreading over the seaward sky. It was her favourite time of day, when the children grew mellow and love entered through the front door.

Catching sight of her daughter's face in the dressing table mirror, Anita smiled and hummed a nursery rhyme as she added the final touches to Rina's hair, a few pink ribbons clipped in among the springing curls. 'There you are darling, it's all done,' she said, planting a kiss on the child's forehead.

As her mother moved away Rina peered into the mirror and shook her head from side to side, watching her curls spin wildly.

Anita swiftly stepped back and grabbed her daughter by the shoulders. 'Don't do that, child,' she said sternly. 'You'll get dizzy.'

Rina grimaced. She shuffled over to her parent's bed and sat down to watch her mother.

Anita walked over to the two long mirrors she had positioned, allowing her to observe every angle of her dress. She loved the midnight-blue silk fabric, patterned with little starry flowers of jade-green and silver. Ordinary by daylight, but under the night-lights the silk shimmered and shone with every move she made. Her skirt was cut on a full bias, forming a circular flare that danced tantalizingly at the calf-length hemline when she walked. The tightly-fitted bodice, which tapered at the waist, had a wide, off-the-shoulder collar narrowing down to a scooped neckline. A slim, silk-covered belt with a little silver buckle complimented the dress rather nicely, she thought, as she fastened two strands of dainty crystal beads and jade droplets around her neck. Crystal and jade pendant earrings sparkled against her dark, shoulder-length hair that fell in soft waves across the right side of her face.

Her eyes travelled down to her shapely feet, encased in silver, high-heeled soft leather sandals, adding a few inches to her five-foot height. She knew she looked good for her thirty-five years. Running around after five children had certainly kept her trim.

Returning to the dressing table Anita drew close to the mirror and applied the finishing touches to her make-up, well pleased with what she saw. A light olive complexion with a smattering of freckles across the cheeks, a well-shaped small nose, intense dark eyes under arched eyebrows, high cheekbones set in a heart-shaped face, and perfectly full, ruby lips — all contributing to her exotic appearance.

'You're beautiful, Mummy,' Rina sang out again.

'And everyone's going to tell me how lovely my daughters are looking tonight,' said her mother, moving back to the long mirrors. She swirled in front of them and turned to smile at Rina. 'But you're the only one who's got your Daddy's curls.'

'Daddy's curls! Where's Daddy's girls?' a strong male voice called out. Benjamin Roberts entered the room and halted, looking at his wife with unconcealed affection. With quick strides he reached one of the mirrors. Standing before it he announced, with a grand, sweeping gesture: 'Mirror, mirror on the wall, here's a secret known by all, Anita Rose Roberts is the Belle of the Ball!'

CHAPTER ONE

His wife threw her head back and laughed, prompting her husband to gather her in his arms, crooning, *Parlez-moi d' amour, redites-moi des choses tendres.*

Anita joined in, *Tender words of love, repeat them again, I implore you …'*

It was their song. Anita had learned it when she studied French as a young girl and she had taught it to Ben. The two of them sang it often, both in English and French.

Rina was as entranced as her father. She was fascinated with things that glittered and shone, and tonight her mother sparkled with every move she made.

She crept out of the room, tingling. She loved her parents' parties. The one they had held for her brother Michael's christening the previous year had gone on for nearly three days. Her parents had been ecstatic at the birth of a son after four girls. Tonight they were celebrating their thirteenth wedding anniversary and some of the guests had already arrived.

As she went skipping through the house looking for her elder sister, Rina was thinking how much she loved her new, pink taffeta dress. With puffed sleeves, a full skirt, and a folded sash around the waist, she liked the crisp, rustling sound of the taffeta when she moved.

She found Emma at the rear of the house. Surveying her sister's dress, which was identical to hers, Rina said, 'Let's practice walking in for the Bridal March, Emma.'

'Bridal March? Don't be silly, Rina,' said ten-year old Emma. 'They're already married.'

'But Mummy said it's a pretend Bridal March. Please, Emma, let's go outside and pretend.'

Emma was always ready for fun. She grabbed her sister by the hand and together they ran through the house.

Rina gasped with delight as she caught sight of the illuminated garden. 'Look at the lights, Emma! It's like Wesak!' She ran around the garden, weaving in and out of the small groups of chairs and looking up at the strings of coloured bulbs draping the shrubs and trees. A few ladies sought to ruffle her curls but she ducked away from them quite deftly.

'It's like Wesak!' she repeated, jumping up and down. Wesak was an annual, weeklong Buddhist festival in Ceylon, when streets, houses, shops and temples were elaborately adorned with a dazzling spectacle of lights, and a magnificent display of illuminated decorations.

Suddenly Rina recalled the nursery rhyme she had heard her mother humming in the room earlier. Grabbing Emma's hand she swung it wildly and burst into song. *What are little girls made of, what are little girls made of...*

Sugar and spice and all things nice, that's what little girls are made of, Emma piped in.

A few guests in the garden clapped, including Dirk Van Doon. 'I have to agree,' he said as he rose from his chair. He addressed the girls in a kindly fashion, 'Now you have to be quiet, children, Uncle Dirk is going to make an announcement.'

Emma and Rina watched him walk towards the house, moving his portly frame with slow and measured steps. Stopping at the front door he turned around to address the guests in the garden. 'Ladies and Gentlemen would you please come inside now. Ben and Anita will be joining us in a minute.'

They heard their cue — the gardener's tap on the window. Ben reached out and flicked a switch at the wall, plunging the front garden into semi-darkness. He and Anita stepped out through the door of their bedroom and into the garden.

A small band was playing inside the house, and music, laughter and conversation filtered out into the night air.

Aslin, their head servant, had little Michael in her arms while she assembled the rest of the children at the gate. Ben and Anita joined them and got into position behind their four daughters.

There was a brief drum roll from inside the house and the musicians started playing, "Parlez Moi d'Amour."

Emma turned around. 'Is this the Bridal March, Mummy?'

'It's a pretend one, darling. Tonight, this is our Bridal March.'

'I told you,' said Rina, as their mother prodded them to start walking.

Carrying satin-lined baskets filled with fragrant pink carnations, Emma and Rina led the small procession. Esther and Jean followed, in

CHAPTER ONE

apple-green, embroidered organza dresses, and behind them walked a radiant Anita. Ben was at her side, proudly carrying their only son.

The band stopped playing as they reached the front door.

Aslin stepped forward to collect Michael from his father's arms as Ben and Anita entered a smiling throng of relatives and friends. Shouts of congratulations and good-humoured banter started the celebrations in the large, combined living and dining room of the Roberts' home.

The room was generously decorated with paper and foil streamers, glittering festoons and bunches of jade-green and blue balloons. A small team of helpful relatives bustled about with trays of food and drinks, while a trio of musicians played songs from Ben and Anita's courtship years, as well as the popular melodies of the fifties.

Aslin gathered the children together and led them into the garden to be entertained by one of Ben's relatives, a good-humoured "song and dance" man who had got roped into playing the role of magician for the night.

After she had greeted her guests, Anita headed towards a couple of vacant seats beside an open window. Balmy breezes from the nearby ocean carried in the smell of the sea.

She looked admiringly at her husband. He looked particularly handsome tonight in his ivory-coloured suit. Benjamin Roberts was an arrestingly good-looking man, over six feet tall and with wide shoulders that lent an air of dignity to his strong build. He walked with an erect carriage and an upward tilt of his head, epitomizing the eager confidence of a man of vitality. He had intelligent eyes that could be soulful, a broad forehead that brimmed with perspiration when he was hot, and a wide smile that lit his wife's heart. Hospitable and gregarious by nature, he drew people to him with his magnetic personality.

The Roberts family and most of their friends were Burghers — mixed-race descendants of the Portuguese, Dutch, and British settlers in Ceylon.

Ben was of Dutch descent and Anita's grandfather was a man of Jewish ancestry. A convert to Christianity, he had come to the country from Pondicherry, a French colony in India, and had risen to the rank of Chief Inspector of Police in the 1800s, during the British administration of the island.

The Burghers were a minority group in Ceylon. The majority of the country's indigenous people were Sinhalese, while a small percentage were Tamils from South India. A few other minority groups such as Moors, Malays and Parsees were all woven into the harmonious social fabric that prevailed in the island during the 1950s.

Entrepreneurs, entertainers, musicians, singers, radio personalities, sportsmen, judges, barristers, bankers, and a host of other famous and infamous, low, middle and high-class folk could all be found among the Burgher clans, contributing handsomely to the tapestry of life in this tropical island, particularly in the capital city, Colombo. For the most part Burghers were law-abiding citizens who went about their daily lives with no political aspirations or agendas. They excelled in sport, particularly cricket, and the more simple of their kinfolk ascribed to an unfettered philosophy of "eat, drink and be merry." But they graced the field of creative arts with their multitudinous talents for music, song and dance that coursed in their veins.

Anita's gaze shifted to the little band tucked away in a corner of the large room. They were really swinging now. Johnny Nelson, a well-known and accomplished musician was on the piano. Someone Anita didn't know played drums and Earl Gomes, one of Ben's cousins, plucked a soothingly deep, double bass.

Two of Anita's friends, Lydia Wilmet and Mavis Van Buren waved from across the room and made their way towards her. They had all lived next door to each other in Mowdana, a nearby suburb, and though Anita and Ben had moved away some three years before, they maintained a friendship with their former neighbours. Mavis and Lydia still lived in Mowdana.

Mavis looked slender and willowy in a turquoise brocade evening gown and Lydia swished in a red glass-nylon sari, teamed with a green satin blouse.

Both women complimented Anita generously.

Lydia grabbed a seat beside Anita while Mavis kept moving, her long strides leading her away to the front door. 'I'm curious to see how Myrna's enjoying the magic show,' she called over her shoulder as she disappeared into the garden. Myrna was Mavis's ten-year-old daughter.

Anita turned her attention to Lydia.

CHAPTER ONE

Lydia Wilmet was a short and stout woman. She had long, dark, curly hair, and with her bold and flirtatious eyes was best described as coarsely attractive. Her laugh was raucous.

'So what's the latest news in the Roberts household, my friend?' she asked Anita. 'I haven't seen you for awhile.'

A small voice inside Anita's head seemed to prompt, *say nothing*, but being a guileless woman she dismissed the notion. 'We're planning to go to Canada, Lydia.'

'For a holiday?'

'No ... to live there! We're emigrating!'

Lydia's eyes widened. 'Really? That's a huge decision to make all of a sudden.'

'It's not sudden, Lydia. We've been discussing it for some time,' said Anita lamely.

'But why?'

'Ben feels the days ahead in Ceylon are bound to get turbulent, politically,' Anita explained, wishing she'd listened to that little voice. 'A few of his friends are leaving and he thinks we should, too. But please, Lydia, we don't want it known just yet, so keep this to yourself.'

'Don't worry, Anita, I won't say a word,' Lydia promised. 'But what will you do with Irene?'

Anita frowned. 'I don't know. We'll have to think of something.' The very thought of Irene was unpleasant tonight. She was Ben's sister, a quarrelsome spinster who had been living in the Roberts household for some nine years, since the death of Anita's mother-in-law.

Changing the subject, Anita asked, 'Where's Stanley tonight?'

Lydia's shoulders slumped. 'Don't even mention that mongrel to me, Anita. He's getting worse. Card games, card games, card games,' she repeated, twirling a hand in circular motions. 'All he does is gamble away most of what he earns and with the rest he drinks like a fish. My poor children are so neglected.' She looked vacantly at the guests milling around and droned, 'I've even given up going to church. What's the point? For years I've been petitioning heaven to change my plight but nothing happens. So I said to myself I'm not going anymore.' She tilted her head towards Anita and whispered, 'One of the ladies I do some sewing for says she'll take me to see a medium. And after that we're going to get a charm done for my luck to change. Who knows, I may be able to get a better husband and chuck this one out.' A peal of giddy laughter followed.

Anita stood up. She didn't want to hear any more of this tonight. She gently fluffed out her skirt, and said, 'I have to go now, Lydia, I'll catch up with you later. Look, here's Mavis coming in ... why don't you two have a chat?' She placed a hand on Lydia's arm and bent close to her ear. 'Don't trifle with mediums and charm-makers, Lydia. That sort of stuff should be off-limits to you.'

Anita walked over to her husband. 'I'm ready for a dance now, Benjamin Roberts,' she bantered.

Ben looked rakishly at his wife. Kissing her cheek, he whispered, 'Just remember I've ticked off your whole dance card tonight, Miss Anita-Rose.'

Anita chuckled. She had never been to a dancehall in her life. Her strict "Victorian" parents had guarded their only child with fearsome morality, barely letting her out of their sight. It was her husband who had taught her to dance once they were married.

Ben walked across to the pianist and conspired with him.

The music stopped and Johnny Nelson stood up. 'Ladies and Gentlemen, Ben and Anita will dance their anniversary waltz now, and Ben dedicates this song to his lovely wife.'

Anita was whisked away. As they waltzed in perfect step, Ben picked up the refrain. '*Nita, Juanita, always linger by my side. Nita, Juanita, be my own fair bride* ... Why are you trembling, darling?'

'I don't know ... just felt a bit of a shiver, then. I think the sea breezes are a bit cooler tonight.'

Ben gathered her close. 'I'll keep you warm, Juanita.'

Enveloped in her husband's arms, Anita smiled as she remembered how he had called her his "Jewel" at the beginning of their courtship. A few months later he switched to "Juanita." 'Why?' she wanted to know.

'Jewel and Anita,' he explained, with a triumphant smile.

His wedding gift to her was an ornate, silver jewellery box, engraved on the inside of the lid: *You'll always be my Jewel, my dove-hearted Anita.*

Their opening waltz was over and Ben called out with a boyish shout, 'Come on everybody! Get dancing!'

Their guests didn't need another prompt.

After some time Johnny Nelson switched his piano playing from western music to the beloved traditional dance of the island, the

CHAPTER ONE

Ceylonese Baila. A man Anita didn't recognize — a friend of Johnny's — she surmised, stood next to the piano, singing the familiar songs.

In an instant everyone was on the floor.

The children abandoned the magician and came running in to observe the transformation of sedate ballroom dancers into a frivolous group of calypso-style swingers.

Even the servants and waiters left their chores and gathered in a cluster to watch, with undisguised delight, as ladies young and old picked up their skirts and swung them provocatively from side to side.

Anita looked at her servants and smiled. She knew Mary, the cook, would soon be dancing too, hidden from view.

The Baila had an almost, but not quite, calypso-style rhythm, with satirical lyrics in Sinhalese (the country's indigenous language), and a smattering of English.

Baila composers masterfully mirrored to the people of Ceylon the broad panorama of their lives, in an entertaining medium of catchy tunes and parody. Politics, love and marriage, social customs, domestic life and even crime and religion weren't spared from being caricatured in their witty lyrics.

It was two in the morning when Anita sank into bed, weary, but happy. Sighing with contentment she snuggled up against her husband, as she settled in under the large mosquito net. Moonlight shone through the open window, and sea breezes rustled the muslin curtains.

Anita fell asleep listening to the sound of the ocean in the distance.

It was the morning after the party. The Roberts home was astir with the patter of little feet, morning chatter and the clang and clatter from the kitchen as the servants prepared breakfast.

Familiar sounds of Merinda's suburban Sunday morning filled the air. Voices of children and adults in the neighbourhood in Sinhalese, Tamil and English (the three main languages of the island), lyrical outbursts from peddlers announcing their merchandise as they traversed up and down the street, and the sounds of tooting horns from cars and buses on the busy Galle Road were all picking up a pace now.

Merinda was a sprawling seaside suburb on the southern outskirts of Colombo. The Roberts family lived down Clifford place; a small lane that ran from the main thoroughfare, the Galle Road, down to the beach.

Anita walked briskly into the large double bedroom that housed her four daughters, her sister-in-law Irene and the sleeping quarters of the female servants.

Seeing Rina still lolling in bed, Anita called out, 'Wake up *curly-tops*, everyone's up and nearly ready for church, except you.'

Rina lay very still, an arm shielding her eyes.

Almost simultaneously Aslin approached with a towel, ready to do business. 'C'mon Rina-baby, time to get washed and dressed,' she said firmly, in Sinhalese. Adhering to local custom, the servants addressed the children by their first names, followed by the term "baby."

Rina was out of her bed in an instant. Meekly she followed the servant.

Aslin was a widow of about forty; a tall, slim, gaunt-faced woman, fiercely loyal to her employers. She and Anita shared a wonderful rapport, but Aslin was strict with her young charges, balancing the doting affection of their father and their mother's preoccupation with her only son.

Anita was overly anxious with Michael. From the day he was born she had developed the habit of watching him almost every breathing moment of his little life. She had lost her first-born son some six years before, and the trauma of his death a few hours after birth had affected her deeply. A coronial inquest found that the midwife had cut the infant's umbilical cord too short.

At last the five Roberts children were washed, dressed and fed, and Anita called out to her husband that they were ready.

Ben carried Michael in his arms as they leisurely walked the short distance to their local Catholic Church. When Father Cyril, the parish priest of St Lucia's stepped into the pulpit to preach his Sunday sermon, his eyes sought the Roberts clan. The priest nodded and smiled when he caught sight of Ben and Anita. "*A* fine model of an upstanding Christian family" was how he had described them in the Parish Register. He made an announcement that after the Mass he would confer a special blessing on the Roberts family on the occasion of Ben and Anita's thirteenth wedding anniversary.

On returning home Anita headed for the kitchen. The servants were bustling about preparing the usual Sunday special ... 'Yellow Rice' and the accompanying delicious dishes.

CHAPTER ONE

Opening a few of the pots, Anita tasted the food. 'Very good, Mary,' she said, patting the cook on her back.

'Lunch will be ready in half an hour, Missie,' promised Mary, when she saw Anita glance at her watch.

Anita had four servants. Besides Aslin, who had charge of the children, there was Danny who did the gardening. He was Aslin's seventeen-year-old son. They took up residence with the Roberts family in 1947. Mary, the cook, who was separated from her husband, joined them with her two children a year later. When her son grew up he left to take up a trade and now lived with his father.

Mary's daughter Nanda, who had just turned eighteen, helped Anita in the general upkeep of the house until the time came for her to be married. Anita, Mary and Aslin were on the lookout for a prospective suitor for Nanda.

The servants called Anita *Missie*, a title given to a young woman. Ben was addressed as *Mahaththaya*. Loosely the term meant mister, but it translated more accurately into English as gentleman. Ben's sister was referred to as Irene *Nona* — the term for an older woman.

Anita's servants played a significant role in the loving and nurturing atmosphere of the Roberts home, and Ben and Anita treated them as part of the family.

'Ah! There you are,' said Dirk Van Doon, as Anita strolled into the living room. Dirk was sprawled in an armchair reading the Sunday papers.

Anita was glad the Van Doons had decided to stay overnight. Dirk, his wife, Clare, and their five children had travelled some distance to attend the party the night before.

'Be seated, child,' Dirk bantered. 'I'm sure your little feet are tired after last night.'

'More than just last night, Dirk, I've been rushing around for the last few weeks.' Anita dropped into a teak and rattan recliner and swung out the wooden footrest. *I don't have to do a thing today,* she thought as she put her feet up on a couple of cushions, *the servants will take care of it all.* It was a most pleasurable thought.

'Where's Clare and Ben?' she asked Dirk, taking the glass of homemade ginger beer he held out to her.

'Clare's getting dressed, she'll be here soon, and Ben's gone out to the garden with Danny.'

19

The Van Doons were Burghers too. Most Burghers were practising Christians of varied denomination, the majority Roman Catholic, but Dirk and his family were Jehovah's Witnesses.

Dirk and Ben often debated religion. Such polemics didn't interest Anita and she never got involved in their friendly arguments. The two men enjoyed each other's company. Dirk had served in the army and Ben loved listening to the army jokes and stories Dirk would tell in his resounding military voice. Dirk had a commanding presence, with a natural bent towards the theatrical. Anita often thought he would have made a splendid stage actor. Contrastingly, his wife Clare was slightly built, soft-spoken and shy. Though Ben and Anita weren't related to Dirk or his wife, their respective offspring customarily referred to their parents' friends as "uncle" or "aunty."

Ben came in from the garden. 'I had to cut down a couple of branches from the mango tree,' he told his wife, ruefully. 'One of our magician's tricks misfired last night — literally.' Mopping the dripping perspiration off his brow with a handkerchief, Ben gratefully accepted the cool glass of beer Dirk held out to him.

Ben and Anita had no fridge in the house, but a large metal drum filled with sawdust and ice had kept the drinks chilled for the party the night before. Their floating "ice-box" was still functioning adequately.

Ben grabbed the newspaper and fanned himself as he sprawled into an armchair.

It was a warm and lazy Sunday afternoon. The Van Doons and Roberts children were having their usual "concert" in the front garden and the sound of their happy voices and singing drifted into the living room where Ben, Anita and Dirk sat, sipping their drinks and chatting amiably.

Clare soon joined them. 'I love the way you've re-arranged this room, Anita,' she said, admiringly.

While Anita and her family were at church, the hired party chairs had been stacked away and the servants had moved the furniture back into place.

Brass urns with luxurious tropical foliage sat on a cluster of tables of varying height near the front door. A collection of teak and rattan upright chairs were scattered around, encircling Anita's lounge suite, which was box-styled, with deep seats and padded arms. Anita and Ben reupholstered the suite every few years, a craft they both enjoyed. Ben

CHAPTER ONE

had just bought their splendid dining table. Made of solid Rangoon teak and capable of seating ten, the base of the table, which sat under the mid-section, was a sturdy two-door crockery cupboard. An elegant European chiffonier stood to the right of the table and on the left was an old John Brinsmead piano, with real ebony and real ivory on the keyboards. The polished, red cement floor complemented the tropical ambience of the well-proportioned room.

'It was nice seeing Mavis and Lydia last night,' Anita said conversationally to her husband. 'I hadn't seen either of them since Easter.'

'Stanley's probably boozing again,' Ben speculated. 'Can't think why else he kept away.'

'He is,' confirmed Anita. 'Lydia complained bitterly about him last night. And she said something that gave me quite a shock, Ben. She wants to get a charm done for her luck to change, and I don't think she was joking. Apparently she's stopped going to church too.'

Ben was disturbed by the news and said so.

Lydia and Stanley were Sinhalese folk, and Catholic. Although the majority of Sinhalese people in Ceylon were Buddhists, a small number in urban areas and some coastal villages were Christians, mostly Roman Catholic — a legacy of the Portuguese who had colonised the island in the sixteenth century.

Consulting mediums and soothsayers was a common practice among the non-Christian populace, when people thought their lives were not bringing them the success they believed they should have, or if some calamity had befallen them. Often they got charms (occult hexes) made through sorcery, in an attempt to bring about a change of fortune.

Anita knew it was her husband's love for children that compelled him to say, 'I think we should invite Stanley and the family to come over for Michael's birthday next week, dear. I'll try and talk some sense into him. The man needs to realize what he's doing to his kids.'

Lydia and Stanley had five children.

Anita was taken aback when she saw Dirk lean forward and grip Ben's arm.

One to never mince his words, Dirk said, 'If you ask me, Ben, you should leave these folk to manage their own affairs. I know you're a perennial do-gooder, son, but a grown man won't change his ways because Benjamin Roberts thinks he should. Besides, you've got your own wife and children to look after.' He released his grip, pointed a

21

chubby finger to his head, and added, solemnly, 'You hearken to my grey hairs now.'

Ben sighed. 'I suppose you're right.' He looked pensively at his friend. 'Sometimes I want to fix all the ills in the world, Dirk.'

'You're not Jehovah, sonny boy,' Dirk responded, looking at Ben with affection. 'You're only his witness in a crazy world.' He chuckled at his joke.

Ben, Anita and Clare joined him in a moment of relieved laughter, which, almost imperceptibly, lifted the heaviness that had descended into the room.

CHAPTER TWO

1954 – September

A glance at the wall-clock prompted Anita's dutiful call, 'You'd better keep an eye on the time, Ben, or you'll miss your bus.'

'Be there in a minute,' Ben shouted, from somewhere in the house.

Anita sipped a cup of tea and read the front page of the "Daily News" as she waited for her husband at the breakfast table.

It was a sunny September morning, some weeks after Ben and Anita's anniversary celebrations. Their two younger children were still asleep, and the three older girls were getting ready for school.

'I'm not catching the bus this morning, dear, Wally's picking me up,' announced Ben as he emerged from the front room slicking back his dark wavy hair.' He took his usual seat and reached for the bread and eggs. 'We're heading off to the airport. Johnson's flying in today, remember?' he reminded his wife.

Anita waved a hand, dismissively. 'Of course, I completely forgot! If he's going to be staying a bit longer than his usual three days, invite him home for dinner, Ben.'

'He's not staying at all, darling. This is just a stopover on his way to Hong Kong. Wally and I are only meeting him for a chat.'

Herb Johnson, who was flying in from London was one of the directors of Harringtons, a well-known British paper manufacturing company. They had branches in a number of current and former British colonies, including Ceylon.

Ben had begun his career at Harringtons as a sales representative in 1946, and in eight years he had tripled the company's profits and their customer base. He had just been promoted to the position of manager and his salary had also peaked dramatically. Harringtons were now the chief importers of high quality stationery and other affiliated products into the island, and they had no competition of any significance.

Anita was proud of her husband's achievements. She believed he had the essential prerequisites for a successful businessman: a dignified but charming personality, integrity, honesty, and a "gift of the gab."

Emma, the eldest of the Roberts children, joined her parents at the breakfast table. Esther soon followed. Both girls were dressed and ready for school.

Anita looked at Emma. 'She's still asleep is she?'

'Or pretending,' said Emma, with a mischievous glint in her eye.

As usual, Rina was the last of the school-going children to wake up. She opened her eyes and squinted at the morning sunlight streaming in through the metal-trellised windows.

She peered over the side of her bed to check on her slippers. Relief! They were still hidden where she had tucked them away last night.

Emma often teased her younger sister by putting on her slippers. Sometimes she would do a little mock dance in them, causing Rina to shriek in anger. The two girls had celebrated their birthdays in May. Emma, the dancer, got a tambourine decorated with coloured ribbons and Rina got her slippers. Embroidered and padded, shiny red satin slippers — all the way from China, her daddy informed her.

Bleary eyed, she got out of bed and walked out to the breakfast table.

'Oh-oh,' said her father, as he heard the dragging sound of her "sleepy" feet. He put the newspaper down. 'You're going to be late for school, Miss *Cinderina*! Better take off those shiny slippers and let Aslin get you ready.' He leaned forward to kiss his daughter.

Rina was playing Cinderella in the junior-school concert coming up at the end of the year and Ben called her *Cinderina* on occasion.

She ambled up to him, loving the familiar smell of his laundered white shirt, the fresh cologne on his cheeks and the faint whiff of Brylcream in his dark, wavy hair.

Ben hugged his daughter and ruffled her tangled curls.

'That's Wally,' said Ben, at the sound of a car tooting at the gate. He rose from the table and kissed his wife goodbye. 'I'll be home early today,

CHAPTER TWO

dear,' he told her, as he moved towards the front door. 'We're not going back to the office.'

Standing at the door, Ben called out to Emma, Rina and Esther. He was about to perform a daily ritual, handing out money for sweets to his school-going girls.

With a mock sombre look on his face, Ben pulled out his wallet while the girls watched, pretending to be serious too as befitting the ritual. He made an exaggerated attempt to coax three ten-cent pieces out of his wallet and carefully placed one in each little upturned hand.

The girls clasped the coins and reached up with smiles as their father bent down to collect his kisses.

'Today I love you from the sea to the sky,' said Esther earnestly.

From the back of the house Aslin was calling out for Rina. She ran off with the coin in her hand, shouting to her father as she ran, 'I'm going to love your forever and ever till after I die.'

Coming up with some fresh saying occasionally, besides the daily 'Thank you, Daddy,' was part of the game the children played with their father.

'I'm going to buy cigars today with my money and I'm going to smoke them after school,' said ten-year-old Emma. She waited for a reaction.

Ben looked over Emma's head and grinned at his wife. Their eldest daughter was a bit of a handful, but Aslin had already informed both parents of the new chocolate-flavoured candy cigars in the school tuckshop.

'Make sure you bring one home for Daddy,' said Ben, winking at Anita as he stepped outside. His long strides took him to the gate in seconds.

He waved as he entered the waiting car.

Emma and Esther blew him kisses till the car was out of sight.

It was mid-afternoon and the Roberts household was quiet. They were having their daily siesta.

Anita felt a kiss on her forehead. Opening her eyes, she looked into the face of her husband. 'You're back already,' she murmured drowsily. 'Did Johnson arrive?'

'Right on time,' said Ben, changing into his home clothes. 'The old boy looked tired, but he soon perked up after a few cups of tea. We had a good chat about the company's plans for the future, my promotion and the office in general, and then he was off. But before he left he said, "Give that lovely wife of yours, my warm regards."'

Anita smiled, enhancing the compliment. 'Why don't you go and open the mail, Ben, and I'll make us some tea.' She got off the bed and made her way towards the kitchen.

The cook was having an afternoon nap on the kitchen floor. Anita leaped over her, stealthily, but Mary was a light sleeper and she was upright in a flash. Bundling her long black hair into a knot, Mary hurriedly put away her reed mat and pillow and shooed Anita out, promising to have the tea ready in a few minutes.

'Have a guess who I met at the airport today, you'll be surprised,' Ben said to Anita, as she joined him at the dining table. He was opening the mail with an antique, ivory handled, silver paper knife — a family heirloom handed down from his Dutch grandfather.

Anita gave her husband a puzzled look. 'I can't even think who.'

'Lydia Wilmet, with little Jaya! She looked like she was going to a party.'

Anita was more than surprised. 'What on earth was she doing at the airport?'

'She said an aunt was returning from a pilgrimage to Lourdes and she'd come to meet her.'

'I wonder whose aunt?' Anita conjectured, aloud. 'Probably Stanley's. I can't see Lydia having aunts with that kind of money. What a coincidence!'

Mary brought in the tea, set it on the table and returned to the kitchen.

'Nothing from the Canadian Embassy?' asked Anita as she poured out two cups of tea.

'Nothing yet, but we should hear something before the month is over.'

'Do you think we'll really go if we get passed, Ben?'

'Of course, Anita!' Ben's voice expressed surprise that she should think otherwise. 'We've got to, for the children's sake. What are we going to do when English gets dumped? You know that's on the cards.'

Ceylon was in the throes of post-colonial recovery. A search for national identity after centuries of foreign domination was being danced out with high theatre in the country's political arena.

CHAPTER TWO

But the biggest challenge facing the Burghers was the looming demotion of English, which had been the lingua franca of the island for more than a century.

Ben and Anita Roberts' middle class lifestyle was on par with their Sinhalese, Tamil and other ethnic counterparts in the country's urban strata. They were all English educated folk, the offspring of British colonialism, but unlike their counterparts, the only language the Burghers knew was English, though some could speak Sinhalese quite fluently, as Ben and Anita both did. Burghers were sensing the days ahead would not be kind to them, so early migration to the West had begun. The day would arrive when they would be perceived as the unwanted remnants of colonialism.

'I met Moira Redlich the other day,' Anita told her husband. 'They're off to England next month. She says there's not much of a future left for the Burghers and they weren't waiting around to find out, they were leaving early.'

'And that's what I'm trying to do, Anita. Get in early and be prepared. I've even got our two passports ready.'

'What about the children's?'

'Their names are included in mine.'

Despite the serious nature of their conversation Anita's well-trained ears picked up the sound of her son stirring in his cot. 'Michael's up,' she said, and hurried from the table.

A few weeks later Anita greeted her husband with her usual kiss as he got home from work. 'You'll have to include another name in your passport, Mr Roberts,' she told him, coyly. 'We'll be taking a new baby with us to Canada.'

Ben dropped his briefcase. 'Anita! You never said a word! When did you find out?'

'Today. I went to see Dr Ratnam to get the results of my blood test from last week, and as I walked into his room, he said, "You'll have to get that son of yours out of the cot soon, Mrs Roberts. Baby number six is on the way."'

Ben led his wife into their bedroom. 'Now you just lie there on that bed, Mrs Roberts, and rest ... Your husband's orders, okay? I don't want you tiring yourself unnecessarily. We can get another servant if the work gets too much for Aslin and Mary.'

27

Anita lay down, obligingly. She was used to this act. Each time she broke the news of her pregnancies to Ben he treated her like fine china for a few weeks, until it dawned on him that his wife was carrying another child quite capably and without any fuss.

Taking off his shoes, Ben lay down beside Anita. He clasped her hand in his and offered a prayer of thanksgiving, then leaned over her and looked into her face. 'What's your guess, darling? A girl or a boy?'

Anita smiled up at her husband. 'A girl. Somehow I have this strange feeling I'm meant to have an only son.'

'You mean we,' Ben corrected quickly. Lying back on the bed, he lay quiet for a few moments. 'And another May baby,' he said with a chuckle.

'Good arithmetic, Ben. Early May, says Dr Ratnam. Wouldn't it be a treat if she arrived on the seventh? We'll have three May birthdays in a row.'

Rina's birthday was on the fifth of May and Emma's was on the sixth.

'Our darling buds of May,' mused Ben. 'That'll be quite a feat, my sweet.'

'You'll have to start thinking of a nice girl's name,' said Anita.

Ben always picked their children's first names.

'May,' he said, spontaneously. 'If she's a girl, let's call her May.'

'That was easy. Well, I've been busy dreaming up a middle name all afternoon.' Waving an arm in a dramatic flourish, Anita announced, 'Benjamin Frederick Roberts, your fifth daughter will be called May Bernadette. I think that's got a nice ring to it, don't you?'

Ben pondered for a a moment. 'Hmmm ... yes, I like it. But I think we should pick a boy's name too, Anita, just in case you're wrong.'

He sat up suddenly. 'I've got an idea ... let's visit Aunty Florrie and give her the news, and then we can go off and watch the sunset from the beach.'

Anita reached up and gave her husband a smothering kiss. 'You think of everything, Benjamin Roberts. What a lucky wife I am.'

Florrie Adams was a long-time friend of Anita's mother who had passed away some ten years before. Both Anita's parents were deceased and being an only child she had no other family; Florrie was now like a mother to her. She lived only a few streets away from the Roberts home and her house was a mere stone's throw from the ocean.

CHAPTER TWO

The sunsets of Ceylon were spectacular, and beloved to Anita. The western coastline turned on a dazzling show every evening when the weather was fine, which it was for most of the year. In Merinda there would be a few dozen people sitting on the large rocks at the ocean shore, mesmerised by the glorious scene before their eyes. Vivid shades of pink and orange, magenta, mauves and purples transformed the tropical sky into a breathtaking spectacle of colour.

After they had visited Florrie Adams, Ben and Anita sat on the rocks and watched it all, until a glowing sun caressed the ocean's horizon and slowly sank into the sea.

The sky above them was a canopy of glowing, burnished copper and deep shades of purple. Anita took off her sandals and sank her feet into the warm, wet sand, as she and Ben strolled along the beach. When the sound of the seagulls wheeling and turning faded from the shore, they headed for home.

CHAPTER THREE

1954 – December

Anita looked around her garden, wondering what she could pick for the vase on her dining table. She made a mental note to get Danny a special gift for Christmas.

When Ben and Anita had moved into their newly built house in Merinda, some three years before, young Danny had helped Ben transform their arid garden full of builders' rubble into a wonderful tropical oasis.

The once poor soil was now a fertile loam abounding with tropical crotons, coleus, canna-lilies, hibiscus, and other exotic plants. Baskets of orchids hung from the branches of several trees.

Even the lawn had finally yielded to Danny's wooing. It had taken a couple of years to get started and Anita thought he was wasting his time, but the boy persisted, and then suddenly last April the lawn began to flourish. Now it was a beautiful carpet of green.

Glancing at a corner of the garden where her children were playing, Anita was thankful that the old mango tree on the property hadn't been cut down during the building of the house. Ben had tied a swing on a sturdy limb of the large mango tree. He had also fitted a painted blue seat to the swing, which gave his daughters hours of safe enjoyment. Their little feet had tramped a long canoe-shaped hollow in the earth beneath it.

Anita walked back towards the house with an armful of ferns and clusters of fragrant pink-petalled araliya blossoms (frangipani). She was in the fifth month of her pregnancy now and her waistline was beginning to expand.

CHAPTER THREE

'Girls, you'd better come in now,' she called out to Rina and Esther who were playing on the swing. 'We're going to make the Christmas cake.'

'I'm booking the spoon first,' shouted Rina, as she guided the ropes to a halt and helped Esther clamber down.

Emma came flying out of the house. 'I want the basin!' she announced.

'Emma, you can't have all of the basin,' protested her mother, stopping at the front door. 'Esther will want some too, won't you, darling?'

Esther, running across the lawn towards her mother, parroted, 'I want the basin.'

Soon Ben joined the chorus, mimicking his daughters, 'I want the basin, too.'

'Emma, Esther and Daddy can each have a third of the basin and Rina gets the spoon,' declared Anita, firmly. 'And that's settled. No fights, okay?'

'What about Jean?' persisted Rina. 'I can't share my spoon with her, there isn't enough.'

'You won't have to, Rina,' said her mother, 'I'll give her a little bit in a cup.'

'What are you making this year, Mummy?' asked Emma, as the three girls trooped behind their mother. 'Is it love cake?'

'Clever girl, Emilene! Yes, it's love cake.' Anita alternated between the two traditional Ceylonese Christmas cakes each year.

Three little voices chorused, 'We luuuvvv love cake.'

Last year they had sung, 'We luuuvvv rich cake,' their mother remembered.

Love Cake and Rich Cake were the traditional Christmas cakes of Ceylon. No one really knew how the names originated, but it was firmly established that the making of these special treats at Christmas was a tradition handed down by the Portuguese and Dutch settlers on the island, and their mixed race descendants — the Burghers. Rich Cake, which was filled with dried fruit, including moist glace cherries, cost a lot more to make than love cake. Perhaps therein lay the clue to its name.

Anita and the girls gathered at the back of the house. This was a spacious open room adjoining the kitchen. Aslin had cleared a large area of the floor. She now spread out a reed mat, placed an old bedspread over it and dragged out a couple of low stools, one for herself and one for Anita. The two of them would mix the cake, and the three girls would hold the basin down to the floor. Anita had ruled Ben out of this ritual a few years ago to give her daughters the opportunity of participating in this annual event.

She had diligently prepared her ingredients and they were placed in bowls on a wooden bench nearby. Anita followed the practice of her mother and grandmother before her; handmade and homemade Christmas cakes, a treasured tradition in many households.

'I'll get the basin,' said Ben. He soon returned with a huge enamelled basin and the largest wooden spoon you could find in Ceylon.

Aslin took them away for washing. For a whole year the basin and spoon lay wrapped up in an old sheet on top of a wardrobe in the children's bedroom, and only taken down for the making of the Christmas cake.

During the making of the cake Anita had to keep a watchful eye on her girls. The children were experts at surreptitiously moving little thumbs down past the rim while holding down the basin, and deliberately allowing the rich mixture to swirl over their thumbs as the cake was being churned. They would then wait for an opportune moment to raise thumbs to mouths with lightning speed. It was, after all, a delicious mix of fine semolina, eggs, soft sugar and butter.

After an hour or so of light reprimands, fun and laughter, the love cake was ready. When she finally spooned the cake mixture into two large baking trays, Anita left a generous portion on the wooden ladle and in the large metal basin. This was the much anticipated treat for the older children — finger-licking the delicious residue of the Christmas cake, now enhanced with the addition of chopped cashew nuts, a small glass of brandy, the essences of vanilla, rose and almond, and finely powdered spices such as nutmeg, cardamom seeds, cloves, and cinnamon.

Aslin and Mary changed into their street clothes and ceremoniously carried the two trays of cake mixture to their local bake-house. During the 1950s many middle-class outer suburban homes in Ceylon didn't have ovens in their kitchens, unless of course the housewife was a keen cake maker. Anita wasn't.

At this time of the year bakeries were accustomed to the steady stream of housewives and servants transporting trays of thick cake mixture for

CHAPTER THREE

baking, only to return a few hours later or the following morning, to collect delicious, fruit-filled rich cakes and unforgettable love cakes.

The week leading to Christmas was an exciting and eventful time for the Roberts family. Besides being the season of good cheer it was also the season for minor mishaps, due to the children's high-spirited frivolity as they counted down the days.

Over the last couple of years Anita and Aslin, and even Ben, had to reprimand the two older girls quite firmly as they whooped it up during the pre-Christmas period.

There was the incident the previous year when Rina choked on a bun trying to show Emma how fast she could eat. It happened a few days before Christmas. The two girls raided the food cupboard one night and crept back to their beds with buttered fruit buns. They decided to have a race to see who could eat the fastest.

Suddenly Emma shouted, 'Mummy, Daddy, come quickly! Rina can't breathe. She's choking on a bun.'

Ben was seated in the lounge room, reading. He rushed from his chair, slipped on the polished cement floor, (he had wooden clogs on his feet), collided with the piano and fell heavily, bruising his left hip.

Anita was in her bedroom. She ran into the children's room through the connecting door.

On reaching Rina's bed she thrust her fingers down the girl's throat and pulled out a huge chunk of fruit bun. Tears streamed down Rina's reddened face as she coughed up violently and vomited.

And then there was the more recent incident in the kitchen. As in most homes, food was cooked on a hearth, waist high, about six feet long and four feet deep. The hearth in the Roberts kitchen had four little fireplaces. Each little fireplace consisted of an arrangement of triangularly placed bricks, upon which clay cooking pots called *chatties* would be placed. And under the chatties, small stumps of commercial firewood, about a foot in length, would be arranged and lit to form the heat for cooking.

Firewood, as well as coconuts — a daily ingredient in Ceylonese cuisine — was stored beneath the hearth. Boiled drinking water was kept in a large clay goblet on top of the kitchen hearth.

On this particular night, after everyone had gone to bed, Emma and Rina, feeling thirsty, went to the kitchen to get some water. Rina was pouring out a glass of water from the goblet when the cat sprang out from under the hearth, toppling down a heap of coconuts and firewood.

The girls started in fright.

Emma, the first to recover, and always the prankster, shouted, 'A ghost! A ghost!'

Rina dropped the glass and accidentally pulled down the clay goblet. Shards of pottery and shattering glass clattered to the kitchen floor.

The frightened cat was shrieking like a banshee, trying unsuccessfully to jump out of a closed, wooden, kitchen window.

Both girls ran screaming from the kitchen, which set off the dog in the back yard. Utter bedlam followed as the lively black Labrador ran around the garden, barking furiously.

Being pregnant, Anita didn't rush. She first uttered her most common prayer, 'Dear God.' She was now accustomed to these displays of exuberance from her two eldest daughters. She got out of bed and walked slowly towards the door as Ben turned on the light and ran out of the room.

The servants switched on the lights in the second room and hurried into the lounge room. Mary slipped on the highly polished floor and fell. Luckily she didn't hurt herself much, but as she tried to get up off the floor her legs got stuck in her clothing. Emma and Rina, the miscreants, burst into fits of hysterical laughter as they watched Mary struggling to rise, only to slip and fall again. Aslin grabbed a wooden ruler, smacked both girls on the legs and drove them to bed, while Ben went out into the backyard to pacify the dog.

Meanwhile the scared cat had bolted nervously into the night and shot up a tree in a neighbour's garden, protesting loudly at the indignities he had suffered.

Despite Ben's coaxing calls, the cat refused to come down.

It took a while for the now fully awake household to settle down. Anita could hear the two girls giggling in the dark every now and then until they fell asleep. Worse still, she could hear Ben's muffled laughter, though he tried to smother it with a pillow over his face.

Christmas in Ceylon was a huge celebration for the minority Christian population. Their houses were spruced up inside and out with a fresh coat of paint, whitewash, or *samara*, (a sandstone-coloured water-based paint). Windows got a new coat of lacquer or varnish, furniture

CHAPTER THREE

was polished, floors were waxed, and new curtains made. New clothes and shoes were a must and the city's shopping district, Pettah, was jam-packed with shoppers throughout the month of December.

Colombo's famous gourmet Bakery, Perera and Sons, sold their mouth-watering chocolate Yule Logs and Dutch Breudhers (a type of cake-bread) — essential festive treats that were only made at Christmas. And housewives were busy making cakes, puddings and all sorts of other delectables.

Homes were decorated with balloons, festoons and streamers, and the highpoint was the setting up of the Christmas crib. Great anticipation and excitement was in the air!

The grand finale was the spectacular fireworks that started on the stroke of midnight on the twenty-fourth of December. As church bells tolled triumphantly, noisy firecrackers and dazzling fireworks were set off on that night and every night thereafter for about a week. Catherine wheels, Roman candles, rockets and sparklers were the delight of every child celebrating Christmas, even if a hastily shot rocket landed horizontally in a nearby window, setting a neighbour's curtain alight ... Such things did happen, as little Esther Roberts discovered.

Over the next several days, people visited each other, and in the evenings teenagers went door to door carolling to raise funds for their school or church social programs.

Christians would send plates filled with Christmas treats to their Buddhist or Hindu neighbours, and in like manner, non-Christian neighbours did the same when their festivals came around.

The goodwill prevailing in the land was tangible.

Anita and her family enjoyed their traditional Christmas celebrations. And while they were at midnight Mass, Santa visited, with a little help from the servants.

Each year, the week after Christmas, Ben would hire a car and driver to take his family on their Christmas visiting rounds, calling on friends and relatives in near and far places.

Anita took great pride in dressing her girls in their finery and adorning them with dainty jewellery — gold chains and crosses, gold earrings, and little gold bangles.

The three older girls were often asked to sing. The trio were accomplished little artistes. Esther and Rina harmonised with Emma as they entertained their delighted audiences with the popular songs of the fifties.

Christmas in Ceylon was unforgettable.

The new year of 1955 began with the usual "getting ready for school" activities in the Roberts home. For many days Ben would return from work, laden with exercise books, pencils, crayons, art books, and, most importantly, the textbooks, which the children painstakingly covered with brown-paper jackets.

Anita had her hands full sewing school uniforms. Her friend, Florrie Adams came over to help and stayed for a couple of weeks. The old lady, who could be quite cantankerous at times, had a decidedly sobering influence on the older girls during the long school holidays.

Before the schools reopened Ben and Anita were invited to attend the Canadian embassy for their migration interview. A month later Ben received a formal letter from the embassy notifying him that his application had been successful. They were required to proceed to Canada within the year.

Ben and Anita and a couple of their close friends, who were also migrating, met several times to plan their departures. The three families finally decided they would leave Ceylon together, in November 1955.

The Roberts children received the news of their planned migration with mixed reactions. They had numerous questions for their parents about life in the new country. Esther wanted to know if they could light fireworks at Christmas. Emma was disappointed to learn she wouldn't have someone like "Heen Baba" come home and teach her oriental dancing. But they were considerably cheered to learn that some of their parents' friends and families would be going to Canada with them. At least they would have some old playmates in a strange land. And the thought of building a snowman for Christmas the following year filled Rina with a sense of awe.

CHAPTER FOUR

... *1955*

Eight-year-old Rina Roberts had her own little world, which absorbed her intensely. It was a rich world of discovery, enchantment and endless delight. She was a bit of an introvert, a far cry from her high-spirited eldest sister Emma, and her talkative younger sister, Esther.

Rina's favourite hobby was reading. She loved the enchanting stories of Hans Christian Anderson and Grimms' Fairy Tales, as well as the wide collection of Enid Blyton books she had. But she absolutely adored "Les Miserables." She had a children's version of the story and it broke her heart each time she read of little Cossette's struggles. Monsieur LeBlanc (Jean Valjean) became her hero.

Besides reading, Rina had many other pursuits that equally enthralled her.

The Roberts' house had no ceilings for Ben Roberts had intentions of adding a second storey. Sometimes a gap in the tiles would allow long rays of sunbeams to filter down through the roof. Whenever she was at home during the day, Rina would go looking for sunbeams. To her they were mysterious visitors that came in and sat on the polished floor in little circles of light. She was entranced with the tiny particles that floated up and down this magical, light-filled highway, and convinced that the travelling bits had life. How else could they move, she reasoned? She felt sure they were going somewhere beyond the roof and up into a mystical world she tried to envision.

When she was getting ready for her first communion the previous year she had encountered the word "forever." It had puzzled her and she asked her Uncle Dirk what it meant.

'Forever is the travelling of the soul,' he informed her, loftily. 'It's like reaching up into the sky; beyond the sun, the moon, the stars ... beyond what you can see. A journey to a special place where nothing dies.'

Rina was intrigued. She was sure the sunbeams were going there, and she reckoned the little particles of dust were souls travelling to this special place. Sometimes she would run outside the house and try to spot them going up from the roof. At night she would look up at the dark sky, satisfied that the sunbeams she had seen during the day had reached their destination.

Often, the older Roberts children and their parents would sit out at night after dinner, to enjoy the ocean breezes. At times they would scan the sky for shooting stars. Rina would get excited when she spotted one. She imagined they were angels sending messages to tell her that a sunbeam had made it to heaven. Her daddy had taught her the song, "Jesus Wants Me for a Sunbeam" and she loved to sing it, happy at the thought that one day she would be a sunbeam too.

She told her father once, 'When I become a sunbeam and go to heaven, I'm going to look for Monsieur LeBlanc.'

'Is he so special to you, darling?' Benjamin Roberts asked his daughter.

'He is, Daddy. Look how much he helped Cossette.'

Rina loved listening to her mother's stories. One of her favourites was the one about St Therese — how when she was a little girl she had looked up at the sky one night and said to her father, 'Look Papa, my name is written in the sky.' Whenever Rina was out in the garden at night, the first thing she'd do was crane her neck and look for the Southern Cross. She thought her eldest sister Emma was very special, because her middle name was Therese, and the intial 't' was up there written in the sky. Rina was hoping that one day God would write her name too among the stars.

Her eyes were sharp, always looking out for things that shimmered and shone. The iridescent wings of the dragonflies fascinated her as they flitted about and hung in space for a few seconds, before moving on. There were plenty of them in her garden and she often wondered if they were fairies.

She loved searching for the golden chrysalis, a rare treat if she spotted one hidden under the leaves of the oleander trees at school. The

CHAPTER FOUR

first time she had seen one was under the leaves of an oleander tree, and so she thought that was where they lived, habitually. Entreating her older sister Emma to go with her, they both risked a caning as they ventured beyond the inner gates of the school, and up into the portion of the convent garden forbidden to them. Hiding low under the large shrubs, Emma would help Rina accomplish her mission — finding the beautiful and rare golden chrysalis, the pupa of an exotic butterfly. Rina thought they were exquisite creatures. All she wanted to do was look at them.

After school she would crouch outside the crafts classroom and carefully search the clean sand that layered the compound, looking for coloured, shiny glass beads that would accidentally be swept out. Whenever she spotted one, she would pounce on it with delight. She hid her precious beads in a small wooden box and decided she would make a chain with them when she had enough.

She had other treasures too. Her most prized possessions in the house were an amethyst-coloured, translucent jar with a glass stopper, and a pair of beautiful glass cake trays. Her mother said the trays were Jacobean and made by Davidson, a famous glass manufacturer in England. They were amber-coloured, wavy-rimmed glass dishes, shot through with the colours of the rainbow.

Rina would wait for an occasion when no one was around in the dining room. She would take her secret attractions out very carefully from the china cabinet, and hold each one up to the window. Watching the coloured glass reflect rays of fiery beams in the sunlight never failed to exhilarate her.

It was a marvellous feat of her ingenuity and determination that she was never discovered, and that she never had an accident with her glass treasures.

The picture of a large guardian angel hovering over two children crossing a footbridge fascinated her. It was hanging on the wall of the large bedroom she shared with her sisters. Her mother had told her the story of the little girl and boy, and how the angel was protecting them from falling into the raging river below.

Rina would sit on her bed and gaze at the picture for long periods of time, thinking about guardian angels and imagining all sorts of heroic things they would be doing to protect children all over the world. She knew she had a guardian angel. Her mother told her so.

She liked it when her parents sat together in the living room after dinner, listening to the radio thriller, "The Dark Stranger." She was filled with both dread and curiosity whenever she heard the signature whistling that introduced the continuing saga every night. She would run to the living room and sit on her daddy's lap. He would cradle her safely in his arms as she listened to the raps and taps, voices, echoing footsteps, doors banging and creaking, and other sounds that conveyed to her that this was a scary story. Often she would fall asleep in her father's arms and he would carry her to bed and tuck her in.

Together with her sisters she looked forward to greeting her daddy at the gate every evening. Aslin would bathe them and have them dressed and ready around five o'clock. This was the time the radio would play, "The Teddy Bear's Picnic," which ushered in the daily children's program.

Emma, Esther and Rina had learned all the words of the song. They would hold hands with Jean and dance around in a circle on the lawn, singing:

If you go down to the woods today, you're in for a big surprise
If you go down to the woods today, you'd better go in disguise
For every bear that ever there was
Would gather there for certain, because
Today's the day the teddy-bears have their piiiic ... nic,

followed by the chorus.

Little Jean would clap her hands and sing the only complete line she knew, *At six o'clock their mummies and daddies would take them home to bed, because they're tired little teddy-bears.*

Rina's world was safe and happy and filled with the magic of childhood.

CHAPTER FIVE

1955 – Mid-April

The southwest monsoon had started early. It was only mid-April and for nearly a week the heavens had poured down torrents of water, but on this Saturday afternoon the sun was trying to push through an overcast sky in Merinda.

Anita was helping the cook prepare a pot of oxtail soup, a family favourite during the rainy season, which usually began in May. A tap on the front door brought her out of the kitchen.

The entrance doors of the house were left open during the day and from where she stood Anita could see her visitor. With a few instructions to Mary to start cooking the soup Anita waddled out of the kitchen to greet her former neighbour from Mowdana.

The two friends greeted each other with smiles and hellos.

Lydia Wilmet lightly touched Anita's bulge. 'So, when's the baby due?' she asked.

'Early May,' replied Anita, leading the way to a couple of chairs.

'Three May births!' exclaimed Lydia, with a broad smile on her face. 'I can hardly believe it.'

Anita laughed. 'The relatives are taking bets with the date, but I'm hoping she'll arrive on the seventh.'

'And are you still convinced it's going to be a girl?'

'Most of the time, I am, Lydia, but you never know. I could be wrong.'

'I've brought your Godson to see you.'

Not seeing the child, Anita asked, 'Where is he?'

'Out in the garden. He went straight to the swing.'

'I don't think it's dry yet. Danny was trying to clean it up for the girls this morning.'

Anita called out to her husband, 'Ben ... We've got visitors!'

The two women were chatting about pregnancies and childbirth when Ben joined them.

He shot Anita a puzzled look. This was an unexpected visit.

'Hello Lydia, where's Stanley?'

'He's visiting his aunt in Kandy for a few days, Ben. Seeing that the rains cleared a bit today I thought I'd come over with Jaya to say thank you for the Easter hamper. The children are thrilled with the chocolates.'

'So where's my little Godson?' Ben asked.

Lydia walked briskly to the front door and shouted for Jaya.

The four-year-old came bounding in and was immediately seized by both his Godparents. They lavished him with hugs and kisses. Ben and Anita had lived next door to Lydia and her husband at the time Jaya was born and they had grown quite fond of the boy.

Jaya hovered around, impatiently.

'What do you want, darling?' Anita asked him.

'Aunty, can I go on the swing?'

'Of course, you can.' Patches of water were showing on the child's clothes and Anita cautioned, 'Just make sure you don't get too wet or you'll catch a cold.'

She called out to Emma and Rina and asked them to give Jaya a few rides on the swing. The children trooped off noisily.

Aslin approached, announcing that afternoon tea would be served shortly.

'My, my, my, being waited on hand and foot,' said Lydia, archly. 'Lucky you, Anita!' She glanced at Ben. 'I wish I had someone to make me a cup of tea at home and do all my cooking and cleaning. Your wife is very fortunate, Ben.'

'And she deserves every bit of it, Lydia. My darling worked very hard in the days when we had no servants.' Ben looked at his darling and smiled. 'I wasn't earning much then and she had to go out to work too during those awful war years ... probably all that hard slog was what caused her to lose our first baby. All I want to do now is give her and the children the best I can afford.'

'I think husbands like you are rare,' sighed Lydia.

CHAPTER FIVE

Her friend's pointed remarks were irritating Anita. 'I know how special Ben is, Lydia, but I have to tell you that most of my friends have husbands who are equally devoted to their families. Isn't that right, dear?' She turned to Ben for confirmation.

Rarely did Benjamin Roberts disagree with his wife. Whenever she gave an opinion or made a point it was a considered one. 'Of course!' he said, wholeheartedly. 'It's a natural thing for a man to take care of his family. Well, for most of the men I know, anyway.'

Lydia's nostrils flared. 'What a miserable wretch am I to have got one who gambles and drinks and doesn't give a damn about his kids.'

'Ah! Here comes the tea,' said Ben, rising to help Aslin.

Timely intervention thought Anita. She didn't want another *I hate Stanley,* outburst from her friend. They all moved towards the dining table.

Aslin lured the children in from the garden with a plate of vanilla and chocolate wafers. They rushed in and settled themselves around the table, reaching for the cream-filled biscuits with gusto.

'I'll be back in a minute,' said Anita, 'I've got to check on my soup.'

When Anita returned from the kitchen, Emma and Rina had disappeared and Lydia was in earnest conversation with Ben. Jaya was sitting next to him.

'Where are the girls?' asked Anita.

Lydia flashed her a smile, dimples showing. 'I told them to go and get their drawings to show Aunty Lydia.'

She continued her conversation with Ben, waxing lyrical about some herbal medicine she'd discovered. 'Stanley is already taking the stuff … Of course he thinks it's for his headaches.' She tapped Ben on the arm and laughed throatily. 'But I can tell you his drinking is down to half a pint a day now, if not less.'

Anita observed her friend and thought she seemed quite elated.

Lydia turned to Anita, 'Truly Anita, this stuff can cure just about anything.'

'Where did you get it?' drawled Anita out of politeness. She was more interested in looking at her daughters' drawings. The girls had their large art books open and were waiting patiently for Lydia to stop talking.

'There's this man down in Kurupita who makes the stuff,' Lydia was saying. 'Apparently his remedies are the best you can get.'

'And how did you hear about him?' Ben wanted to know.

Lydia hesitated for just a second. 'Through a friend of mine. She says he can fix anything.'

Anita noticed the lagging response and wondered if this was the woman Lydia had mentioned to her on previous occasions — the one who consulted mediums.

'The lady who dabbles in charms?' Anita asked, unable to stop the anxious query.

'Yes,' answered Lydia brightly. 'She knows about a lot of things.'

Anita looked at her husband. 'If you want to try herbal remedies, Ben, why don't you consult the Ayurvedic doctor at the top of Clifford Place? He must be good … Whenever I go past I see his waiting room full.'

'Might be worth a try, dear.' Ben told his wife. 'All I want to do is stop this wretched sneezing in the mornings.'

'Now let me see what these clever girls have drawn,' said Lydia, turning her attention to the chaotic spread of paper and drawing books on the table.

Looking at his children's world in watercolours and crayons never failed to captivate Ben.

He was quite the artist himself.

He picked up Esther's drawing of "Daddy Goes to Work."

'Do I really look like that?' he asked, scratching his head.

'Yes,' said his daughter, quite seriously.

'With a green brief case?'

'My brown paint got all finished up, Daddy, so I thought green was the best colour for your *beefcase* because it looks just like grass,' she said with the delightful conviction of a six year old.

Ben ruffled his daughter's hair. 'Looks like I'll have to get you a larger box of colours. And since we're all going to the beach tomorrow, if the rains hold off, I'll have to buy you some extra blue paint too. I'm sure you'll want to draw the sea.'

'I've already drawn the sea,' piped Esther, sitting up straight in her chair. 'And the sea is not blue, Daddy,' she informed her father. 'It's green and blue, with white on all the wavy bits.' Her fingers rippled across the table to demonstrate the waves.

Her father laughed heartily and planted a kiss on the top of her head. He whispered to his wife, 'What a little grandmother!'

CHAPTER FIVE

She whispered back. 'With your gift of the gab!'

Lydia rose from the table. 'I'd better be going home folks before it gets dark.' Carefully adjusting the pleats of her sari, she turned to Anita. 'So when's your final appointment with the gynaecologist?'

'Twentieth of April,' replied Anita, rubbing her tummy as she got out of her chair.

They sauntered to the front door.

'And what time are you seeing him? I can come with you if you like.'

'Thanks, Lydia, but I've already asked Aunty Florrie. We're planning to leave here about eleven o'clock.'

Lydia put an arm around Anita. 'But don't forget I'm here if you need me, okay?' She kissed the Roberts children goodbye and wished them all a happy Easter.

Anita and Ben accompanied their visitors to the gate and stood watching as Lydia and her son walked up towards the Galle Road.

Halfway up the street, the boy turned around and shouted, 'I'll get Mummy to bring you a toffee next time, Aunty Anita.'

Lydia increased her pace. Holding up her sari, she sprinted, dragging the child behind her. 'I think that's our bus,' she called over her shoulder, before they disappeared from view.

Ben took his wife's arm as they ambled back towards the house. 'I feel sorry for the poor devil.'

'Me too, darling, but what more can we do? We are helping them. Perhaps if Stanley gets cured of his drinking, things might improve. But I thought she looked a lot happier today, so something must be going right.'

Once inside the house Anita moved towards the table and loaded the cups and saucers onto a large wooden tray. She noticed Ben trying to pick something out of his mouth.

'What is it, Ben?' she enquired.

'Oh it's this sweet Jaya gave me. It was chewy and there are bits stuck in my mouth.'

'Well go and brush your teeth then and get the girls to brush theirs too. They've probably got bits of toffee stuck in their teeth as well.'

'The girls didn't get any. Jaya just had one toffee for me.'

Anita was walking to the kitchen. She halted with the tray. 'Only one sweet for you? That's odd.'

'Actually Lydia gave the girls a bag of lollies, but Jaya said his toffee was specially for me. He asked me to close my eyes, open my mouth, and in went the toffee.' Ben chuckled. 'Didn't taste all that great, but I didn't want to hurt his feelings.'

Anita smiled. 'So that's what he was shouting to me about when they rushed up the street. I wasn't sure what he meant ... probably some sweets he got at school.'

Ben was already walking out the back door. He didn't appear to have heard his wife.

CHAPTER SIX

1955 – Late-April

'It's going to bucket down any minute,' said Anita, looking up at the darkening sky. She and Florrie Adams were hurrying towards the taxi stand.

The old lady agreed. 'But I think it'll hold off till we get home.' They had their large black umbrellas in readiness for a monsoon storm.

Anita had just visited her gynaecologist for her final pre-natal check up and the doctor had been satisfied. 'Everything's fine with you, my dear. I don't foresee any birth complications. Now you've got yourself a good midwife, haven't you?' he asked.

'The very best in Merinda,' Anita told him with a smile.

'Excellent! Your baby should arrive anytime after the fourth of May.' Dr Ratnam congratulated her warmly.

A brief taxi ride brought Anita and Florrie to Merinda. Anita dropped her companion off first and headed home. She was famished and looked forward to a good lunch and an afternoon nap.

The winds had turned blustery. Garden debris was swirling across the lawn as Anita opened the gates and walked up the footpath. She entered the house calling out to Aslin.

The servant approached, looking decidedly irate. 'Come outside with me, Missie,' she whispered, 'I have something to tell you.'

'What is it, Aslin? Are the children okay?'

'Yes, yes,' said the servant, impatiently. 'It's nothing to do with them.'

Puzzled and curious, Anita followed Aslin out to the garden, which was growing darker by the minute. Low rumblings of thunder were announcing the imminent storm.

'Your former neighbour from Mowdana came here while you were at the doctors,' said Aslin, somewhat indignantly.

'Which one? Mavis-Missie or Lydia-Missie?' asked Anita.

'Lydia-Missie!' answered Aslin, in an exasperated tone. 'She went into Irene Nona's room. They talked and whispered for about an hour and then she left. What sort of a comedy is this, Missie?' Aslin was using a local idiom.

The news disturbed Anita. Irene had hardly ever spoken to Lydia before, and besides, Lydia was well aware of the woman's hostility towards Anita.

'That's very strange, Aslin,' Anita said to her servant. 'I distinctly recall mentioning to Lydia the last time she was here that I'd be visiting the doctor today. She even asked me what time I was going. Now why would she come here knowing I won't be at home?'

Flashes of lightning streaked through the sky as Anita rose from the bench. 'I'm going to speak to Irene Nona.'

The first wind-driven drops of rain fell as the two women hurried indoors. The sound of thunder fairly exploded through the house.

Mary's daughter, Nanda, was rushing about placing metal buckets on the floor where the roof leaked. During the monsoons nothing could be done to fix cracked tiles. The moisture-laden clay tiles had to dry out completely before anyone could climb onto a roof.

Mary was closing all the windows in the house. Monsoon storms could be fierce. Not as fierce as Irene Roberts.

Anita braced herself as she entered the second bedroom.

A corner of the large room including a window had been partitioned off with a curtained screen. This was Irene's quarters. The woman was bone-idle. She ate, drank, performed her daily ablutions and was unfailingly ill-disposed towards everybody.

As usual Irene Roberts was lying in bed, humming a tune and shaking her feet.

Anita stood at the entrance to her sister-in-law's cubicle. 'Irene, what did Lydia come to see you about? The servants are saying she was here for about an hour.'

Aslin and Mary stood behind Anita.

Irene took her time to answer. She rose from her reclining position, put her feet down and into her slippers, then stood up and clipped her

CHAPTER SIX

hair back on either side of her head. Straightening herself, she pointed a bony finger accusingly at her sister-in-law. 'Your servants are interfering busybodies. Haven't they got anything better to do?' she asked, angrily. 'It's nobody's concern what Lydia and I talked about. Do you hear me? It's none of your business.'

'I think what goes on in my house is my business,' answered Anita evenly. 'And anyway when did you and Lydia become friends?' She had to make the point. 'You always criticised her and poked fun at her. You even said the only thing she needed was a basket on her head and people would mistake her for a fishmonger. So what's going on, Irene? What did she have to talk to you about for an hour?'

'Didn't you hear me the first time, woman? I said it's none of your damn business,' snarled Irene. 'This is my brother's house and I don't answer to you. You're nobody to me!'

'Now you listen to me,' said Anita. 'Whether you like it or not I am your brother's wife, and this is MY home.' Anita's pent up anger over her sister-in-law's constant hostility spewed forth. 'You're an ungrateful woman, Irene. No one wanted to take you in after Mama died. No one! Not Earl, not Freddy, not Elaine, not even Ben. They all said you'd make life hell for them and they wanted to dump you away somewhere. It was I who felt sorry for you. It was I who pleaded with Ben to give you a home. But now I regret the day I brought you into my house. You've given me nothing but trouble.'

Irene stung back. 'And I regret the day my brother married you. You're just a common bitch.'

Anita recoiled as if slapped. She walked away.

Aslin and Mary took turns reprimanding Irene. 'Why did you speak to Missie like that? All she wanted was an answer to a question.'

'Can't you talk to Missie like a human being after everything she's done for you all these years.'

'Don't you go upsetting her now. She's a mother just about to give birth.'

Irene shrieked at the servants, 'Get out! Get out, all of you. Leave me alone and get out of here.'

'Aslin! Mary!' Anita shouted from the living room. 'Come away from there. It's useless talking to that woman.'

Anita was reclining in a chair and looking rather pale when the servants joined her.

The storm outside and the altercation inside had disturbed little Michael who had been asleep in the front bedroom.

Aslin rushed to his cot. 'Hush now my *Raththarung Putha*, don't cry my Raththarung Putha,' she cooed.

Despite herself, Anita smiled weakly. *Raththarung Putha* was a Sinhalese term of endearment Aslin often used on little Michael. The words meant "son of gold ... of very precious worth."

Aslin came out of the room with Michael toddling beside her. She brought him over to his mother for a kiss.

Anita hugged her son. 'This is my *Raththarung Putha*, isn't he Aslin?' She covered Michael's face with kisses, comforting herself from the emotional bruising of her encounter with Irene.

With bitter irony Anita recalled how when she had taken her sister-in-law into her home nine years before, a year after her own mother had died, she had hoped Irene would be the sister she had never had.

On the rare occasion that she poured out her complaints to Ben he would remind her that Irene was merely jealous of Anita's happiness and the abundance of her life, which contrasted glaringly with the paucity of his sister's barren existence. 'Don't let it hurt you like this,' he would say.

But Anita did get wounded. Her view was that Irene should be grateful to be living in her brother's home. It was a happy home, filled with children, laughter, music and friends. Besides, Irene contributed nothing to the Roberts household in any way, shape or form, and yet she was well looked after. She was clothed, fed and sheltered. She could do as she wished and come and go as she pleased. Therefore Anita could never understand Irene's behaviour. And she didn't concur with Ben's assessment of his sister. Rather, Anita believed that Irene had an intrinsic wickedness in her nature. She was able to hate without a cause.

Aslin was seated on the floor with Michael on her lap, lulling him back to sleep. It was customary for servants to sit on the floor. She looked up at Anita. 'Missie, don't trouble yourself too much over Irene Nona, just concentrate on the new baby.'

Mary nodded in agreement. 'Don't take any notice of what she says, Missie. She's mad, that's what I reckon,' Mary said, in her simplistic fashion. 'And I don't like that Lydia-Missie either. I didn't take any notice of her when she came into the kitchen to see what I was cooking.'

CHAPTER SIX

'She came into the kitchen to see what you were cooking?' echoed Anita, incredulously. 'Did she speak to you?'

'Yes, she asked me what I was preparing, then looked around the kitchen and walked away.'

Anita and her servants were speaking softly so Irene wouldn't hear them. 'I'll tell you what,' said Anita, 'we won't worry about this now. The next time I see Lydia-Missie I'll find out why she came here today.'

She got to her feet and moved towards the kitchen. 'Come along now,' she said to her servants. 'Let's have some lunch, I'm starving.'

'Missie! Missie!' Mary called out. 'We forgot to ask you. What did the doctor say?'

Anita turned around and smiled at her servants. 'Everything's fine. We'll be having a new baby in the house in a couple of weeks.'

It was the ninth of May, four days after Rina's ninth birthday. Dressed and ready for school, she hurried to the dining table for breakfast and halted in surprise. The table was bare.

Emma wandered in from the back of the house. 'Mummy's new baby was born last night,' she whispered to her younger sister. 'Aslin told me it's a girl.'

Breakfast was forgotten momentarily. 'Can we have a look?' Rina asked Emma.

'No, we can't. I've already asked Aslin. She says we have to wait till we get home from school, 'cos Mummy's not feeling well,' said Emma. She left her sister standing at the table and walked away.

Rina saw her father emerge from the front bedroom and head towards the table. 'Daddy, what are we going to eat for breakfast?' she asked him, in a happy singsong voice. The thought of a new baby sister excited her.

'Your mother's mad!' her father announced ominously, not looking at his daughter. 'You'll have to ask Mary or Aslin.' He picked the newspaper off the table, grabbed his briefcase and walked out of the house.

Rina sat down in shock. She had never heard her father say anything bad about her mother before, and she had never seen such an angry look on his face. She gasped as she realised he had forgotten their pocket money, and he had gone off to work without kissing any of his children.

Rina was bewildered. And for the first time in her life she experienced a strange sensation. Fear.

Where is everybody, she wondered? She went to the kitchen to look for Mary and found her cooking something on the hearth. 'Mary, what's wrong with my Mummy? Is she mad?' blurted Rina.

'What nonsense are you talking, child?' answered the servant, roughly. 'Your Mummy's not mad, she's just not well. But I'm making some *thambung hothi* for her and when she drinks this she'll feel a lot better.' Mary kept stirring the pot of steaming herbal soup. The fireplace beneath it was roaring with flames.

Rina stood awkwardly in the kitchen, staring at the fire.

Mary glanced at the child and her expression softened. 'Your Mummy had a bad night last night with the new baby and she's tired. She's having a rest, child, that's all.'

'But what about our breakfast, Mary? And who's taking us to school?' asked Rina, still disturbed by her father's odd behaviour.

'Everything will be ready in five minutes, Rina-baby. Five minutes. Go and sit at the table like a good girl and Nanda will fix everything. Breakfast, school, lunch … everything. Just go and sit down now.'

Rina walked back to the table and sat down.

She desperately wanted to see her mother.

It was a hot afternoon and the Merinda Post Office was crowded. Anita felt sweaty and irritable as she pushed through the queues of people lining up at the counters.

She headed for the phone booth in the corner.

Shutting the door firmly behind her, Anita dialled the number of her husband's office.

'Harringtons here, this is Wally,' said the voice at the other end.

'Wally, it's Anita. If Ben's around please don't mention my name.'

'Hello, Anita. No Ben's not here, he's out of the office. What's the matter, girl?'

'Can you spare me a few minutes, Wally?'

'Of course, my dear … what's happened?'

'Wally, do you know if anything's troubling Ben?' asked Anita. 'His behaviour has been strange over the last couple of weeks.'

'Yes, I know what you mean, girl. He hasn't been his happy self just lately.' Wally Fernando and Benjamin Roberts shared a long-

CHAPTER SIX

standing friendship. 'I thought it must have something to do with the new baby and going to Canada and all that ... Do you think he's having second thoughts?' Wally asked.

'He doesn't talk about it, Wally. More than once I've asked him what's bothering him, and whether he was having any doubts about leaving. He says, no, and that there's nothing wrong. Do you know where he's gone?'

'He's visiting one of our major buyers.'

'Wally, is there anything happening in the evenings to do with work?'

'What do you mean?'

'Well Ben goes out in the evenings now and when I question him about it he says there are things he has to do, and doesn't explain. I thought it must have something to do with his new position.'

'No, not at all Anita. Work for Ben finishes at five.'

Anita sighed dejectedly. 'Okay, Wally, I'd better be going.'

'Wait a second ... If you're troubled Iris and I can come over for a chat.'

'You know we won't be free to talk with Irene around. She sees and hears everything.'

'Come over to our place then. Iris will be glad to see you.'

'Thanks Wally, but I can't spare the time right now. There's too much to do at home.'

Ben went out again that evening. He returned late.

Anita waited till he got changed into his nightclothes and slipped into bed beside her. 'Ben, can you tell me where you're going in the evenings? Surely this can't all be work.'

Ben was slow to respond. 'Anita, I want a bit of freedom for myself. I'm exploring a few things.' His voice was cold and harsh. He pulled the sheets up to his chin and turned away.

'Like what? I think as your wife, I have a right to know.'

Again he was silent for a few seconds before answering morosely, 'I've been attending some meetings of the Rosicrucians.'

'The what?'

'The Rosicrucians!'

'And what the hell is that?'

'I'm not supposed to talk about it ... it's a secret organisation.'

Anita sat up. 'Ben, what's happening to you all of a sudden? Why are you acting so strange?'

'Go to sleep, Anita. I'm tired.'

The dismissal hurt. And Anita couldn't fall asleep. Questions and answers chased around in her head as she tried to come to grips with what was happening to Ben. She struggled to accept the awful truth she'd been trying to evade for weeks. Her beloved husband had distanced himself from her physically and emotionally.

After the children were despatched to school the next morning Anita went looking for Aslin. She found her washing nappies at the well.

Most homes beyond the metropolitan boundaries of Colombo didn't have water on tap. They had wells in their back yards. These were constructed like large wishing wells, with waist high retaining walls. A large area around the well was cemented and a drainage system put in place to collect the run-off.

Aslin was sitting on a low stool with two metal washtubs before her, scrubbing and rinsing.

'Aslin, I'm going to visit Florrie Nona for a little while,' said Anita. 'Can you keep an eye on things while I'm gone?'

Aslin nodded. 'Sure, Missie, I'm nearly finished here.'

Anita was deep in thought as she walked the short distance to Florrie's house. Vendors on the hot and dusty street, the busy traffic and people milling about in the morning sunlight slipped by, unnoticed.

'Goodness! What's the matter?' asked Florrie Adams, as she answered the knock on her door. 'Come and sit down, my dear, and let me get you a cup of tea.'

Anita entered the spacious living room and headed for the large couch. 'Don't worry about tea, Aunty, I just want to talk to you.' She sat on the couch, leaned back with a sigh, and closed her eyes.

Usually Anita loved this bright and sunny room.

French windows opened out onto a well-tended and verdant lawn. Further ahead, graceful palm trees and expansive views of the ocean were delightfully refreshing. But today Anita's eyes and heart weren't attracted to any pleasant sights.

'What on earth's the matter, child?' asked Florrie. Settling into a chair, she faced her visitor, 'Are the children ok?'

CHAPTER SIX

Anita's eyes flew open. 'It's Ben. He hasn't been himself for a couple of months now. He gets angry with me and loses his temper with the children ... We're all getting afraid of him.'

'Ben ... Angry? Impatient? You can't be afraid of Ben, surely.' Florrie came over and sat on the couch beside Anita. Putting an arm around her, she asked, 'And when did all this start?'

'I noticed it a couple of weeks before May was born. I thought it must have something to do with his new position and our plans to leave Ceylon and all that, so I tried not to let it bother me. But with Lydia and Stanley coming over all the time now he's getting worse.'

'Your old neighbours from Mowdana? What do they want?' asked Florrie, taken aback by the news.

'I don't know ... my home seems to have been disrupted by them.'

Anita unburdened herself and began to recount several troublesome incidents surrounding Lydia and Stanley's visits. 'They come around at least twice a week and stay till late into the night. I'm tired of it all.'

'Twice a week!' Florrie thumped the chair. Her plump and fair face grew flushed. 'For God's sake, haven't they got a home? Don't they have any sense to realise that you've just given birth and need all the rest you can get?'

'Rest? I haven't had much of that since May was born.' Anita's voice was edgy. 'I get so tired these days, Aunty. Most of the time I leave them and go about my business attending to the children, but Ben expects me to sit with them. I can't even go to sleep. He says it's rude for me to go to bed when we have visitors.'

'What on earth have they got to talk about so much, girl?'

'Mostly it's idle chatter — rubbish really. And Ben's got involved in some secret movement called the Rosicrucians.' Anita rolled her eyes. 'God only knows what that is. I suspect Stanley's in it too. They discuss it sometimes, guardedly. But worst of all Lydia has convinced Ben to get all the children's horoscopes cast by some astrologer she knows.'

'Rosicrucians and horoscopes and astrologers!' exclaimed Florrie, 'Ben must be mad! Look, Anita, I think you should see Father Cyril and tell him what's happening.' Florrie got up off the chair with some difficulty. She was a heavy, thickset woman. 'I'm going to make some tea, darling. Come over to the kitchen with me.' She took a few limping steps.

Anita followed her.

'Does Ben go to church with you?' asked Florrie, leading the way to the back of her house.

'He hasn't for the last few weeks. He makes flimsy excuses and tells me …' Anita stopped. A long-forgotten memory from the days of the war suddenly and vividly claimed her attention.

Easter Sunday 1942 — the day the Japanese had bombed the harbour in Colombo. Anita and Ben had been married for just under a year and Anita was pregnant with their first child. They were attending Mass at a church in the north of the city when the bombs fell. The church shook with the blast. People shouted and ran in every direction. Some fled to the street, but a few stayed inside and prayed, including Ben and Anita. Even though he was afraid, he told her later, Ben had put an arm around his trembling and pregnant wife and bowed his head. When the sirens ceased and the turmoil subsided he told her with conviction, 'I made a promise to myself and God today that nothing would stop us going to church together, darling. Nothing, except sickness and death.' Throughout the fourteen years of their marriage they had had an enduring faith that was solid and strong until now. With an ominous feeling Anita realised something strange must surely be happening to her husband to cause him to forget his sacred pledge. She mentioned it to Florrie.

'Anita, you must speak to Father Cyril … soon,' urged Florrie. 'Ask him to have a talk to Ben. Can you promise me that?'

Anita promised.

'Good. Now how about a cup of tea?'

'I can't stay, Aunty.'

Florrie came over and stood before Anita. Grasping her shoulders firmly, she said. 'Now listen, girl. You're like a daughter to me. If there's anything I can do to help, you let me know. But I'm sure this will all blow over in time. Your husband's a wonderful man. This is just a rough patch you're going through, darling. It happens in every marriage. Things will be all right again. You wait and see.'

Anita's step was much lighter as she walked home. Talking with Florrie Adams had eased her mind. She felt more hopeful now and reassured that everything in her marriage would be back to normal soon.

Rina could hear their conversation … mostly in Sinhalese, but with traces of English. Though unable to understand any of it, she felt uneasy.

CHAPTER SIX

She went over to Emma's bed and lay down beside her. 'Why are they coming to our house all the time now?' she whispered in her sister's ear.

'I don't know,' said Emma, tersely. 'Go back to your bed, Rina.'

'I don't like it when they're here,' said Rina, ignoring the command. 'I like it better when Uncle Dirk and all of them come.'

Her sister didn't speak.

Rina lay beside Emma, listening. She looked around the semi-darkness of the room and saw Aslin on the floor. But the servant wasn't asleep. She was sitting up on her mat.

'Emma? Emma, are you crying?'

'Go away, Rina.'

'Emma ... I'm afraid.'

Aslin called out, softly, 'Rina-baby, come over here and lie down with me like a good child.'

In a few swift moves Rina was on the reed mat with the servant. Aslin grabbed a pillow and laid Rina's head on her lap.

'What are they saying, Aslin, and who's that crying?' Rina whispered. 'Is that my mummy crying?'

'Go to sleep, Rina-baby,' said Aslin, gently. She put her arms around the nine-year old and stroked her head. 'Go to sleep. What you're hearing is coming from the radio next door.'

Anita woke up with a thundering headache. Her heart started thudding as she recalled the events of the night before. She had never been so distressed in her life.

Over the previous few weeks she had found herself getting increasingly agitated whenever Lydia and Stanley came around. She never knew which direction their conversation would take. Sometimes Ben would find fault with her in front of them. And Lydia or Stanley would, as well. Last night had been intolerable. Her visitors had sat in her lounge for two whole hours, and Ben and Stanley had been drinking for nearly the whole time. Anita was bone-tired. She sat holding her sleeping infant in her arms, reluctant to put her down in the cot. Her baby was an anchor of comfort in this hostile setting.

The "attack" started at about nine thirty. Lydia criticised her for being so besotted with Michael, saying she was spoiling him, and Ben agreed.

Anita held back the tears.

That conversation ended after a while, then Lydia launched at her from another angle.

'Anita, Stanley says you used to go to the beach with some Merinda boys when you were young.' Lydia laughed derisively.

Anita had grown up in the 1930's when this was improper behaviour for any decent young girl in Ceylon. The implications of Lydia's remark were serious and Anita was shocked. 'Stanley's off his head! I've never been to the beach with any boys in my life. My mother would have killed me. Ben knows how strict she was.' She turned to Ben for confirmation.

He ignored her.

And Stanley smirked, 'Didn't you go gallivanting with the two Simmond boys who used to live near the church?'

Anita was deeply insulted. The Simmond brothers had been well known in Merinda. Their besmirched reputation was legend in her hometown, in the whole of Colombo in fact. Any girl who had been in their company was tarnished forever.

Anita's heart sank at the malicious assault on her good name. 'What rot are you talking, Stanley?' She looked pleadingly at her husband for support.

Ben leered drunkenly at his wife. 'So you weren't the innocent little jewel I thought you were, Anita? Your mother did a good job making out you were a saint, didn't she?'

'I don't know why you're saying this to me, Ben.' Anita's voice faltered badly. 'You knew my mother and you know my history. I never went out with any boys. My mother wouldn't even let me even go out with my cousin Noel, that's how strict she was. And she chaperoned me everywhere I went.' Anita was in tears.

The three of them ignored her and talked as if she wasn't there. Stanley continued his veiled slander, prodded by Lydia wanting to know more, while Ben spoke disparagingly of Anita and her parents.

Liars, Liars, why are you doing this to me? Anita screamed silently.

She felt degraded by their insinuations and enraged by Ben's callous insults of her dead parents.

He knew how much Anita adored them, and he also knew, first hand, that they had lavished her with protective love.

Suddenly it was all too much. The weeks of unrelenting stress Anita had endured since the birth of her baby took its toll.

CHAPTER SIX

She burst into tears and ran out of the house with her infant in her arms. Unmoved, her three "attackers" watched her go.

Sobbing wildly, she rushed out through the open gates and ran down Clifford Place, heading towards the sea.

Desperation swept over her and she hadn't gone very far when an insane idea took hold of her. She would leave her baby on the ground at the bottom of the street, and throw herself before a train.

The city's coastal rail link, between the capital city of Colombo and distant Galle in the south, ran parallel to the ocean at the bottom of Clifford Place. It transported thousands of city workers each day.

But the railway lines served a more sinister and tragic purpose. Desperate people chose to kill themselves on the steel tracks, either by jumping in front of suburban trains, or calmly lying across the sleepers before the approaching Galle Express. Their suicides brought agony to train drivers, who blew their powerful horns continuously when confronted with the looming disaster, especially in the latter scenario, hoping to startle and dissuade the desperate men and women seeking death under the screeching metal juggernauts.

Anita ran swiftly into the night, guided by the faint illumination from the scattered street lamps.

Halfway down the street, a voice behind her called in the dark, 'Mrs Roberts, Mrs Roberts! Stop! Stop!'

She kept running with her baby in her arms.

When Ebert Vidhana, her neighbour's son, caught up with Anita she was almost at the bottom of the street, close to the railway tracks. She cried aloud as Ebert took hold of her roughly.

In an emotional outburst she poured out all that had taken place in her home. Her baby was howling now, startled by the sound of a hurtling train.

A few people had come out into the street, disturbed by the barking of the neighbourhood dogs.

Anita felt ashamed as Ebert murmured some response to their anxious queries. He gently led her up the street and back into the house.

Ben, Stanley and Lydia were still chatting in the living room, unperturbed.

Barely containing his fury, Ebert addressed them contemptuously, 'You should all be ashamed of yourselves! This lady has just given birth. I happened to be in the garden and noticed Mrs Roberts running down the street. She was going to throw herself before a train. I'm flabbergasted that you've all been sitting here unconcerned and that none of you went looking for her. In a little while this would have been the police knocking on your door, Mr Roberts, to tell you that your wife and baby daughter had been killed.'

Ebert looked accusingly at Ben. 'Have you people got no heart?' he asked angrily.

No one said a word.

'Mrs Roberts, please go inside and rest with your baby,' Ebert pleaded before he left.

Anita went into her room, trying to placate her crying infant.

Lydia and Stanley hurried from the house.

Ben remained in the lounge, brooding.

CHAPTER SEVEN

1955 – October

They walked down the lane in silence.

Crossing over the railway tracks the two women took off their sandals and headed towards a shady spot on the beach, under a clump of palm trees.

Anita's feet sank into the soft, golden sand. She could almost taste the salty sea spray settling on her face in a fine mist. It was ten thirty in the morning and the wind blowing in across the water was warm. A couple of weathered logs — old, fallen coconut-tree trunks that were part of the landscape — provided rustic seating to Anita and her friend.

She glanced sideways at Mavis Van Buren and wondered what was troubling her. 'What's wrong girl?' she asked, with concern. 'Couldn't we have talked at home?'

'No, Anita, I didn't want Irene to hear us.' Mavis looked distressed.

'Why? What's happened?' asked Anita, frowning.

Mavis stared out to sea, then looked briefly at Anita and lowered her glance. 'I'm sorry to bring you this news, Anita, but I can't watch it any more without letting you know.'

'Know what?'

'Over the last few months Ben has been visiting Lydia almost daily.' Mavis rattled on. 'He arrives at about one o'clock in the afternoons in a …'

'Stop it Mavis! You're talking rubbish,' interrupted Anita. 'Ben works in the afternoons. He's got a very responsible job, you know.' She brushed away the hand Mavis held out to her. 'Why are telling me such a dreadful lie?'

'Anita darling, I'm not lying, please believe me … It's been going on for five months. I didn't know how to tell you and I've agonised over it, but finally made up my mind today that I had to let you know.'

Anita was stunned into silence.

Encouraged, Mavis continued quickly, 'I've been watching it all through my bedroom window. Ben arrives in a taxi — always around one o'clock. Usually he brings groceries and unloads them onto the veranda, and as soon as the cab leaves Lydia comes out to greet him. You should see her, Anita.'

Mavis's voice descended into a tone of contempt. 'She wears this cotton dressing gown, partially unbuttoned. Half her breasts are exposed and her legs are showing … you can tell she's had a bath just before he arrives; her long hair looks damp and hangs loose down to her waist. They go inside with their arms around each other, and after a couple of minutes they come out to the veranda and take all the groceries inside. Then Lydia closes the front door.'

The scene was indescribable torture to Anita. How could it be possible? 'But where are the children, and what about Stanley?'

'Stanley gets home late in the evenings — after his rounds of gambling and drinking no doubt. And all her children go to school now remember? So no one's around when Ben arrives, and by the time the kids get home he's gone.'

'Mavis are you sure it's Ben?' Anita's eyes pleaded for a response of hope.

Mavis looked away. 'Of course it's Ben.' Her voice was pained. 'Do you think I'd be so cruel to tell you this if it weren't true … if I wasn't sure?"

'Does he know you've seen him?'

'I don't think he cares. Surely he must know I'd see him sooner or later.'

Every vestige of restraint deserted Anita. She broke down and wept uncontrollably.

Mavis cried with her.

A few people walking past looked at the two women in alarm. A couple stopped, their faces showing concern. Mavis waved them on.

From one of the nearby fishermen's huts an old woman came hobbling up the shallow sand bank. Her brown face was weathered by the sun and the sea. With a sense of alarm, she asked, 'Has there been a death in the family?'

CHAPTER SEVEN

Yes ... it's me, thought Anita as she wept.

Mavis assured the old woman that no one had died. She hurried away and returned with two glasses of water.

With great difficulty Anita controlled her weeping, willing herself to see the faces of her children, rather than the scenes playing in her mind.

She spoke in indeterminate whispers. 'He has been so difficult. I didn't know what was wrong ... like a stranger in the house, and now he's decided we won't be going to Canada. She comes around all the time, dragging the children, even Stanley.'

'Stanley!' Mavis spat out the name. 'He's just a pimp, Anita. A bloody pimp! He doesn't care what she does as long as there's food on the table — the rotten sod!'

Anita grew silent.

Mavis continued, a note of urgency in her voice. 'Listen, girl, I'm convinced Lydia has done a charm to hook Ben. I'm absolutely sure of it. You've got to get it broken! God forbid there's no way Ben would fall for that creature. He has always adored you.'

Anita was holding her head with both hands. 'I can't think anymore, Mavis. I can't think! I must go home now.' She put her sandals back on and got to her feet, aided by her friend. 'I'm going to question him tonight.'

'No, don't do that!' shouted Mavis. Lowering her voice, she urged, 'Not tonight. We don't know whether Irene saw me or heard me when I was at the house. Wait a couple of days, please!'

For most of the day Anita wept, alone in her room.

Her servants were deeply disturbed. They pleaded with her to tell them what was wrong.

How could she?

Aslin and Mary kept the children away from their mother when they came home from school, but Anita's strong maternal instincts found her attending to her newborn baby and her little son with her usual tenderness.

Though everything inside her was screaming for confrontation, Anita decided she would keep away from her husband when he got home from work.

Emma and Rina helped their mother rearrange the second room and tidy up the children's clothes cupboards for most of the evening.

Around two pm the next day Anita was in the phone booth at the Merinda Post Office.

'It's Anita here, Wally. Don't mention my name if Ben's there.'

'He's not, Anita. Is everything okay?'

'I have to ask you something, Wally, and it's very important. Does Ben go out a lot in the afternoons?'

'Actually he does, almost daily. I've even asked him about it. As you know he's not a sales rep anymore, but he says he likes to keep in touch with our buyers. By the way, your friend Lydia popped in yesterday. Said she was shopping and wanted to give Ben some gift she'd bought for the baby. But Ben was out and she didn't want to wait.'

'Did she leave the gift with you?'

'No, she said she'd take it to you at home.'

'I see.' Anita's sigh was more of a groan.

'I heard that, girl. What's up? Is she causing you grief?'

'That's something I'm trying not to think about, Wally.'

'Be careful, Anita, I'm a bit wary of her after that airport incident.'

'What incident?'

'Remember when Ben and I went to meet Herb Johnson last year?'

'Yes, of course! Ben mentioned Lydia was there … I thought it was a strange co-incidence, but what happened?'

'First I have to tell you what happened at your anniversary party.'

'Tell me.'

'Ben and I were standing around, chatting. We were discussing his promotion and some company business and so forth, and then we went on to talk about Johnson's trip. We even mentioned the date and time of his arrival, when suddenly I became aware of this woman in a red sari standing next to us, listening intently to our conversation. When she knew I'd noticed her eavesdropping she moved away. I asked Ben who she was and he said she was Lydia Wilmet, a former neighbour. Bumping into Ben at the airport was no coincidence, Anita. She knew he was going to be there.'

'Did she spot him first?'

'What do you think? She made a beeline for him as soon as we entered, as if she'd been waiting for him. She was all dolled up and giggled and carried on with Ben like a teenager. I even joked with him about it later. "You'd better watch out for that woman, she's making a play for you," I told him. He laughed at my concerns. "Wally, no woman can get my affections. My heart belongs to my wife and it always will." That's what he said.'

'I have to go now, Wally.'

'Anita, what's wrong? Please tell me what's wrong?'

'I can't talk about it right now.'

'Listen, shall Iris and I come over?'

'No, Wally. I'll come around to your place if I need to. But thanks for telling me abut the airport stunt. I'm getting a better picture ... I'll see you later.'

'Bye Anita, you take care now, girl.'

It was around six in the morning — two days after Anita's phone call to Wally. Ben was out in the backyard having his morning bath at the well, and the paperboy was at the front door waiting for his monthly account to be paid.

Anita was in her room getting the money ready, but found she was short of change. Seeing Ben's wallet on the dressing table she opened it up to get some coins. A small black and white photograph fluttered to the floor. She stooped to pick it up thinking it was one of her old pictures, pleased that he still carried it around.

Her heart lurched. It was a photograph of Lydia. Turning the picture over she recognised Lydia's handwriting: *Heart to heart, though far apart, my love for you will never depart.* Anita slipped the photo into the pocket of her dressing gown and left the room. After she had paid the paperboy she hurried to the kitchen and stayed there till Ben had gone to work.

Anita returned to her room, sat on her bed and pulled out the photograph.

Over the last couple of days she had found herself questioning Mavis's story, wondering whether it had been concocted. She wanted to believe anything rather than the heartbreaking picture of betrayal Mavis had revealed at the beach.

It was ludicrous, she told herself. Ben and her friend Lydia having an affair! But what Wally had told her was disturbing ... and now this photograph!

She thought of how much she had helped Lydia over the years. Every Easter and Christmas she would send a rickshaw over to her house, filled with a huge parcel of food for the family. She even took Lydia's children shopping at Christmas to buy them gifts and clothes. She couldn't believe her friend could do this to her.

The two-fold betrayal was shattering.

Stanley and Lydia came visiting that night.

Anita waited until they exchanged greetings and were seated. She went into her room, came out again and walked over to her friend. 'Lydia, I want to know why you've given your photograph to Ben,' Anita demanded, thrusting the picture in Lydia's face.

The woman was brazenness personified. She looked up at Anita, with insolent eyes. 'Don't be so narrow-minded, Anita. I just gave it to him because we're friends.'

'Friends!' hissed Anita, 'with this verse you've written on the back? *Heart to heart, though far apart, my love for you will never depart.* That doesn't sound to me like something you'd write to a friend, Lydia.' She was breathless, trying to control her rising anger.

Ben was out of his chair in a flash. He slapped Anita hard and grabbed the photograph out of her hand. In tears she ran into the bedroom and threw herself on the bed.

Ben entered the room, shouting abuse. His loud and angry voice woke the sleeping infant. Aslin came running in, picked the crying child up from the cot and ran out again.

Lydia and Stanley made a quick exit.

'Why didn't you ask me about the photograph?' Ben yelled, threateningly. 'Why did you humiliate me like that?'

'Humiliate you?' Anita rose to her feet and faced him squarely. 'I am your wife and you slapped me in front of that bitch!'

'I can explain that picture, you should have asked me.'

'Explain it to me!' she shouted, shaking with anger.

'That verse was not written for me, it was an old photo she gave me. She had …'

'You're a liar, Ben! You're a rotten, bloody liar. You've been visiting that bitch for months now. Yes … I know all about it. You've been sleeping with that whore. That's right, that's all she is, a slut and a whore!' The words felt acrid on her tongue.

Ben hit her again, throwing her to the bed.

The children's loud cries drowned their mother's screams. The four girls came running to the door of their parents' bedroom, too afraid to enter. Esther was jumping up and down, wringing her hands and screaming, non-stop. Aslin held the baby out to Nanda and grabbed hold of Esther.

Mary was carrying Michael in her arms, hushing his mournful wailing.

Ben shouted at them all to go back to their room.

They fled.

Anita got up from her bed and looked at her husband with contempt. She pushed past him to the second bedroom where the servants were trying to calm six terrified children.

They rushed around their mother, sobbing wildly. Anita hugged them and stroked their heads, consoling them with kisses till they quietened down.

They were all on Emma's bed, except the baby. Aslin had May in her arms, lulling her back to sleep.

'Why is Daddy so angry, Mummy?' asked Esther, twisting her hands nervously.

'Sshhh darling, it's all right. I'm here now, it's all right.'

'Did he hit you?' asked Emma, anxiously. 'Is it hurting?'

Rina clutched her mother's arm and leaned against her trembling body.

Anita pulled two of the beds together and turned out the lights. She lay down beside her children, coaxing them to sleep.

After some time they heard the sound of furniture being dragged about in the living room.

Three heads lifted off the pillows. Anita reached out to reassure Emma, Rina and Esther.

Mary peeked through the doorway curtain and whispered that Ben had moved the spare bed out of the front bedroom. He was placing it behind the dining table, she said, alongside a wall.

They heard Ben call out roughly to his sister, 'Irene, come over here and gimme a hand.'

Ben brought out his dresser, his clothes, and his writing desk and set up a little room behind the dining table. And Irene pulled a panelled, folding screen across the floor to separate Ben's quarters from the dining area. After re-arranging the furniture they sat around the table.

Encouraged by his sister, Ben insulted his wife out loud as he continued to drink.

As she listened to them, Anita's heart filled with dread. She knew her sister-in-law's wickedness would be triumphant now under this reign of evil that had entered her home.

The next morning Ben left for work, quietly and early, before anyone in the household had woken up.

Anita came out of her room to find Aslin hovering around. 'Missie, Hahminay wants to talk to you,' whispered the servant. 'She's asked if you could come over.'

Hahminay was Mrs Vidhana, an old widow who lived next door. Everyone called her *Hahminay* — a Sinhalese title of respect.

Anita had just finished nursing her baby. She handed the infant over to Aslin and hurried next door.

Hahminay's creased and faded eyes filled with sadness, as Anita embraced her, and greeted her in Sinhalese. Hahminay didn't speak any English. She held Anita's face, observing the split lip, the bruises and the swollen black eye. 'Anita *duwa*,' she said, addressing Anita as daughter, as she always did. 'This grey head is hurting and these old eyes can't believe what's happening to Ben. We've been watching your house for some time now. Ebert couldn't tell you the night you ran down Clifford Place, but Mabel and Shanthi saw everything … they'd been looking through the fence. They came rushing into the house, shouting to their brother, "Ebert Aiya! Quick … quick … run! Mrs Roberts has taken off down the street with the baby." Hahminay's lips quivered, and her aged voice was hoarse. 'With that infant in your arms, what were you trying to do, *duwa*?'

Mabel and Shanthi Vidhana joined their mother in attempts to comfort their distraught neighbour. After much effort, Anita composed herself sufficiently to listen to what the two young women had to say.

Mabel and Shanthi were in their mid-twenties. Ebert, their older brother, was around thirty. Mabel was a schoolteacher and Shanthi worked as a salesgirl in a bookshop. Hahminay's children spoke English fluently.

Anita learned that Mabel and Shanthi, and their mother, had grown suspicious of Lydia some months before. They found her frequent visits to Anita's home disturbing, and the girls began snooping at the fence sometimes when Lydia came around.

CHAPTER SEVEN

Between their two houses there was a thatched fence of cadjun (dried, woven coconut palms), while a row of shrubs separated their front gardens. A flourishing antignon vine had draped itself along the cadjun fence forming an effective screen, but Mabel and Shanthi had poked holes in the thatching to see what was going on in Anita's home when Lydia was there.

The girls told Anita that when Lydia and Ben sat with decorum at the dinner table, while Anita was bustling about serving the food, Lydia would stretch out a bare foot and slide it over Ben's feet, with sinuous motions. And sometimes, even while Anita was seated at the table Lydia would place a hand on Ben's thigh, 'and there have been worse improprieties,' said Mabel, blushing.

Anita was astounded to hear of her friend's impudence.

The girls recalled an incident when Lydia appeared to be feeling hot one evening and had pulled down the top half of her sari, exhibiting the little cropped sari jacket she wore. It gaped in the middle. She had only fastened the body-hugging blouse at the top and bottom, wantonly revealing breasts barely concealed in a brassiere. Ben had sat on a stool beside her, fanning her attentively. 'That was on a Saturday evening, Mrs Roberts,' said Shanthi, 'when you had had gone down to the beach with the servants and the children, including a couple of Lydia's kids.'

'I remember the day,' Anita recalled. 'We were ready to leave, when Lydia suddenly said she wasn't feeling well, and stayed back. And Ben said he'd keep her company.'

Anita recounted all that had transpired in her home since the birth of her baby, including Mavis's shocking disclosure at the beach.

'*Duwa*, please listen to me,' urged Hahminay, 'I'm convinced that Lydia has done a charm to lure Ben. There's no doubt of it in my mind. We've got to consult a good medium first and then arrange to have it broken.'

It was a widely held belief among rural folk that unexplainable misfortunes were the result of malevolent charms. However, in the 1950s, such beliefs existed even under the veneer of the more urbanised populations. But in the westernised and Christian circles Anita moved no one knew much about charms. She was now anxious to find out.

Mabel and Shanthi went off to the kitchen to make a pot of tea while Hahminay began to educate Anita about charms.

'People use different methods to do charms, *duwa*,' Hahminay started. 'Sometimes they use human ash. Sorcerers charm the ash and get it thrown on the roof of a house. They're the worst kind! The ash gets embedded in the tiles and even if the rains wash it off, it still remains in the soil doing its deadly work. You can never retrieve it.'

'Why would you want to retrieve the ash?' asked Anita, puzzled.

'Let me explain ... you've seen amulets, haven't you?'

'Yes, of course. I've seen lots of folk wearing them around the neck or round an arm.'

'The amulet or talisman is only a container,' explained Hahminay. 'And most of the talismans you see people wearing are benevolent. They contain scrolls with protective inscriptions to ward off evil and bring prosperity or healing to the wearer. But in the case of malevolent charms, the scroll is inscribed with a hex, which has first been ritually uttered by a sorcerer over and over again — sometimes even up to ten thousand times to reinforce the effectiveness of the hex. The scroll is then rolled up and placed inside the amulet.'

'Now to break a charm, the amulet needs to be retrieved and the scroll inside it recovered. Whoever is going to revoke the charm needs to know what kind of hex was written down so that it can be effectively countered. After that the scroll is destroyed ... Only then can the charm be broken.'

'But with human ash, once it is hexed and thrown on the roof of a house you can never recover it ... that's why they are the deadliest of charms,' said Hahminay.

She continued, after a pause. 'It's becoming a common practice now for people to throw dirty dishwater and kitchen waste onto a funeral pyre after a body has been cremated, to prevent sorcerers from stealing human ash. Once the ash gets polluted they won't use it, you see.'

This was incredibly astonishing information for Anita to grasp. She could hardly believe what she was hearing. While she was trying to understand it all, the girls brought in some refreshments.

Sipping a cup of tea, Anita told her neighbours of the incident with Jaya's toffee and Lydia's surprise visit to Irene just before May was born. Though Lydia had made out to Anita that she had visited Irene to talk of herbal remedies that was now highly questionable.

Hahminay and her daughters speculated on what type of charms Lydia might have done.

CHAPTER SEVEN

'*Duwa*, as soon as you go home, do a thorough search and see if you can find any amulets,' said Hahminay. 'Usually they're buried under the ashes of the kitchen hearth. And also dig around the fence posts at the four corners of the garden. That's another place where charms are buried ... I'm sure you'll find at least one. Bring it to me and we'll visit this medium I know.'

When Anita got back to her house it was mid-morning. Her older children had gone to school, May was asleep in her cot and young Nanda was playing with Michael.

Despite her lack of appetite and the heaviness in her heart, persuaded by Aslin, Anita sat at the table and forced down a bit of breakfast. She ate slowly, gathering her thoughts.

She was now sufficiently convinced that Ben was under the influence of a deadly charm. There seemed no other explanation for the drastic change in her husband's behaviour.

Anita knew she would have to confide in her servants. She needed allies. After breakfast she summoned Aslin and Mary and they retreated into the front room.

The servants sat on the floor, Anita perched on her bed, and in hushed tones she told them of the discussions she had had with her neighbours, and what was going on between Ben and Lydia. 'We have to find these charms,' she concluded, feverishly.

The servants were already devastated over the events of the night before. They were now horrified. Mary offered to examine the kitchen hearth, and Aslin said she'd get her son Danny to dig up the four corners of the garden.

The servants dispersed and embarked on their hunt.

They found four brass amulets. Two were hidden in the fireplace, buried under the hardened ashes of the cooking hearth. One was in a corner of the backyard near a clump of banana trees, and the last one was discovered in a shallow hole at the fence post next to the gate.

Anita tied the amulets in a piece of cloth and took them to Hahminay.

The next day the two women visited the medium.

Anita felt uneasy. Never in her life had she done anything like this. But the horror of what was happening to her marriage, and the urging of her servants and neighbours to get the charms broken as quickly as possible, drove her to act speedily.

The medium was an agreeable woman in her mid-fifties.

Anita listened as Hahminay conversed with her in Sinhalese, saying they wanted to find out whether any charms had been planted in Anita's home, and if so, by whom. She didn't reveal that they had retrieved the amulets.

The seer brought out a small lamp and lit it. She closed her eyes, held Anita's hands over the flickering flame and made some invocations.

Soon she was describing a woman — her features and her appearance. Anita was stunned! Clearly, the clairvoyant was seeing a vision of Lydia. 'I see this woman going to a certain house. This is your house, lady,' the medium said to Anita. She went on to describe it. 'It's close to the ocean and it has a high front façade. I see a nice garden with a swing tied to a mango tree. But this woman doesn't reside there, she's only a visitor. I see her burying an amulet in the left corner of the backyard and one in the front garden near the gate. This is happening on a stormy day … I can see dark clouds.'

Anita looked at Hahminay and raised her eyebrows.

The medium paused for a while, uttered more invocations and continued. 'I see an older woman now — she is a part of your household.' A good description of Irene followed. 'It's late at night and I see her in the kitchen. She's digging up two of the fireplaces in the cooking hearth and placing an amulet under the ashes of each.'

Hahminay brought out the four talismans. She showed them to the medium and told her about Lydia and Ben.

The woman murmured her sympathies and was eager to help. 'Lady, I know of a famous Buddhist priest at the Galkade Temple,' she said, addressing Anita. 'He's the chief priest there, and I am confident he can break these charms. Please go to him as soon as you can.'

Anita got home in a daze. Caught up in a tide of conflicting emotions, she thought of what she had done and what she was about to do. She knew her parents would have been appalled. They would never have allowed her to delve into the supernatural realm. But panic and fear gripped Anita now. She was desperate to save her marriage and break the power of the charms. And only Hahminay and her servants knew how that could be done and they urged her to do it without delay.

CHAPTER SEVEN

The following morning Anita took Aslin with her and headed for the Galkade Temple.

It was a hot and humid day, and the small single-decker bus was overcrowded. The two women sat in silence, while Anita's mind continued its journey of confusion and foreboding, mixed with hope. Her children, her marriage, her home, her husband, and her very existence were all in the balance. She couldn't believe such a day had come upon her.

On arriving at the Galkade temple, Anita and Aslin hurried into the residential quarters and asked to see the Chief Hamudhuru. Buddhist priests were addressed as *Hamudhuru* — a title of honour.

An official led them to a waiting room.

When the priest arrived Aslin spoke to him fluently in Sinhalese, explaining the purpose of their visit. She told him about Lydia and the charms and what the medium had said.

The priest turned to Anita. 'Lady, tell me what has happened to your marriage.'

He listened empathetically as Anita told him of the tragedy that had befallen her once happy home, and of the dreadful change that had come over Ben. She gave him the four amulets.

The priest laid them out on the table and carefully opened the brass cylinders. He extracted the rolled copperleaf scrolls and using a magnifying glass read the inscriptions in complete silence. After he had scrutinized them several times he put them down on the table and addressed Anita. 'As long as this woman is not wearing a talisman on her body I can break these charms, lady. But it will cost you four hundred rupees.'

'I don't know whether she's wearing one or not, Hamudhuru, but I want these charms broken. I've brought some money with me now, it's only three hundred, but tomorrow …'

'I've got the rest,' interrupted Aslin.

Anita looked gratefully at her servant.

The priest rose to his feet. 'Let's do it now.'

CHAPTER EIGHT

1955 – 1957

Three weeks went by without a quarrel in the Roberts' home and Anita grew more hopeful by the day.

This time it was a good report Mavis brought her. Ben had stopped visiting Lydia.

Bolstered by the news Anita moved her husband's bed back into her room and he raised no objections.

The charms had been broken!

Wally Fernando proved a formidable ally. He knew the whole story now. And when Lydia had rung Ben's office he refused to let her talk to him. With uncharacteristic fury, Wally had launched into a tirade, demanding that she leave Ben alone. 'You should think of your young daughters and put an end to this shameless behaviour, woman. Stop trying to destroy Ben's marriage,' he had shouted at her.

Lydia was spitting mad. 'You'll pay for this,' was her parting promise to Wally.

'Dear Fred and Ethel,' penned Anita one morning, two weeks before Christmas. She was seated at the table, writing to Ben's eldest brother. 'You'll be glad to hear that things have improved enormously over the last few weeks, and I'm sure it would do Ben a world of good if you all joined us for lunch on Christmas Day.'

Fred's reply came speedily. 'Anita my dear, we're thrilled to hear the good news. Shall certainly be there. Charmaine is over the moon that she'll be spending Christmas with the girls. She's missed her cousins.' Fred and his wife had four sons. Charmaine was their only daughter.

CHAPTER EIGHT

It was a bit like old times at the Roberts home on Christmas day. Ben played the harmonica and the girls and their uncle Fred took turns playing the piano. They sang carols and other rousing favourites, with Ben's rich baritone voice poignantly rendering the old familiar songs. Once again it was a happy home.

The new year of 1956 began with the renewal of hope and joy for Anita and her children. There was fun and laughter in the house again, and Anita and her servants turned out their fabulous Sunday lunches. Friends and relatives gladly resumed their weekend visits, enjoying being around the entertaining and hospitable family where singing and music was the order of the day.

Six months later disaster struck like a vicious monsoon storm.

Ben quarrelled fiercely with Anita. Again he moved his bed out of their room, drank heavily and verbally abused her. Now he demanded a written account of the housekeeping money he gave her, and questioned her relentlessly about expenses — every single cent of it.

Mavis Van Buren brought Anita the dreaded news. Ben was visiting Lydia almost daily, and Stanley had left his wife.

On Anita's pleading, the parish priest visited again.

Ben insulted him shamefully. 'If you don't leave this house right now, I'll wrap your robe around your neck and send you naked down the street,' he threatened the priest.

Father Cyril urged Anita to keep praying. She did, despairingly. She made novenas and vows in all the notable churches, well known for miracles: All Saints, St Anthony's, St Jude's. Even her bedroom had become a shrine, with candles, altar lamps and holy pictures. Every night she stormed heaven's gates for mercy.

But Anita didn't mention to the priest or to anyone else that Ben was forcing her to drink a bitter concoction, seeking to destroy the new life she was now carrying in her womb. That was her dark and painful secret.

Hahminay kept urging Anita to consult the clairvoyant again. After days of agonising indecision, Anita agreed.

The medium commenced her rituals. Within a few moments of her invocations she shook her head in dismay. 'This is going to be very difficult for you, lady. That woman is now wearing an amulet. You won't be able to break this charm!'

But before Lydia had done that, the medium said someone had placed a hexed twine under the front door rug of Anita's home. 'I see this man approaching your house. He's selling clay pots and I see him embedding a yellow twine into the underside of the rug, but I see a woman giving him money to do this.

Anita had no recollection of the incident. She figured it must have happened on a day when she was out. 'I'll check it with my servants,' she said, staggered at what she was hearing.

That was the first charm Lydia had done to lure Ben back, said the medium. The second was the deadly snare. 'With the amulet this woman is now wearing around her waist, your husband has been totally enslaved.'

Like a python was how the seer described the potency of the charm that had swallowed up Ben.

Anita returned home in a state of emotional exhaustion.

The first thing she did was question her head servant about the pot seller.

'Yes, Missie,' said Aslin, nodding her head vigorously as she recalled the incident. 'He lingered for a while at the door, pestering me to buy pots. And I kept telling him we didn't need any, and that in any case the lady of the house was away.'

'Aslin, what is it with the twine under the rug? And why are these charms only affecting *Mahaththaya*?' Anita wanted to know.

Aslin explained. 'Missie, when a charm is being done, only the name of the person or persons being charmed are written on the scroll and pronounced when the hex is uttered. So the charm only affects those people. That is why, Missie, in our rural culture, we have two names. One is a proper inherited name, which we keep very private, and then we have our common names. My common name is Aslin, but not a soul outside my family knows my real name. So for instance if someone does a charm against me using the name of Aslin, it won't work.'

'And placing a hexed twine under the front door rug is a well-known method of doing simple charms. Every time the person being charmed crosses the threshold of the house, the charm takes effect. But it's a very ordinary charm, and people usually detect the twine and discard it. But if that pot-seller embedded it deep into the underside

CHAPTER EIGHT

of the rug, our Nanda would never have noticed it when she swept the floors.'

Anita walked over to the thick coir rug. Aslin followed her as she took it out of the house, where Irene wouldn't see them. Their intense scrutiny revealed a soiled, yellow twine pushed deep into the stands of fibre. Anita extricated the twine and burned it.

Ben repelled every attempt by relatives and friends to bring reconciliation between him and Anita. And his open hostility ensured their reluctance to visit.

Anita felt isolated. Even her old friend Florrie Adams had left Merinda. Due to illness and her advancing age Florrie was now living with her only son in the hill-country. But Anita had one ready ally — her neighbour, Hahminay. She advised and consoled, becoming Anita's trusted confidante. When Ben's daily arguing and haggling over expenses wore her down, Anita moaned about it to the old lady. 'He has never done this before, Hahminay. I'm convinced Lydia is behind it.'

'Of course she is, *duwa*. That *veysi* (prostitute) knows you spent money to get the earlier charms broken, and the bitch is rightly guessing you'll do so again,' said Hahminay, angrily. 'If Ben wants an account of every cent he gives you, you're not going to be able to siphon off money to revoke charms!'

Ben and Anita's quarrels over money intensified until the day Ben handed over the running of his home to his sister, Irene, leaving his wife penniless.

Anita's survival instincts overrode her despair.

Despite being in the fourth month of her pregnancy she was able to get herself a job as a stenographer. And she went out to work blessing her dead mother for having had her trained as a secretary when she left school.

In the fifth month of her pregnancy, when she felt the baby kick in her womb, Anita resolutely refused to drink the concoctions Ben forced upon her in his attempts to get rid of their unborn child.

Meanwhile Lydia's evil manoeuvres worsened, undoubtedly inflamed by Anita's pregnancy. She sent an open and obscene postcard to Ben's office, purported to have been written by Anita. *You bastard, you crawled on me like a drunken cockroach and made me pregnant for the seventh time,* was the opening slur on the card, which contained other lurid obscenities. It was signed, *Your longsuffering wife, Anita.*

In the 1950s in Ceylon, a "poison-pen" letter on an open postcard was one of the most degrading things a person could do to denigrate someone. It demoralised the recipient, and more so in this instance as it appeared to have come from Ben's wife. And of course all the staff at Harringtons would have read the open postcard, and the contents would have been discussed. This was customary.

The day he received the postcard, Ben was murderously furious with Anita when he got home from work. He flung the card at her in a screaming rage, accusing her of having disgraced him at Harringtons.

The servants gathered the frightened children into the second room, as Anita grabbed the postcard off the floor and fled to her room.

She was horrified to read the malicious slander. But she didn't take the accusation quietly.

'You're blind, Ben,' she shouted from behind the locked doors of her bedroom. 'You know I'd never write such filth, and you can't see the truth. I've been pregnant nine times, not seven. I lost two babies — our eldest daughter and our first son,' she sobbed. 'I didn't write that postcard. Can't you see that it couldn't be me? It's that bitch Lydia.' Anita became incoherent. 'I would have written nine, not seven … nine not seven,' she repeated, sinking to the floor in her room, as despair like a prairie fire threatened to engulf her again.

Over the next few weeks Lydia's evil intensified.

You'll pay for this, she had threatened Wally Fernando when he had refused to let her talk to Ben on the telephone, at the time the earlier charms had been broken. She now kept that threat. She boldly visited Wally's house while he was at work and managed to convince his wife Iris that Anita was having an affair with her husband.

The day Iris visited Anita and accused her of having an affair with Wally, Anita felt she was going mad.

Lydia planted the lie in Ben's head too and he added the accusation of slut and whore to the other verbal abuses he daily hurled at his wife.

The unfolding drama heightened as Ben walked out on his job.

Wally informed Anita that Herb Johnson had made a special trip to Colombo from London, when he heard of what was happening to

CHAPTER EIGHT

Ben. Of course Herb was totally unaware of charms and hexes. He simply thought it was the matter of a married man having an affair with another woman.

'My personal life is none of your business, Herb,' Ben stridently informed his boss, when Herb confronted him.

'My dear Ben, it becomes my business when you spend company time, for which you are being paid, on gadding about and seeing a woman who we all know is not your wife,' was Herb's acid reply.

Ben promptly resigned. And within a week he set about dismissing the servants. Aslin, Danny, Mary and Nanda who had been with the family for nearly ten years were all given notice and informed that their master couldn't afford to keep them any longer.

Anita's heart was heavy with the loss she was about to face.

'It's just a ploy, Hahminay,' she cried to her neighbour. 'Ben has plenty of savings, plus the money he gets from two houses we've rented out. And besides that he gets a good monthly income from the bookkeeping and income tax work he does for a number of wealthy clients. But I know what he's doing. He's taking this opportunity to get rid of the support I have in the house.'

Anita's home was enveloped with grief the day the servants departed. Nanda was crying as she embraced Anita. Aslin was trying to pacify Esther. Mary was sitting on the floor in the children's bedroom, holding her face in her hands; her tears sliding through her fingers as Emma and Rina sat beside her, sobbing. Only Irene remained in her cubicle, unmoved.

As the servants filed out of the house, the children cried and clung to them all the way to the gate, begging them to stay.

Anita was right. It was a ruse. Within twenty-four hours, Ben hired a day servant to do the cooking.

'I don't want you taking any instructions from that woman in the front room,' he told the servant, referring to Anita. 'She's only here to look after the children.'

The new servant's duties were to cook and clean the kitchen. She did nothing else. And she went home in the evenings.

Undeterred, Anita hired another woman, Alice, to take care of her two youngest children so that she could still go out to work. May was only a year old and Michael had just turned three. Alice was also a day servant.

Anita's tenacious spirit wouldn't give up on her husband or the hope of saving her marriage. She spoke to the nuns at St Lucia's, pleading with them to do something, perhaps reason with Lydia, whose two daughters still studied at the convent.

Mother De Sales, the school principal, wrote a letter to Lydia, summoning her to the convent. When she arrived, the nun despatched one of the servants to the parish church to fetch Father Cyril.

The nun and priest sat in the school parlour and spoke quite sternly to Lydia. They demanded that she put a stop to her harrowing evil of trying to break up Anita's marriage, and they asked her to end her liaison with Ben. Lydia was openly defiant. She said she would be removing her daughters from the school and that she had no interest in going to church anymore, and finally, she told the priest and nun that she would never give up her relationship with Ben Roberts.

'I've never seen anything like it,' said Mother De Sales to a bitterly disappointed Anita, who visited the convent a few days later to hear the outcome of the meeting.

'I've reached the conclusion that Lydia Wilmet is an utterly amoral woman,' said the English nun to Anita. 'She has no fear of God left in her, Anita. And she has lost all sense of decency and charity.'

The school principal was deeply affected by Anita's seemingly hopeless struggle to reclaim her marriage. 'It's a tragedy ... a tragedy,' she whispered, her eyes glistening. 'And you with your next baby on the way. May the Lord give you strength.'

Anita was in the seventh month of her pregnancy when the cook Ben had hired, left. He refused to hire another servant and the pressure on Anita to stay home and manage her household intensified.

'I'll never give up my job, Hahminay,' Anita told her neighbour. 'I am not going to be reduced to a penniless slave in my own home.'

Anita still had Alice, who looked after Michael and May and cleaned the house. The kindly old servant agreed to do the cooking for a small increase in her wages.

Anita now trained her two eldest daughters to do some housework, such as sweeping the floors and tidying up the house every day. Emma and Rina took their tasks seriously. Anita had some light relief when they showed her a timetable they had drawn up, which included such

CHAPTER EIGHT

chores as polishing the brass and silver, sweeping the floors and tidying the rooms, plus an ample period allocated for playing hopscotch!

After the birth of her baby in March 1957, Anita stayed home for a few weeks before engaging the services of a young woman named Roslyn to care for her infant, so she could return to work

Anita's baby daughter was born with cyanotic heart disease. Referred to as a "blue baby," Cecily Anne Roberts was ill from the first week of her birth.

Her death at five months was shattering to her mother.

On the day of the infant's funeral a number of mourners called in at the house to pay their respects, and Cecily's burial at the Mount Lavinia cemetery was attended by a large gathering of relatives and friends.

As the priest read the order of service, Anita looked around for her husband. Ben stood a good distance from his wife, mingled in among the crowd. His sister Irene, dressed in black, was holding onto his arm, with a feigned look of sadness on her face. Anita was incensed at the woman's hypocrisy. She stared at her sister-in-law, who furtively glanced in her direction once or twice.

Anita recalled the drunken insults of her husband, aided and abetted by his sister. The two of them would taunt Anita with mocking laughter. 'The bitch has given birth to a mongrel,' they would say, referring to Cecily, who was also stricken with Down's syndrome.

Anita had to explain to her questioning older daughters that people commonly called such children "Mongols." And the hard-hearted callousness Irene displayed at the time of Cecily's death was heinous. The servants had asked her for two fifty-cent coins to weigh down the infant's eyelids. Little Cecily had been so weak her eyes hadn't closed at death.

The whole household knew Irene hoarded money. She had a large box filled with coins in her cupboard, but she refused to part with two fifty-cent pieces for Cecily.

Anita came out of her reverie as the nuns drew close. They encircled her, and she wondered why.

The gravesite sloped upwards and Father Cyril was standing on the crest of the hill. Anita noticed the deacon, a family friend, whisper to the priest.

Father Cyril stopped the service. He raised his head and looked steadily at something or someone.

Anita turned to look in the direction of his gaze and her heart lurched violently. Lydia was standing at the back of the crowd. Their eyes met, briefly. *It's like looking into the eyes of a cobra* thought Anita, ravaged by the woman's impropriety in turning up at Cecily's funeral.

Mother De Sales put an arm around Anita and firmly held her trembling body.

Father Cyril continued staring at Lydia until she walked away, to the sound of an angry murmur from the crowd of mourners. Only when she was out of sight did the priest continue with the burial service, under skies that were darkening by the minute. Storm clouds were gathering in from the nearby ocean.

The threatening squall had petered out to a steady drizzle by the time a few mourners returned to the Roberts home to stay around the family, as was the custom.

Anita looked around at the small group gathered in her living room. Her children, the old servants who had come to visit and a few relatives were sitting around in an atmosphere heavy with grief. Rina was missing.

Anita went in search of her and found her outside, sitting alone on the garden seat.

Oblivious that she was drenched to the skin, Rina's face was dripping wet as she stared up into the dark and stormy night sky.

'What are you doing out here in the pouring rain, child?' Anita gently chided, touching her daughter's cold and rain-drenched face.

'I'm trying to find a shooting star, Mummy.'

'You won't see any tonight, darling, not in this weather. Come inside now.'

Anita embraced Rina and led her into the house.

CHAPTER NINE

1958 – August

A year had past since Cecily's death and Anita's "Troubles" continued, with no respite.

She was grieved over the loss of privileges forced upon her children. Emma's dancing and drama classes were halted. Rina's music lessons had ceased. The private tutors who instructed her three older girls in maths and Sinhalese were dismissed, and all the other extra-curricular activities the Roberts children had once enjoyed, for which their father had paid so willingly, had now been cancelled.

To Anita it was war, and she was the only soldier staunchly defending her bastion. She held the ground admirably, despite the overwhelming odds pitched against her.

To the outside world she had to pretend that everything was fine. Such were the prevailing protocols of society at the time. Only her neighbours, and a few close friends and relatives knew of the horrors that had descended upon Anita and her children in the hidden precinct of their home

Anita recognized Mimi Rizad from a distance as she walked towards the bus stop one evening at the end of her working day. When Anita was in her early twenties she had tutored English to a few girls from non-English speaking backgrounds, and Mimi had been one of her students. Anita had often met up with Mimi over the years.

The Rizad family belonged to a small minority group in Ceylon known as Parsees, whose origins were in Persia. Parsee men were mostly shop owners and affluent merchants.

After they had greeted each other, Mimi caught Anita by surprise. 'When did you start wearing saris, Miss Anita? I saw you coming out of the Pindula Temple with your husband the other day.'

Clearly, it was a case of mistaken identity. Mimi was nearsighted and wore large, thick-rimmed glasses.

Recovering from the shock, Anita said, 'A friend of mine gave me a couple of saris, dear, and I wear them occasionally.' The Burghers, for the most part, wore western clothes.

Mimi knew Benjamin Roberts well. Her father was the owner of a large textile shop in Colombo, and Ben did his bookkeeping and income tax returns. 'I didn't see you very clearly as your back was towards me,' said Mimi, 'but Mr Roberts turned around and I recognised him. So what were you doing at the temple?' she asked with curiosity, knowing Anita was a practising Catholic.

'Actually we were taking a shortcut, dear,' said Anita, unfazed by her duplicity. 'We were visiting a friend who lives behind the temple.' Her words felt like nettles in her throat. She wanted to scream, *that was my husband with his rotten whore*, but instead, asked smoothly, 'Was that when we were there last month?'

'No, Miss Anita, it was last week.'

The two women chatted for a few minutes before parting company, with Mimi saying she was on her way to her father's shop.

Anita waited for the weekend, and on the Saturday afternoon she took thirteen-year old Emma with her on a little investigative journey.

On reaching the well-known Pindula Temple, she asked to see the Chief Buddhist Priest and was politely shown into one of the sitting rooms in the priests' quarters.

It took a while before the old priest appeared, garbed in the usual saffron coloured robe. He was a plump and bald-headed man with a kindly face. He didn't appear to be in any hurry.

Anita stood up as he entered the room. The priest offered her the traditional greeting ... hands clasped together and a bowing of the head. Anita greeted him in similar fashion.

Lowering himself into a chair, the priest asked, 'What can I do for you, lady?'

'Hamudhuru, I came to enquire whether you make any medicines here, and what other services you provide in the temple,' she told him.

CHAPTER NINE

The chain and cross around Anita's neck clearly revealed she wasn't a Buddhist.

'We do all sorts of things here, lady,' said the priest. 'Besides the usual *pirith* ceremonies and *poojahs*, (invocations and offerings), I chart horoscopes, and some of our priests who have studied Ayurvedha make some fine herbal remedies.'

He continued talking of the temple and what they did for the neighbourhood, but kept looking at Emma from time to time, which disconcerted Anita. After several glances at Emma, the priest asked, 'Lady, is this your child?'

'Yes, she is,' said Anita, taken aback by the strange question.

'Is she your own birth child? I mean ... she's not adopted?' His forehead creased in a frown.

Anita was astonished. 'No, she's certainly not adopted, she's my very own. Why do you ask?'

The priest shook his head as if to clear away a thought. 'I'm sorry if I upset you, lady, but there's a man who comes here with his wife — a Mr Roberts. He's a tall handsome man. And this is an amazing coincidence, but your daughter's face bears a striking resemblance to him.'

Anita's lips quivered.

'What's the matter?' asked the priest, moving forward in his chair.

'Hamudhuru, that man is my husband and this is his eldest daughter. I am Mrs Roberts,' said Anita.

'That's not possible,' declared the priest, drawing back in his chair. 'I've known his wife for well over two years now. She's married to this man and they have five children. Surely he can't be married to the two of you!'

'That man is my husband, Hamudhuru,' insisted Anita.

The priest stood up, ending the meeting. 'Lady, you'll have to prove to me what you've just said. Please bring me some evidence that this man is your husband, then we'll talk further.'

Anita was desperate not to alienate the priest. She had to think fast.

'Hamudhuru, I'll return with my wedding photograph, and I'll bring my husband's friend who was the best man at our wedding,' she told him, earnestly. 'You'll see both him and my husband in the photograph.'

'You do that,' said the priest. 'I can't comprehend what you're telling me.'

'Can I come on Monday?' Anita asked, doggedly.

'Yes, yes ... come at three pm. We have to sort this out.' Shaking his head, the priest left the room.

Anita heard him muttering laments as he disappeared down the outer verandahs of the temple residence.

'What's happened, Mummy?' asked Emma. They were walking to the bus stop.

'Don't worry, darling, I'll explain it to you later ... Mummy's trying to find out what's causing the "Troubles" at home.'

Anita always referred to what was happening in her marriage, as the "Troubles." She frequently reminded her children, 'You must never forget that your daddy was a wonderful man before the "Troubles" began.'

The first thing Anita did on the Monday morning was telephone Joe Page. He and Ben had been old school mates at Wesley College in Colombo.

'Joe, this is Anita.'

'Hello, my dear. Are things any better?'

'No, not at all Joe, in fact they're getting worse. But I need a big favour from you.'

'Go ahead, ask.'

'I want you to meet me at the Pindula Temple this afternoon. I've made an appointment to see the Chief Buddhist Priest at three o'clock and I want you to be there.'

'Buddhist priests and temples? What's going on, Anita?'

'I can't tell you now, Joe. But you must come to the temple.'

'Okay,' said Joe. 'I'm mystified.'

'You won't be after you hear what this priest has to say.'

They were seated in a small room at the Pindula Temple — Anita, Joe Page, and the priest. Anita handed her wedding photograph over to the priest. It was wrapped in brown paper.

He unwrapped it and stared at the picture. He looked up at Joe, then at Anita and stared at the picture again.

He did this several times before silently handing the framed photograph back to Anita.

The priest struck his forehead several times with the palm of his right hand. 'What have I done? What have I done?' he lamented.

'What is it you've done, Hamudhuru?' asked Joe. 'Please tell us.'

CHAPTER NINE

The priest looked agonised. 'Wait here a moment,' he said. His bare feet thudded heavily on the cement floor as he hurried away. Soon he returned with a large folio of bound pages. He spread it out on the table in front of them and turned the leaves over until he came to a particular page. Joe and Anita drew near.

The date on the page was June 1956. Hieroglyphics and words of an ancient text, as well as a picture of a man and woman were drawn on the large sheet of paper. The couple were standing together, locked in an embrace, their feet trampling seven heads.

'This lady came to see me with a sad story some two years ago,' said the priest, 'how a friend of hers (a woman with six children), was trying to take her husband from her. And she wanted us to do a charm that would make her husband hate her friend and her friend's six children.'

The priest leaned forward and pointed to the page. 'That's the meaning of their feet crushing the seven heads. And the figures of the man and woman embracing each other shows the charm bonding this woman and Mr Roberts in strong affection as husband and wife.'

Anita burst into tears.

Joe put an arm around her. 'I'm shocked, Hamudhuru. I'm in total shock. This family has been one of the loveliest I've known. My best friend Ben is the man affected by this charm. He's a fine human being, who loved his wife and adored his children. But now they've been torn apart. And from what you're telling me I understand your charm has done this.' Joe was exceedingly angry.

'Sir, I'm very upset about this myself,' said the priest, striking his chest with a closed fist. 'How could I know that this woman was not telling me the truth? She was in great distress when she came to see me, saying how much she loved her *husband,* and that he was neglecting her ... not giving her money, not feeding her children. She was in tears. And she wanted this man — this Ben Roberts who she claimed was her husband — to love her again, and to love and care for her five children. That's all in the charm and it's an extremely strong charm.'

'But can't we break it?' Anita asked, through tears.

'Lady, for us to break it you'll have to retrieve the talisman she's wearing.'

Joe looked at the priest in disbelief. 'I've heard that charms can be broken, Hamudhuru. Are you really telling me you cannot break this charm?'

87

'No sir, we cannot break this charm,' said the priest. 'The sorcerer who performed the hex did it under the patronage of Kali, the avenging Hindu deity. It is a very powerful and destructive charm.'

The priest turned to Anita. 'Lady, this woman also got the sorcerer to utter *vas kavis* (vengeful curses) against you. And she asked him to charm some human ash so that she could get it thrown on the roof of your house.'

Joe and Anita were flabbergasted. Neither of them could utter a word as the priest made his conclusions.

Addressing Anita, he said, 'Lady, the amulet this woman is wearing contains a very potent charm, bonding her to your husband. To break it we need to get the scroll out of the amulet and destroy it.' The priest closed the book. 'She's wearing it around her waist twenty-four hours a day. I asked her never to take it off, not even when she's bathing.'

'Phew,' said Joe, 'Anita, I don't know what to think and I can't think what to say. My head is reeling! I've never heard anything like this in my life.' He and Anita had left the temple and were having a cup of tea in a nearby café.

Anita was equally shattered. 'But Joe isn't it obvious that Ben is under the influence of some horrible evil? Not only is he raging with us, he's stopped going to church. And he insulted the parish priest and ordered him out of the house. We all know this isn't like Ben. He's never behaved in this fashion. I've never heard him speak rudely to anyone, not even to the servants or a beggar. The children are terrified of him.'

'You're absolutely right,' said Joe. 'This isn't the Ben we all know and love.' He couldn't hide his distress. 'What are you going to do, girl?'

'I won't give up, Joe. I'll try to break the charm, despite what this priest says. And I'll keep praying. That's all I can do. But it's the children I'm worried about — they're going through hell.'

CHAPTER TEN

... *1958*

Rina admired Emma. She was always brave. Some nights their father would shout, 'Emma! Come here!'

Dutifully, Emma would present herself in the dreaded domain — the dining room. It was now a nightly theatre of terror.

'Who do you love more, your mother or your father?' Ben would ask Emma, gruffly.

'Mummy,' she would answer.

Drunk to the point of falling over, Ben would make the same compelling demand, night after night. And Emma's unflinching response never changed, met by an angry discharge from her father: 'Get out of here.'

Emma would walk away, proud and unafraid.

Next, he would shout, 'Rina!'

And Rina trembled. In their bedroom they had a chamber pot the children used at night, rather than risk going through the house to the toilet in the back yard. Rina would run to the pot and sit on it.

'I can't come. I'm on the chamber,' she would squeak, too afraid to face her father and say she loved her mother more.

In the beginning she had tried to be diplomatic. 'I don't know,' she answered him.

The dreaded growl followed, 'Get out of here. You're a rotten bitch like your mother.'

On another occasion she judiciously replied, 'Both.' But that hadn't pleased him either.

Rina wished she could be courageous like Emma. She could never forget the day their aunt Irene had a fight with their mother. Anita, who was pregnant with Cecily at the time, was wearing a pink maternity smock, threaded at the neckline with a silk cord. Irene lurched forward and grabbed the cord, strangling Anita. The children watched in horror as their mother collapsed into a chair, yet Irene wouldn't let go of the cord. Anita was choking.

Emma raced into the kitchen and raced back with a fork. She stabbed her aunt's arm until she released the cord.

Irene retreated with a bleeding arm, and the children rushed around their shaken mother.

Rina's fear of her father was made worse by the frequent dismissals she received from him. One that cut deep was the time she had played the part of a bride doll in a junior-school concert. She was ten at the time. Her mother had sewn her a beautiful bridal dress, and after the play the roads leading away from the school were filled with concertgoers. They were admiring the little bride doll still dressed in her pretty gown, walking home with her mother and Emma.

Ben was at home when they entered the house. This was in the early days of the "Troubles."

Anita whispered to Rina, 'Go and show Daddy your costume, darling.'

Skipping with delight, Rina ran over to her father. He was lying in bed in his little room, behind the dining table.

'Daddy, look at my dress, I'm the bride doll,' she sang out.

'Switch off the bloody lights and go to sleep,' roared her father, angrily.

There was another humiliating dismissal the following year.

Four months after her baby sister, Cecily had died, Rina failed her exams and had to remain another year in sixth grade. It was a crushing blow to the eleven-year-old who usually did well at school.

With trepidation she had given her father her report book to sign.

He reprimanded her over her miserable performance and flung the book out of the house. Rina fled to the garden in tears. It was a rainy day and her report book was lying drenched in the mud.

She couldn't bear looking at her father's face anymore. There was no longer any love left in his eyes. Gone was the adoring man who used to

CHAPTER TEN

tuck her into bed at night and teach her beautiful songs. This was now a snarling stranger, with a wicked face and cruel eyes.

As time went on Ben grew more demented and violent.

Anita often walked into the house after work only to be confronted by her raging husband, spewing forth a volley of abuse. His constant threat was, 'I'll kill you, you bitch.'

At first she tried to stand her ground. Hurling abuse back at him she would retreat into the front room with her terrified children and slam the door shut. But that didn't deter Ben. He would force the door open and Anita would flee to Hahminay's house next door with the children at her heels.

The front bedroom of the Roberts home became a virtual prison for Anita and her children. The spacious room had three doors and one window. One door led into the living room. Thankfully it had a key and was now permanently locked. Anita had also placed a bed alongside the door and it couldn't be breached.

Another door connected to the large second bedroom, which was once the children's room. Now it was virtually abandoned. It only housed Ben's sister Irene and the children's wardrobes and cupboards. It was through this door that Ben came charging in at night seeking to harm his wife.

And there was a third door, painted blue, which opened out into the front garden.

If Ben sensed that Anita was in the front room he would force open the door — the one that led into the second bedroom. There was no lock on it. A small rectangular wooden block, which could be moved horizontally across the door and doorjamb, served as a fastener. And there were no strong men to ward him off, only a weary mother and her frightened children.

They tried barricading the door by placing a wardrobe against it, but that didn't stop Ben. Once the peg gave way he would push open the door, moving the wardrobe with it. And the children would flee, scattering like mice as their father entered the room breathing murderous threats. If Anita was in the room, the older girls made sure their mother was the first one out through the blue door, often running shoeless into the night. The blue door mercifully provided them with an escape route.

Usually Ben would be asleep in a drunken stupor by about ten thirty, but it was close to midnight on one particular occasion when he was still hollering threats and pacing the house. Eventually he wearied himself and fell asleep.

Anita had left her neighbour's house since they were retiring for the night, and to pass the time she walked down the street.

While she was away Emma ran next door and found the lights out. She knew Hahminay and her family had gone to bed. Emma hurried back to the front room and whispered to Rina and Esther to start praying.

Anita came back up the street and entered her front garden in the dark. Although she couldn't hear Ben's ravings, she wasn't sure if he had fallen asleep yet. Ben's sister had forgotten to turn the lights out in the main part of the house as she usually did when Ben went to bed. Anita figured he could still be awake … perhaps waiting up for her.

She hid near the fence behind a clump of palm bushes, directly opposite the blue door. The girls had left it partially open. Anita could see Esther, Rina and Emma kneeling and praying. All three of them were crying as they recited the rosary.

The girls didn't know their mother was hiding in the garden and that she could see their distress. Anita desperately wanted to reassure her daughters that she was safe. Picking up a few small pebbles she threw them towards the blue door, praying the stones would strike their target. She watched, as the girls heard the pelting and cautiously approached the door, peering out into the night.

'Emma, Rina, Esther … Mummy's here!' a voice softly called from behind the palm bushes.

The girls ran to her, whispering through their sobs that their father was asleep and that it was safe for her to come home. Anita hugged her daughters as they stealthily walked back into the front room. They had learned from bitter experience the danger of rousing Ben from his drunken sleep.

Anita had to comfort Rina. 'I was so afraid, Mummy. I thought you had jumped in front of a train and committed suicide,' sobbed the twelve year old. Her mother hugged her and stroked her head till she fell asleep.

Finally it was Emma who came up with the clever idea of setting up a signal for their mother.

CHAPTER TEN

They had several shoe-flower bushes near the gate. The hibiscus was commonly called shoe-flower in Ceylon, a reference to the crushed flowers that could be used as a shoe polish. The large shrubs were covered with a multitude of blood red, double-petalled flowers that blossomed and fell all year. Emma thought of placing the flowers on the gate as signals for Anita.

One red flower: *Mum, don't come home; go to Hahminay's house.*

Two red flowers: *Mum, he's at home but he's fallen asleep; it's safe to come home.*

Anita's three elder daughters hovered round the gate each evening, playing, but more importantly, keeping vigil.

Ben came home every evening in a taxi. As soon as the girls saw the cab slowing down, one of them would place a red flower on the gate, while the other two would shield her from being observed. Emma, Rina and Esther became experts at twisting the red flowers into the metal-trellised gate in a matter of seconds. This was their grim daily pantomime. Their father was too drunk to notice their little ritual as he stepped out of the cab and gruffly ordered them into the house.

But sometimes they got caught playing away from the gate. Ben would march the three girls indoors and command them to stay in their room.

On such nights Emma took great risks as she crept out through the blue door. To avoid detection she had to take a circuitous route, behind bushes and shrubs and around the borders of the fence, to reach the gate and place a red flower on it: *Mum, don't come home.*

When Ben fell asleep after his ranting and raving Emma would dash next-door first to check if her mother was there. If Anita hadn't arrived yet at Hahminay's, Emma would run to the gate and place a second red flower on it.

If there were no flowers on the gate and no sign of her three older girls, Anita stayed away. She knew the scene was bad.

The children were desolate the night their father smashed their beautiful spinning top. It was the top that Ben's boss had brought over from England when Michael was a baby. Little May loved seeing the red, blue and yellow top swirl around the floor like a graceful ballerina. Whenever she was distressed, her older sisters could stop her cries by distracting her with the spinning top.

In one of his rages, as he burst into the room, Ben saw the colourful top lying on the ground. He picked it up and kept hurling it to the floor.

The children fled; Emma and Rina carrying Michael and May with them. Much later when they returned, Michael cried. So did May. They all did. Their beautiful spinning top lay in pieces on the floor.

Anita treasured her "holy pictures." They hung on the wall in her bedroom. One was a portrait of the "Madonna and Child" and the other was a picture of Jesus, which had to be reframed twice.

'Don't let him get at my holy pictures,' Anita constantly reminded her daughters. The three elder girls would race around the room when the door was giving way, hiding things that could be smashed or broken.

Anita wasn't home one night when Ben burst through the door thinking she was. Emma grabbed the picture of the "Madonna and Child" and raced out through the blue door. Rina didn't have time to run. She barely managed to hide the picture of Jesus under the bed covers before she sat over it. She heard the glass crack, but didn't budge. The others had all escaped. Rina cowered on the bed as her father screamed an abusive tirade at her absent mother. He smashed everything in sight. Splinters of glass and other breakables were flying in every direction. Rina sat trembling, her head bent low and covered with her arms.

After his rage was spent, Ben left the room and Rina ran out to Hahminay's house, leaving the shattered picture under the bedclothes.

Later, they cleaned up the room, trying to keep the noise low. Emma and Anita carefully picked splinters of glass from Rina's curly hair. Anita considered it a miracle that she and her children never cut themselves on any shards of glass, china, or whatever else that lay shattered on the floor after Ben's rampaging visits.

Every evening the servant Alice would feed the three smaller children before she left. She would also serve out four plates of food for Anita and her three older girls and leave them on the dressing table in the front bedroom. But Emma, Rina and Esther were too anxious and worried to even look at food until their mother was safely in the room with them.

Sometimes the dramas in their home ensured that the girls and their mother went to bed without dinner.

In the morning the servant would remove the four plates of food, covered with ants ... or worse.

CHAPTER ELEVEN

1959

Rina stirred in bed, faintly aware of sounds from the house and sunshine flooding in through the open window. She'd always had difficulty opening her eyes from sleep. It had earned her the nickname "pasted eye" from her tomboyish, elder sister, Emma.

Bleary-eyed, she looked around the room. Their blue Bakelite radio was lying in pieces on the floor. 'Oh God,' she whispered, remembering the night before. It had been the worst episode of their father's violence to date.

The room was still in a mess. What used to be a beautiful photograph of their mother taken on her twenty-first birthday was lying in shreds on the floor. It had been swept into a corner of the room together with broken glass and other debris. The picture, dating back to 1937, had been a sepia study of a slender beauty gazing shyly into the camera, her long hair neatly braided and set in a coronet around her head.

The girls had witnessed their father hurl the picture to the floor. And they watched helplessly as their aunt Irene stooped to the ground, extricated the portrait from its shattered frame and handed it to their father. He tore it to shreds.

Recalling the terror of the previous night, Rina sat up quickly. Seeing Emma, she asked, 'Where's Mummy?'

Emma put a finger to her lips and looked at her sister, saying nothing.

Rina heard her father's voice. *He's still in the house,* she thought, fearfully. She noticed the blue door was open, so she knew her mother was at Hahminay's house. On such mornings, after really bad fights,

Anita would wake up early, slip next-door and stay there till Ben left the house. Only then would she return, get dressed and go off to work, and the children would get ready for school.

But these were the August school holidays, so the Roberts children weren't going anywhere.

Suddenly, the door leading to the second room flew open. The feeble wooden wedge securing it had split apart the night before.

'Daddy,' exclaimed Rina, jumping to her feet. She was terrified as she saw the cruel expression on her father's face.

Ben Roberts didn't utter a word as he entered the room. He didn't even glance at his daughter. His sister Irene followed him. The two of them marched over to the blue door. They closed it, bolted it, and nailed it down with metal strips.

Irene left the room.

Rina was still standing rigidly by her bed, her heart palpitating as she realised their escape door had been sealed.

Her father spoke. 'I don't want to see your mother here when I come home tonight. And you lot can go with her.'

With those heartless words, Benjamin Roberts dismissed his wife of eighteen years, and his six children, and walked briskly out of the room.

Rina turned and saw Emma. She wasn't even aware that her sister was in the room. *Surely Emma wasn't here before,* thought Rina, *she must have just come in.* That moment of rejection was so vividly etched in her young mind that throughout her life Rina had the impression she was alone in the room that morning, and that it was only she who had heard the awful words of denouncement.

Emma and Rina walked through to the living room as their father strode out of the house, cold sober and darkly grim as he always was in the mornings. As soon as he was out of sight, Emma took off like a rabbit. Rina stood at the door and watched her sister creep through the gap they had made in the shrubbery fence to gave them easy access to Hahminay's house.

Soon her mother came into view. Anita bent low under the shrubs and with a few quick strides through the garden, she entered the house.

Rina looked at her mother and marvelled. There were no tears. She suddenly noticed Esther standing beside her. Where was Esther earlier? Everything was still a blur.

CHAPTER ELEVEN

Anita hugged her three older daughters. 'Get all your clothes together and bring them to my room,' she whispered. 'And hurry!'

The girls fled to the second room and pulled out all the clothes from the wardrobes and cupboards. Bundling them in their arms, they rushed to the front room, dropping a few bits along the way in their haste. They dumped it all on their mother's bed and watched, as she spread two large sheets out on the floor.

Anita sorted out the clothes including her own, gathering some garments into two heaps on the floor and leaving the rest on her bed. It wasn't long before she tied up the sheets into two large bundles.

'They look like *dhobi* bundles, Mummy,' said Esther. *Dhobis* were paid laundry contractors who visited homes and carried away bundles of soiled clothes tied up in large sheets for washing.

'Yes, I know, darling,' said Anita distractedly as she hurried round the room. 'Get your school books and things together,' she told her daughters.

She made no attempt to hide from them the fact that she was scared. If Ben returned now she'd be trapped.

'Just leave that, just leave that, children, it won't all fit in a taxi.' Anita directed what her children could take and what they had to leave behind.

She carefully checked her mother's tortoise-shell jewellery box, making sure her children's gold chains and crosses, earrings and bangles, and her own precious pieces of jewellery were safely stored in the little compartments.

'Get the small three ready,' she whispered to Emma. Anita always referred to her younger children as her "small three." May was only four, Michael had just turned six, and Jean was seven. Her older girls, Emma, Rina and Esther were now fifteen, thirteen, and eleven, respectively.

In a little while five of the children were dressed and ready in the front room.

'Where's Jean?' Anita asked them.

Emma answered. 'Aunty Irene is talking to her.'

Ben's sister had doted on Jean since she was a toddler. And in her characteristic magnanimity, Anita had allowed Irene to almost claim the child as her own, hoping it would somehow soften the austere and quarrelsome spinster.

It hadn't.

'I'm going up to the Galle Road for a taxi, Emma. Get some crockery and cutlery together,' Anita instructed her eldest daughter. 'And don't forget May's baby chair.'

'What about Alice, Mum?' asked Emma. 'Aren't you going to wait and tell her what's happening?'

Alice, the servant, reported for work around eight o'clock in the mornings. But during the school holidays she arrived much later.

'I can't take the risk, Emma. If Daddy comes back now I'm trapped. We can't wait for Alice.'

As soon as Anita left, Emma hurried to the back of the house with Rina tagging behind her. Picking up May's baby chair, Emma put her arm through the top bar, so that the chair hung down from the crook of her elbow.

The girls jumped in fright as their Aunt Irene, who had been watching them, swooped like a hawk. She plucked the chair out of Emma's arm. 'You're not getting that,' she said, firmly. 'You're not allowed to take anything.'

Irene prevented Emma and Rina from taking a plate, a mug, a fork or a spoon. They weren't allowed to take May's baby crockery with the little pictures of Brer Rabbit on them, not even the old tin mugs of the servants! Emma bravely tried, then gave up. 'Curse you, you bitch,' she swore at her aunt.

The five intimidated children stood silently by the front door. Soon they saw their mother alighting from a black Morris Minor with the bright yellow taxi sign on top.

Emma rushed to the gate. 'We're not allowed to take anything, Mum. Aunty Irene won't let us.'

Anita clenched her fists and her dark eyes flashed with anger. She stood thinking for a moment before walking boldly through the house. She went out into the backyard and returned with a crowbar in her hand.

Her sister-in-law tried to take it from her. 'You can't have that. You can't take anything from this house.'

'Get away from me, you wretch,' said Anita, menacingly. 'This is my mother's crowbar, you're not having it.' She carried it to the boot of the car. The three older girls followed with their few belongings, which they also placed inside the boot.

CHAPTER ELEVEN

Anita and the girls returned to the house and staggered out with the two bundles of clothing.

The taxi driver came running up the path and grabbed one of the bundles. 'Is everything all right, lady?' he asked, as he took in what was happening.

'Yes, driver, everything's all right,' replied Anita automatically.

After Anita and her children finished loading up the taxi they gathered at the gate.

Irene was standing at the front door with little Jean, observing them.

'Stay here,' Anita commanded her children. 'I'm going to get Jean.'

She strode purposefully to the entrance of the house. Stretching a hand towards her daughter, Anita called out, 'Come along, Jean. Come with Mummy, darling.'

Irene clutched Jean's hand and took a step back with the child. 'Jean is staying with us,' she announced haughtily

From near the gate, Emma, Esther and Rina kept calling to their sister, urging her to come and join them, but their aunt firmly held on to Jean's hand.

Anita walked away. A fight with her sister-in-law was the last thing she wanted now. 'Let's go, children, I'll get her later.'

As they settled down in the cab, the driver asked again, 'Is everything all right, lady?'

Anita smiled at him briefly and nodded. She gave him directions for Granadene, a suburb far beyond the northern outskirts of the capital city. It was a good distance from their southern beachside home.

'We're going to Aunty Alma's house,' Anita informed her children.

There was a weighty silence in the cab as it set out on the Galle Road for its long journey to Granadene.

Alma Anderson was Ben's cousin. She had always been fond of Anita and was deeply concerned over the appalling situation in the Roberts' home. She was now shocked to see Anita and the children on her doorstep.

Anita controlled her emotions as Alma hugged her and helped bring her things into the house.

She told Alma what had happened that morning; how Ben had sealed her escape door and had given orders that his wife and children should leave their family home like beggars.

Alma shook her head in disbelief. They were sitting together in the lounge room.

'I have no home, Alma,' Anita sobbed. 'My children and I don't have a home. We have nothing!' The tears she had held back poured forth.

Alma put her arms around Anita and held her close. 'It's okay, darling, it's okay. You have a home here with us. You can stay here as long as you like. I'm sure Ben will come to his senses in a day or two. He must be mad to do this to you.'

Alma tried to console the children too. The five of them sat huddled together on the edge of a large sofa, with their bundles of clothes and few belongings at their feet. They were all crying.

Alma's own two children hovered around, awkwardly. She asked them to take little Michael and May out to the garden and play with them.

Though Alma's house was large, the only free space she had available was a small room with an army field cot in it. She showed the room to Anita.

'I'll let Rina sleep on that,' said Anita, glancing at the cot. 'The rest of us can sleep on the floor.' She explained to Alma that Rina had suffered several bouts of bronchitis and an episode of double pneumonia. 'She's always been a bit of sickly child, so I'm extra careful about her health.'

Alma went away and returned with her arms full. 'I've got a few mats and pillows here, Anita, you can have them. And there's plenty of food in the house too, so please stay in and rest today.'

It was the worst day of Anita's life. Her heart felt like stone, her mind unable to form a single, coherent thought. She cried intermittently. Her face was swollen, her eyes were red and puffy, and her nose dribbled constantly.

Later in the afternoon, together with her older daughters Anita sorted out the few things they had brought with them as she tried to organise their little room. She folded a mat, lengthwise, and placed it alongside a wall. This was their clothes cupboard. Six little piles of clothes were soon lying on the mat, in staggered heights.

How she longed for the day to be over, but the hours dragged on. Eventually, a short while after dinner everyone retired for the night.

Six of them were in the one confined space.

Anita left the door open and through the cotton curtains in the doorway a faint bit of light illuminated the room.

CHAPTER ELEVEN

The house was quiet.

Looking around her Anita could see that Michael, May and Esther were fast asleep, but she knew Emma was awake.

Her heart smote her to see her children sleeping on reed mats on the floor — that was the domain of their servants back in Merinda. Her children had once been pampered. Their father had cherished them and had given them every luxury he could afford.

Suddenly, from the camp cot above, Anita heard Rina reciting softly:

> Do you remember an Inn, Miranda?
> Do you remember an Inn?
> And the tedding and the spreading
> Of the straw for a bedding,
> And the fleas that tease in the High Pyrenees
> And the wine that tasted of tar ...

Emma joined in, and their young voices rhymed the Hilaire Belloc poem they had learned at school.

> Do you remember an Inn, Miranda?
> Do you remember an Inn?
> And the cheers and the jeers of the young muleteers
> Who hadn't got a penny,
> And who weren't paying any,
> And the hammer at the doors and the din
> And the hip hop hap
> Of the clap of the hands
> To the swirl and the twirl
> Of the girl gone chancing,
> Glancing,
> Dancing ...

The poignant recital stopped, as Emma burst into tears. Her mother moved over swiftly to embrace her as she wept. With a wrench in her heart Anita recalled how in times long ago her eldest daughter would pirouette and dance to the poem's pithy rhythm, watched by her adoring father. Ben would clap his hands and click his fingers, keeping tempo as Emma swirled with her ribboned tambourine, while Anita and Rina recited "Tarantella" with laughter in their voices. They had all loved the poem's clip-clop rhythm. Now it etched their sad plight.

Anita keenly felt the sorrow of her daughters' laments. For a long time she lay awake thinking of her gifted children. Their future had held such promise. She wondered what would happen now to all their talents and accomplishments.

Above her, Rina was crying in the camp cot. Anita rose from the floor and sat beside her sensitive, second daughter, who had turned to the wall to hide her tears. Anita gently stroked her back till she fell asleep.

Rina woke up disoriented, not knowing where she was. Then she remembered.

This wasn't home. They weren't at Merinda!

Her eyes were instantly drawn to the rays of sunshine beaming in through the small ventilation grill set high on the wall. Several feet beneath it was a closed wooden window.

In the distance she could hear the morning cry of the roosters. It reminded her of the story of St Peter's betrayal of Jesus. Her mother had often told her the story while she was growing up, and each time she'd heard it she was saddened. 'Before the rooster crows, you will deny me three times,' Jesus had prophesied to his disciple at the Last Supper. And despite Peter's passionate protests that he would never abandon his Master, he did do just that … and then went out and wept as he heard the awful reminder at daybreak. Rina recalled her mother saying she imagined St Peter having furrows on his cheeks by the time he died, from all the crying he must have done each time he heard a cock crow.

Would her Daddy ever cry over what he had done to them Rina wondered? When he looked at all their things in the house would they remind him that he had abandoned his children, denied them their privileges and driven them out of their home?

'You lot can go with her.' She could still hear the words and still see his cold, harsh face. She wondered whether he knew where they were. She was hurting badly in the deepest place of her heart, to know he'd given orders that they should leave with nothing — like beggars — without a plate or a cup … not even the servants' tin mugs! She thought of all her treasures she had to leave behind: her books, her beads, and her collection of beautiful pictures that her father had given her over the years. The years when they were happy, when he had loved them all.

CHAPTER ELEVEN

At thirteen, Rina had learned to hold back her tears and suppress her pain. She climbed out of the camp cot and walked over to the window. Unclipping the latch, she swung open the wooden shutters. Daylight flooded in. She went looking for her mother.

Anita was sitting in the large family room at the back of Alma's house. Emma, Esther, Michael, and May were gathered around her. Rina joined them in time to hear her mother say to Emma, 'I have to talk to my boss today and get a few days off work, and then I've got to figure out how we can get some money from daddy through the courts.'

Anita was dressed and ready to leave. 'I'll go up the road first and get us something to eat.'

She looked at the faces of her five children. They would never know, she thought, just how much strength she derived from having them around. They made it possible for her to push through the anguish and despair, and face this new day with courage.

After breakfast the children walked out to the street with their mother. She gave them instructions, reminding Emma and Rina that this was their first day without servants, and that the two of them were completely in charge of Michael and May.

It was dusk when Anita returned in a taxi. She had bought a small, single-burner kerosene cooker, a few tin plates and mugs, two cooking pans and some groceries. With help from her three older girls Anita quickly set up a makeshift kitchen in the additional room Alma had cleared for them. Soon they were having their first prepared dinner away from home. Anita had cooked a beef and vegetable soup, and she boiled some rice. It was a simple meal, but the rare pleasure of physically sitting around a dinner table with her children — something she hadn't done for nearly three years — felt like a special benediction for Anita.

Alma's husband, Albert, worked on a tea plantation, many miles away in the cool hill-country, but within a few days of Anita and the children's arrival he came home on leave.

Rina didn't like Albert. He drank a lot. She was afraid of men who drank. He often lunged forward from his reclining chair and tried to grab her when she walked past. He caught her by surprise the first time he got hold of her and forced her to sit on his lap. She looked desperately at her mother as she cried, 'Let me go.'

'Let her go, Albert. Please ... let her go,' Anita pleaded.

But Albert had merely laughed and held onto her, until his wife reprimanded him and ordered him to 'release the girl.'

He freed her reluctantly, but still tried to contain her as she wriggled out of his embrace.

Rina hated his alcohol-laden breath and the way his eyes would follow her. She always sought to hide from him.

The August holidays were soon over, and the Roberts children were travelling long and far to St Lucia's Convent in Merinda.

Little May was only four and under the school entry age. Back at Merinda she had been in the day care of the servant, Alice. Anita consulted the school Principal regarding her dilemma.

The nun was eager to help. 'Just sew her a little uniform, Anita, and send her to school,' said Mother De Sales. 'We'll let her join the Kindergarten class. May wouldn't need to take part in any activities unless she wants to, but at least she'll be safe here till her sisters take her home in the afternoon.'

What used to be a ten-minute walk for the Roberts children from home to school was now an hour's ride by bus. The daily bus fares burned a hole in Anita's purse. The children had to take turns staying home from school when their mother didn't have enough money for fares.

On one particular day, the lot fell on Rina and Michael.

Having discovered a small cache of books in the house Rina spent most of the morning reading. After lunch, instructing Michael not to venture outside, she headed to their small room for an afternoon nap.

Through her sleep infused unconsciousness Rina felt a weight pressing down on her body. Blearily, she opened her eyes and was instantly terrified to find Albert sitting on the edge of the camp cot leaning over her. He reeked of alcohol. His face was an inch away from hers, and his hands groped under her skirt.

She couldn't move.

He was a big man, and though she struggled and pushed with all her strength Rina couldn't break free. When in desperation she bit him on the arm, Albert was caught off-guard and fell off the edge of the narrow bed.

Rina rushed out of the room and looked for Michael. He was nowhere to be seen.

CHAPTER ELEVEN

She ran out to the street.

There was a high parapet wall at the front of the house so she felt safe and hidden from Albert's sight.

In a little while Rina timidly ventured beyond the wall and looked down the side of the garden, relieved to see Michael playing in the backyard.

'What are you doing out here on the street?' Emma asked Rina, when she got home from school with Esther and May in tow.

Knowing how feisty her elder sister was Rina was afraid to tell Emma what Albert had done. 'I just want to wait here for Mummy,' she said.

A good hour passed before she saw Anita getting off the bus.

Rina rushed over to her. Clutching her mother's arm she re-entered the house propelling Anita straight into their room.

In tears, she told her what had happened.

Anita summoned her children and asked them to stay in the room until she had prepared their dinner.

Rina questioned her brother angrily, 'Why did you go outside and play, Michael, when I asked you to stay inside the house?'

'Uncle Albert asked me to go and play out in the garden,' came the innocent reply.

In a little while Rina heard the other members of the household returning. Earlier she had wondered where her young cousins were, when they hadn't come home from school. Then she remembered! They were going to meet their mother for a bit of shopping. That explained why Albert had been so daring. No one else had been in the house.

Anita returned from the kitchen and spoke to Rina. 'I can't tell Aunty Alma what happened today, she'll be too upset, and for now we have nowhere else to go. But I've found out that Uncle Albert is going back to the estate tomorrow morning,' Anita informed her troubled daughter. 'I promise you, darling, you will never see him again. We'll be gone from here before his next trip down to Colombo.'

That night Rina saw her mother crying as she earnestly prayed that they would 'find a place and leave this house, before Albert returns from the estate.'

CHAPTER TWELVE

1959 – 1961

Anita edged her way along the narrow, crowded streets of Hultsdorf — the old Dutch legal district of Colombo. She could sense how overwhelmed her children were at the hustle and bustle around them. They practically clung to their mother as she entered the large courthouse.

Three months had passed since Anita had been driven out of her home and she hadn't received a cent from her husband. She was now suing him for maintenance.

When her case was called, Anita walked into the dock with May in her arms. Emma, Rina, Esther and Michael stood around her. At the last minute she ditched the rather ineffective solicitor who had helped file her case and decided she would speak for herself, if questioned.

With profound sorrow Anita looked at her husband, standing a few feet away. He could have been any stranger. He didn't even glance in her direction.

People of Anita's social standing were conspicuously absent from the milling crowds in the courthouse, which was probably the reason why the distinguished-looking Burgher judge looked long and hard at Anita and her children before reading the papers in front of him.

The judge turned his direction to Ben Roberts. 'Are you willing to be reconciled with your wife?'

'No, your honour.'

'May I ask why?'

'She's temperamentally unsuitable.'

CHAPTER TWELVE

The judge looked steadily at Ben. 'Did it take you eighteen years and six children to find out?' he queried, sternly.

Ben made no response.

The magistrate asked him how much he was earning. He mentioned an amount and was asked to provide evidence. His lawyer handed over some papers to the Bench.

Anita was incensed! The amount Ben said he was earning was a fraction of his wages. Whatever information his solicitor handed over to the judge had to be rigged. Despite her anger Anita didn't raise a protest. She knew enough of the law. Perjury was an indictable offence and she still loved her husband.

The judge ordered Ben to pay his wife fifty rupees for each child, every month.

Ben protested that the amount was too high, 'I have two sisters to look after, your Honour.'

Pointing to Anita, the judge said, 'That's no fault of hers. If you bring forth children into the world, you've got to maintain them.'

The court decree was finally resolved. Ben was ordered to pay thirty-five rupees as maintenance for each of his children every month till they turned eighteen. If Anita was unemployed at any time he had to pay her a monthly allowance of one hundred and fifty rupees. For the record Ben informed the magistrate that he had one child with him and she would remain in his care.

By the time Anita and her children came out of the courthouse, Ben had disappeared. There was much confusion and shouting on the hot, sunlit streets and Anita asked a small group of people what all the commotion was about. She was shocked to learn that the Prime Minister, Mr S.W.R.D. Bandaranayake, had just been shot. He later died from gunshot wounds.

It was the country's first political assassination, and the day was marked with great significance in the nation's calendar. Anita and her children were, therefore, destined never to forget the 26th day of September 1959, the day Benjamin Roberts publicly rejected his wife and children, and then deprived them of any hope of a decent living.

'Thirty-five rupees! That's pitiful,' said Alma, when she heard what had transpired at the courthouse.

'It's beyond pitiful, Alma,' said Anita, heatedly. 'A pair of decent shoes cost that much, so the month I buy Emma or Rina some shoes, I have no money to feed them.'

Nevertheless Anita confessed she was grateful for small mercies, and relieved that monthly maintenance from her husband was now legally ratified.

Anita's children soon adjusted to their new routine at Alma's house. The suburb they were living in now was very much inland, and the surrounding vegetation markedly different from the beachside terrain of their former home.

Together with their cousins they explored the rice fields at the back of Alma's house on weekends, and even after school sometimes. With great excitement they would show their mother the tadpoles they would capture in glass jars during their excursions into the watery marshes. And the small farming communities further afield fascinated them. The sight of goats, pigs, and chickens roaming about the dirt tracks was an interesting discovery. The semi-rural folk in the little villages extended their renowned hospitality to the small band of curious, city-bred children, allowing them to climb trees and pluck fruits, and roam about the land at will, while their own kids eagerly played the role of "jungle guides." Indulgently, the older folk kept an eye on them all.

Two months later, as she had promised Rina, Anita moved out of Alma's house and into a little annexe, located within a half hour's bus ride of her children's school in Merinda. Their new accommodation was merely two rooms, partitioned off from the main section of a large house. The entrance to it was through a dark and unkempt kitchen that was also a part of their little unit. It was all Anita could afford.

'Mummy, there are cockroaches here,' complained Esther, who shuddered when she saw the huge and ugly creatures that infested the kitchen, flying around at night. They terrified her.

'We'll soon have it cleaned out, darling,' consoled her mother.

A week after they had moved into their new premises Anita met up with Aslin. The following Sunday their old servant came visiting. Aslin cried aloud when she saw their abysmal living conditions. Murmuring woeful laments she walked around and looked at it all.

CHAPTER TWELVE

There was only one bed in the place. Reed mats provided further bedding. The rest of the furniture was a cheap unvarnished table and four chairs, while three rattan seats were an apology for a lounge suite. A spindly wooden plate rack stood in the kitchen bearing a few enamelled plates and mugs.

Aslin hugged the children and wept.

But soon her practical nature took over and she set about helping Anita and the three older girls clean out the filthy kitchen. They threw out swags of dried coconut husks that the owners had stowed under the hearth. It had become a breeding ground for colonies of cockroaches.

'If you can give me the money for my bus fares, Missie, I'll come here and cook for you every day,' offered Aslin. She now had another job accompanying a child to school and back in the mornings and afternoons, she said, but she was free for a few hours during the middle of the day.

Aslin did come and cook for them for a few weeks, but Anita was so hard pressed financially she couldn't afford to part with seventy cents for Aslin's bus fares on a daily basis.

Besides coping with financial hardship and their impoverished living conditions, Anita was dismayed to discover that the owner of their annexe was a sorcerer. He lived in the main section of the house with his wife and daughter.

Anita and the children would hear the man jumping up and down, getting into a trance and invoking all kinds of spirits, while conjuring up his spells and charms, morning, noon, and well into the night.

The front room of Anita's annexe adjoined a small verandah where the man's clients would be seated, and at the opposite end of the verandah was a room he used for his sorcery. The children were curious. When they got home from school they would take turns peeping through the keyhole in the front room, intrigued by what was going on next door.

But their mother was worried. Her parish priest advised her to take the children away from their occult surroundings. And so, within a few months, Anita moved again.

Once they had settled into their new home Anita took Rina with her to visit one of her former neighbours in Merinda. This was the first time she was venturing close to her old home.

With their customary friendliness, Edith de Silva, her husband Alfred, and their three daughters, greeted Anita and Rina warmly and invited them to stay for lunch. Soon Rina was out in the front yard, happily romping about with her old playmates.

Meanwhile inside the house, Anita was asking Edith if she could get one of her servants to do a little spying from their backyard to check whether Ben was at home. The servant came back from his reconnaissance and said he had seen Ben.

Anita summoned Rina. 'Darling,' she coaxed, 'we've found out that Daddy's at home. Why don't you go and ask him for the piano? You know if we have the piano, at least you can still keep practising.' Though Emma, Rina and Esther had all learned music, only Rina had continued with her lessons and exams, until her father had abruptly terminated them some two years before.

'I'm scared, Mummy,' said Rina.

'He won't harm you, child,' Anita assured her daughter. 'Just go and ask him … I'm sure he won't refuse you.'

Rina was terrified at the thought of facing her father, but driven by her love for music she walked down the street to her old home.

As she drew near the gate she felt her heart knocking against her ribs — her father was seated on a chair near the front door.

Ben Roberts observed his daughter walking up the footpath. Without a flicker of emotion on his face Rina heard him say, 'Look who's here, Irene!'

Rina was at the door. Her wicked Aunt came out from the back of the house and stood beside Ben.

'Hello, Daddy,' ventured Rina, timidly.

'Hello.' No mention of her name. No kiss, no hug, no welcome. No invitation to come in and take a seat.

Rina stood on the doorstep, afraid, and not knowing what she should do next. Noticing the large sunbeam on the floor a few feet away, the girl who loved sunbeams was drawn into the living room. Her eyes travelled up the ray of light, all the way up to the roof. She gasped. 'There's a hole in the roof,' she said, aloud.

'Sly bitch, like her mother,' snarled Irene.

Rina started. She backed away from the sunbeam and returned to the front door.

CHAPTER TWELVE

Irene's face was a grotesque mask of fury. 'Look at her, Ben ... pretending not to know that her bloody mother got the house stoned.'

Rina's heart was palpitating. 'Daddy, can I have the piano?' she asked, wanting to get it over with quickly.

'No, you can't! Get out of here. Go back to your bitch of a mother.'

Rina ran back to Mrs de Silva's house.

Anita embraced her daughter as she sobbed. 'Don't ask me to go there again, Mummy, I won't,' declared Rina passionately.

'What happened, child?' asked Edith.

Rina told them of her father's heartless dismissal, and what Irene had said about the hole in the roof.

'Oh yes,' said Edith, rolling her eyes, 'that was a bad day.'

'Why? What happened?' asked Anita, with great curiosity.

'Sundasa's men!' said Edith, dramatically.

Sundasa was the most feared gangster in Colombo. The very mention of his name terrified the local underworld. He and his parents who had always lived in Merinda had known Anita and her parents for several decades; they too had lived in Merinda. Although in social ranking they were worlds apart, Sundasa had great respect for Anita.

During the time of her "Troubles" Anita was surprised to learn that Sundasa had bought the house next door. Through the gossip of the servants from both households, Sundasa had discovered what had happened to Anita's marriage.

'Just say the word, lady, and we'll teach that bitch a lesson,' he would frequently say to Anita when he met her on the street. He wanted to get Lydia roughed up.

'I have five daughters, Sundasa,' Anita would respond philosophically. 'I can't let that happen to another woman, no matter how bad she is.'

Edith brought Anita up to date on what had transpired since Anita had left her home. 'After you and the children had gone, Lydia became a frequent visitor ... mostly on weekends. The whole neighbourhood was upset.'

'I'm not surprised that she came, Edith,' said Anita. 'The woman has never shown any shame or remorse over what she's done, and she's brazen beyond belief.'

Edith continued. 'You know how Sundasa has several of his gang members hanging around the place? One Saturday afternoon a few of them stoned your house while Lydia was there. Luckily Ben wasn't at home, or perhaps they knew that.'

The neighbourhood had been agog with what followed, said Edith. Lydia came out to the garden. And with her hands on her hips she faced the direction of Sundasa's boundary wall and shouted, in Sinhalese, 'Who's throwing stones at this house?'

One of Sundasa's men popped his head over the brick wall and glared at her. 'Our hands are too honourable to throw stones at your whorehouse, woman. But if you don't watch your step, we'll strip your sari off you and disgrace you on the street.' A couple of the men had walked over to the gate and looked at her threateningly.

Lydia fled back inside the house.

Stoning a house in Ceylon was an act of public vilification; a shameful indictment that the inmates of the house were worthy of the utmost contempt.

Anita looked worried. 'They probably think I arranged it.'

'Surely Ben must know you'd never do that,' said Edith. 'But really Anita, that wretch has some gall. The neighbours are saying she'll get assaulted pretty soon if she continues to come here, and it'll be one of Sundasa's men who'll do it, that's for sure,' predicted Edith.

'God forbid! I hope they don't. I don't want that on my conscience.'

'For heavens' sake, Anita, don't be so silly! You've done nothing that should trouble your conscience,' said Edith, testily.

'And I was hoping the children could visit their father after church on Sundays,' said Anita.

'No,' shouted Rina who had been listening. 'I won't go.'

'Perhaps later,' soothed Edith. She leaned towards Anita and said in a low voice, 'I think it's good if they visit him from time to time.'

'Not me,' muttered a fretful Rina.

Going home on the bus that afternoon, Anita put an arm around her daughter's shoulders and promised the forlorn youngster, 'The first thing I'll do if I win the lottery is buy you a piano.'

That was another prayer Rina added to her nightly prayers.

Despite their difficulties, Anita was determined to keep things happy for her family. Her children looked forward to their mother's return from

CHAPTER TWELVE

work each day. They relished the freedom they now had to sit with her and have their evening meal together, without the fear and tension and the murderous fights they had been accustomed to for several years.

Often, after dinner, Anita would gather the children around her and tell them stories.

During the last big fight at Merinda, Ben had smashed their small portable radio to bits. Anita couldn't afford a new one. Now the only entertainment the children had was singing songs or listening to their mother's stories, which kept her little brood enthralled for hours.

Anita was a superb storyteller. She had a treasury of fascinating anecdotes of her ancestors and relatives. She knew some scary ghost stories too! And then there were the fairytales for the little ones. She would start her narratives to May and Michael with the familiar, 'Once upon a time …'

One evening, just as she recited the opening phrase, Emma piped in, 'A crow shat a lime!'

The little ones broke into fits of laughter, as did the older girls. Anita reprimanded Emma and asked her from where she had learned such a vulgar line.

'From school,' said mischievous Emma, laughing her head off.

After that day, whenever Anita told them fairytales, Michael and May would look at Emma with anticipation, hoping their eldest sister would repeat the line. Sometimes she did and they would all burst out laughing, as their mother, attempting to keep a straight face, chastised her eldest daughter.

Emma was now sixteen and Rina was fourteen. The two girls had to learn how to cook. Having a servant was out of the question for Anita.

They all had a good laugh the day Emma decided to make "Yellow Rice." It was the day Rina was coming home from hospital after having her appendix removed.

Back in Merinda, "Yellow Rice" was their Sunday treat. A special and expensive kind of rice had to be used, a non-glutinous variety called "samba." The dainty grains looked like the tiniest of little pearls, and the rice was cooked with saffron, coconut milk, a bit of stock, and herbs and spices.

But all Emma did was boil their normal, very starchy rice with a teaspoon of turmeric and salt. The results were revolting. And of course they had to eat it, scolding Emma as they did. Anita couldn't afford to throw out a pot of rice.

Their old servant Aslin had found another full-time job, but from time to time she visited them on weekends. Such was her love for her former charges that Aslin now gave Anita money whenever she came to see them.

The Roberts' former middle-class lifestyle at Merinda seemed like a distant dream. The fabulous Sunday lunches with gatherings of relatives and friends, the music and singing, fun and games, their servants and the pampered life they once enjoyed were lost to them forever.

The realities of daily life bore down upon them fiercely and relentlessly. Anita's biggest hurdle was paying the monthly rent and electricity bill, as well as finding enough money for bus fares and food every day.

Some months she couldn't afford to pay the light bill and the power would be cut off. During those times they had to settle for small kerosene lamps. Unfortunately when it rained, little splatters of rain coming in through the roof or the ventilation grills would shatter the thin glass chimneys. They were then forced to use "bottle-lamps" for lighting. These were crude, makeshift lamps — an old glass jar filled with kerosene, where one end of a wick would be sitting in the fuel, and the other end passed through a metal tube and flange and lit over the rim of the bottle.

The children hated the smell of the bottle-lamp. It emitted a steady stream of black kerosene soot from the unprotected flame, which was snuffed out only when they went to bed. In the mornings they had to clean out their soot-lined nostrils.

Anita would chide Rina for reading under the dim light of a bottle-lamp. 'You're going to ruin your eyes, child,' she would warn the avid reader, to no avail. Fourteen-year old Rina was immersed in books.

Gradually, life took on a new turn for them all.

Laughter and singing could be heard in their humble abode, and they were free of the daily terror they had endured for what seemed like a lifetime.

Anita and her children had been in their new home for some eight months when Ben's older brother, Fred, came visiting on a special

CHAPTER TWELVE

mission. He informed Anita that Ben was willing for the children to return to their family home, but not their mother!

Fred said he had spent many hours on many occasions trying to talk some sense into Ben.

Fred had burdened his brother with the knowledge that his four daughters and only son were living in abject poverty. 'Allow your wife and children to come home,' was Fred's constant plea to Ben. In the end his brother had relented, but refused to have Anita back.

Of course none of the children wanted to leave their mother, but after a while Emma, who had just left school, decided to return to her father's house. She wanted to study bookkeeping at a college of further education in Colombo, which was situated close to their former home. Before she allowed Emma to go back, Anita asked Fred to make sure his brother would pay for Emma's studies. Ben said he would.

When Emma returned to Merinda, Anita's monthly maintenance lessened by thirty-five rupees. Although she missed her eldest daughter, Anita was glad that little Jean would now have a sister living with her. Anita wrote frequently to Emma and arranged for her to bring Jean to church on Sundays, where they all met up together.

Rina was now the eldest and in charge of managing the household for her mother. With help from Esther she prepared dinner each night and soon became an accomplished cook.

Each morning Anita would hand over sixty or seventy cents to Rina and say, 'Can you fix some dinner for us, darling?' Of course they couldn't afford any of the fine fare they were accustomed to in their father's home. This was bare subsistence living.

Rina learned to carefully budget her meagre grocery allowance. She often saved a bit of money after school by getting off the bus with her siblings a few stops before their home and walking the extra distance, so she'd have at least another ten or fifteen cents for their evening meal. But it upset her terribly to see her mother serve most of the food out to the children each night, while she ate the scraps — the burnt remnants of rice and scrapings from the pots.

Some mornings Anita had no money to give Rina for dinner. All she had was enough for their bus fares. On such nights Michael and May went to bed hungry. But Esther and Rina would wait up for their mother, confident that she would bring them food. And she did.

115

Anita would get home late at night, having to catch several buses to reach home after she had visited one or two folk from the small group of friends who helped her regularly. Getting off at the little group of shops at the crossroads, called "The Junction" close to where they lived, Anita would buy bread, butter and eggs, and hurry home along the dimly lit street, her mind filled with despair, knowing her two youngest children would have fallen asleep hungry. While Anita cooked the eggs, Rina and Esther would wake Michael and May and keep them propped up, as their mother fed her sleepy-eyed youngsters. But they never starved.

Sometimes on weekends, Anita would make rissoles and other little savouries, and send Esther and Michael off on a Sunday afternoon to sell them to family friends. If they brought home ten rupees that was a great blessing!

Anita couldn't afford to pay for a *dhobi*. On Saturday mornings while her mother went to work, Rina would trundle off to the washing well, which was a good distance away from their house, carrying about forty pieces of clothing, including bed sheets and pillowcases. The well had no protective wall. It was only a rural spring; a simple water hole dug in the ground with a few logs embedded around it like a raft. This served as a floor. Although they had a proper well in their backyard, the owners of the house didn't want them using it for washing clothes.

Rina would squat on the ground as *dhobis* did, and scrub and beat the clothes on the large rocks placed around, which functioned as washboards. Her hands would be rubbed raw by the tedious chore. She would spread the clothes out to dry in the surrounding grassy fields and return to collect them a few hours later.

Rina was nervous whenever her siblings came near the open well. She would chase them away. 'Mum, I have these terrible daydreams at school,' she confided in her mother one day. 'I see Michael or May falling into the well and drowning, and I see the whole funeral and everything while I'm sitting in class ... I get so scared, Mum.'

Her mother hugged her. 'Cast those horrible thoughts out of your mind, darling. Nothing like that will ever happen to the small two, or to any of my children. I pray for you all, constantly.'

A year had gone by since Emma had returned to Merinda when Anita's old neighbour, Mavis Van Buren, whom she met occasionally in the

CHAPTER TWELVE

city, informed her that Lydia had moved from Mowdana. And the latest gossip in the neighbourhood Mavis told Anita was that Ben had bought a property for Lydia in some distant suburb.

'Do you have any idea where it is?' asked Anita.

'Not really. The woman's been pretty quiet lately, we've hardly seen her. There's a rumour that she's pregnant, but I don't know if it's true.'

'Do you see Ben?'

Mavis noticed the tears. 'Yes, from time to time.' She wasn't going to elaborate.

'I wonder what he's going to do now,' said Anita. Her heartache was constant, only made bearable by the comforting presence of her children.

'He's moving out, Mum,' Emma informed Anita, the next Sunday in church. Ben Roberts sent his family a message through his eldest daughter ... they could all come back and live in the house at Merinda, including their mother.

'I guess he's going to live with Lydia,' said Anita. She gave her eldest daughter the news that Lydia had left Mowdana, but refrained from burdening her with the rumour that her father may have sired another child.

CHAPTER THIRTEEN

1961 – 1964

Anita couldn't believe the sight that greeted her eyes as she alighted from the van with her children. Her once beautiful garden was laid to waste. A few withered shrubs stood like scattered, shrunken scarecrows. Wild lantana brambles had choked off the flowerbeds and the lawn was reduced to patches of sunburnt grass.

The red shoe-flower bushes at the entrance were still covered with abundant blossoms, but the gates were missing. Only the posts were left standing, slightly askew. Anita wondered what had happened to the pair of metal gates that had once served her as faithful sentinels, bearing the blood-red flowers little hands had placed on them.

Inside the house the neglect continued. The floors weren't polished, the walls were in need of paint, and her beautiful furniture wasn't gleaming anymore. Even the curtains looked tired.

The destruction was complete, thought Anita, remembering how the Buddhist priest had described the potency of Lydia's evil charm. Her eyes were seeing it all; her very life scarred by its horror.

Rina's heart thudded as she stepped into the house. Memories of the old terror gripped her. The first thing she noticed was that the piano was gone.

While her mother and siblings unloaded their things from the van, Rina scuttled over to the china cabinet and opened it. The amber glass cake trays and the amethyst coloured jar she had treasured as a child were gone, and so had all their cut-glass crystal ware. She quickly moved to the cupboard under the dining table and swung open the

CHAPTER THIRTEEN

two doors. It was empty. Their beautiful and expensive dinner service was gone. She looked around her ... the chiffonier was missing and the lovely pictures on the walls had been removed. The house has been plundered, she thought, as if robbers had entered and taken away their most prized possessions.

She hurried into the large second bedroom, relieved to find her books, her beads and her scrapbooks still intact inside her little wooden cupboard, but the beloved picture of the guardian angel was gone.

Anita was sad to learn that her trusted old neighbour, Hahminay, had moved away.

Now that she didn't have to pay rent Anita decided to get some hired help. The children were thrilled when their former servant Mary came back to do the cooking. And Aslin visited from time to time. She and Mary would chat together, crying sometimes as they remembered the former days of glory.

Some months later, Ben's younger sister, Elaine, whose marriage had ended, came to stay in the Roberts' home. She was reasonably amenable towards Anita, but Irene remained intractable as ever. She and Anita had occasional outbursts if they crossed paths.

'You have no rights in this house,' Irene would tell her sister-in-law, whenever Anita referred to the house as her home during an altercation. 'This is my brother's house and you don't even own a tile here, woman. You're just a beggar-bitch,' became Irene's constant taunt.

But Anita was wise to the malevolent old spinster. She knew what Irene really wanted was to have them out of the house again. For the sake of her children, Anita did her best to keep the peace.

Rina was delighted to be back in Merinda. She was now fifteen and loved the social life in her hometown, attending birthday parties, picnics, carnivals and the occasional movie with her school friends.

'What you are going to sing on Saturday?' Rina's classmate Anne asked her as they walked out of church one Sunday morning.

Each year in November, St Lucia's Convent and the local parish boy's school held their annual campfire in the church grounds. The next one was coming up the following Saturday and Rina had been asked to sing.

'I'm not sure yet, Anne. I've been practising a few Connie Francis numbers. I might do "Stupid Cupid."'

Rina often sang at various events in her hometown. She was passionate about singing. When she sang she forgot her family traumas, her shyness and her lack of confidence. She entered a different world. The spirit of a song coursed through every fibre of her being, and its pathos or joy became real and personal. She would practice a song for hours until it lived and breathed inside her.

All of the Roberts children had musical talent. Even little May, who was only six, could hold a tune extremely well. And young Michael had instinctive rhythm. He was always rapping on tables or whatever else he could use as a makeshift drum.

It was at the Peterite Carnival late in November that year that Rina saw him.

Most parents allowed their teenage daughters to attend night functions outside their hometown if they were chaperoned by an adult. Rina's friend Anne had a terrific grandmother, a good-looking widow in her sixties who loved socialising. Like Mary's little lamb, wherever Anne went her gran was sure to go, and so, by default, she became the token escort for Rina and her friends.

Anne's grandmother accompanied six schoolgirls from Merinda to St Peters, the popular boy's college in Colombo, for the annual Peterite Carnival, which was held from evening to midnight over a couple of days.

He was strutting around the college grounds with a group of boys, while Rina was with her little bunch of friends walking around the carnival attractions, of which he was the brightest she thought. Tall, dark, and irresistibly good-looking, her eyes were drawn to him instantly. Pointing him out to her school friends, she whispered, 'Who's that?'

'Forget it,' roared her friend, Helen. 'Don't even think about it. He's a born flirt. He's got a new girl every few months ... he'll break your heart.'

'I don't mind being a new girl for a few months,' murmured Rina, unable to take her eyes off him. 'What's his name?'

Anne admonished her. 'Don't be crazy, Rina. Knowing you, you'll fall for him, hook, line and sinker.'

CHAPTER THIRTEEN

'Alright, alright,' muttered Rina, exasperated by her solicitous friends. 'But what's his name?'

'Ivan Schubert,' said Anne. 'He's one of Johnny's best friends.' Johnny was Anne's boy friend.

The carnival atmosphere was heady. A giant Ferris wheel, a merry-go-round, hoopla stalls, a lucky dip and various other forms of entertainment ensured that the college grounds swelled with teenagers from all parts of the metropolis.

The latest pop songs were being played at the jukebox booth and blared out through a couple of loudspeakers. For a nominal charge, anyone could make song requests at the booth. It was a thrilling way for girls and boys to send hidden messages to each other, mostly declarations of teenage love and sweet romance coded in the songs they picked.

'Let's put in some requests,' said one of the girls in Rina's group.

'I'm going to get a song played for Ivan Schubert,' Rina announced.

Helen looked at her with surprise. 'You wouldn't dare.'

'You wanna bet?' Rina asked determinedly, as they headed towards the jukebox booth.

'Are you going to mention your name?' asked one of the girls.

'Don't be silly,' said Rina, trying to sound grown-up.

The girls poured over the list of melodies.

'Help me, girls!' Rina pleaded, impatiently.

'Here's a good one for Ivan,' said Anne, pointing to "Your Cheating Heart." A burst of laughter from the girls was followed by their impromptu rendition of ... *Your cheating heart, will make you weep, you'll cry and cry, and try to sleep* ...

After they had picked their favourite tunes the girls moved away and stood a little distance from the booth. Soon they heard the senior schoolboy manning the jukebox announce that an admirer from Merinda had requested Elvis Presley's, "Can't Help Falling in Love with You," for Ivan Schubert.

A few weeks later, on a Saturday afternoon, Rina was sitting in one of Colombo's cinemas watching the movie "The Young Ones," starring Cliff Richard. Rina had worn her friend Anne out with requests to get her boyfriend Johnny to organise a foursome for a movie. And here they all were.

The starry-eyed teenager had fallen in love for the first time.

Over the next few months, and as she turned sixteen, Rina tried to believe Ivan's reciprocal declarations of affection, but her doubts flowed like a never ceasing tide, brought in on fresh waves of gossip from her school friends. They eagerly rushed to tell her of Ivan's latest flirtatious escapade at some party or social event.

But he kept seeing her, and soon they became a fixed part of the regular dating scene in Merinda — Ivan and Rina, like his best friend Peter, and girlfriend June. The four of them often stole away for romantic rendezvous during picnics or parties, unknown to any of the older folk.

Twelve months later Rina and Ivan were still together. But true to her friend Helen's admonition at the carnival a year before, Rina found herself crying over Ivan's numerous flirtations.

He seemed totally oblivious to the heartache he was causing. His stock line whenever she tearfully brought up the subject was, 'You're the girl I'm going to marry someday, honey. I'm just having a bit of fun, that's all.'

Rina adored Ivan, with all the love-starved emotions of an adolescent who had gone through the traumas she had done while growing up. *I'd rather be with him than without him*, she thought, but wondered at times, rather miserably, what the future held for her with such an incorrigible flirt.

Ivan had now replaced singing as her raison d'etre.

It was two years after Anita and her children had returned to their home in Merinda, when Ben began visiting the house occasionally. He set up a little room again at the back of the dining area, and sometimes he stayed overnight.

Anita wondered what had happened. Had Lydia's husband Stanley returned to his wife? Or perhaps her older children had caused some conflict between the pair. At any rate, Anita never crossed Ben's path. She remained in her front bedroom, totally hidden from him.

Life at Merinda went on in a fashion, and although there were a few flare-ups between Anita and her sister-in-law Irene, nothing too dramatic happened to disturb the peace until the night they had a power failure in town.

CHAPTER THIRTEEN

It was about seven o'clock in the evening and Ben wasn't at home. Anita had returned from work and had just finished dinner with her children in the confines of her room. While she was getting changed into her home clothes the lights went out. The whole street was plunged into darkness. Anita had some candles but she had run out of matches. She knew there would be some in the dining room cupboard. Clad only in her petticoat and blouse, she grabbed a torch and hurried nervously into the living room. This was territory she rarely ventured into in the evenings.

Unfortunately at that very moment, Ben entered the house and saw Anita with the lit torch in her hand. He turned on her in a frenzied rage. Anita and her children fled to the street while Ben stood on the doorstop vowing to kill his wife. The attack was vicious and totally unexpected, made worse by the pitch-black darkness and the screaming of the younger children.

Anita trembled as she hid among the shrubs in a neighbour's garden, embarrassed at her state of undress. Michael and May sobbed as they clung to their mother.

At Anita's frantic plea, Emma and Rina rushed up the street and hailed a taxi. Together with her children, Anita went straight to Ben's brother's house.

Fred Roberts was furious. His wife quickly took charge of the two little ones while Fred paid the cabdriver and asked him to wait.

Once inside the house, Fred summoned his eldest son, Will. Fred and his sons went hunting and they had a few guns and rifles in the house. Fred walked over to a cupboard and got out a small handgun. After he had spoken to Will, Fred handed him the gun and said, 'Make sure they're safe before you leave the house. And shoot him in the wrist if he tries anything.'

Will Roberts was in his late twenties and he owned a powerful Harley Davidson. With their motorcycle escort, Anita and her children returned home in the same taxi.

The power was back on.

They trailed behind Will as he walked up to the front door. It was locked, and the lights in the house were switched off.

'Don't knock on the door, Will,' whispered Anita. Seeing the gun in his hand she was terrified of what might happen if Ben answered the door.

Will went around the side of the house and tapped on Irene's window. She peered through her curtains and gasped in surprise when she saw her nephew. 'Open the front door, Aunty Irene,' demanded Will.

In a few moments Irene partially opened one half of the double entry doors.

Will addressed her sternly. 'Why have you locked the front door while Aunty Anita and the children are still out?'

'Ben asked me to lock it,' she replied, glancing nervously at the revolver in Will's hand. She peered out into the garden. Anita and her children were clearly visible, standing a little distance behind Will.

'Where's Uncle Ben?' asked Will.

'He's asleep.'

'Good. Open up these doors.'

The woman looked scared as she opened the double doors and stood aside.

Will followed Anita and the children into their front bedroom. He saw them safely in and got them to lock the doors before he left.

The next day Ben departed for work, almost at daybreak.

Anita got a few things together. She wasn't going to risk staying in the house after such a violent outburst from her husband. 'We'll go to Aunty Vivien's,' she told her children. 'She'll put us up till we can find a little place close to school.'

Vivien was Anita's first cousin. She and her family were terribly disturbed over Anita's plight, and eagerly made room in their home to accommodate her and the children.

Unfortunately, Vivien's house was some twenty miles away from Merinda, and so it was impossible for Anita's children to travel to school from such a distance.

Under the circumstances, Rina hadn't been able to tell her mother that she had fallen pregnant.

Troubled over what was happening to her family, she struggled to make a decision and toyed with the idea of getting her pregnancy terminated. Her boyfriend, Ivan, urged her not to do it. He wanted them to get married.

Rina had completed a secretarial course and was now working and helping her mother financially. Anita was heavily in debt. During the early days of the "Troubles," she had borrowed a small fortune to pay

CHAPTER THIRTEEN

for her numerous attempts to break the occult charms Lydia had made. Although she had given up on all that activity she was still paying off her burdensome debts.

Rina spent three months agonising over her predicament. Finally she made up her mind. She could not abandon her mother and siblings and go off and get married. She would have an abortion. But she had no idea how to go about arranging for one, and had no choice but to confide in one of her work colleagues, Nita.

After trying her best to dissuade Rina from having a dangerous back street abortion, Nita promised to make some enquiries. A few weeks later she informed Rina that she had located a pharmacist who routinely performed the illegal procedure, but he lived a good distance away from the city.

The two girls made the necessary arrangements. Rina, who had just turned eighteen, was now four and a half months' pregnant.

A few days before her scheduled abortion Rina informed her mother that she had found them a little annexe to rent on the east side of Merinda. 'The place isn't quite ready yet, Mum, so you'll have to stay at Aunty Vivien's for a few more days.'

Rina had paid the bond and advanced rental on the small annexe, and intended staying there after her abortion. But she didn't want her family around until she had recovered from her ordeal. 'I'll be staying with some friends in Merinda, Mum, until we move,' Rina told her mother, explaining that the daily travel from her Aunt's house to the city was arduous, which was certainly true.

On the day of her abortion Rina's friend Nita accompanied her to the house of the pharmacist. The man informed Rina that his wife would be assisting him with the procedure. Rina had no idea what was going to be done. All she knew was that she was ending her pregnancy. Beyond that she didn't know what was involved and the pharmacist and his wife told her nothing. They carried out their grim task in silence.

When it was over they gave her eight tablets. 'Take two of these every four hours for the pain, and if you have any complications you'll have to go to the hospital. Don't come back here,' she was warned.

It was nearly four in the afternoon when the two girls arrived by cab at the little cottage in East Merinda. Nita was going to be staying overnight.

Rina had collected some stuff from her father's home and had moved it into the annexe: a bed, a couple of chairs, some pillows, and a few other things she knew she'd be needing over the next couple of days.

She took all eight tablets in six hours.

The pain was horrendous.

By two in the morning Rina was pacing about, doubled over in agony. Nita, who was sleeping on a reed mat on the floor, heard Rina's groans and clambered up off the floor. 'What's the matter,' she asked, groggily.

'I can't bear the pain,' said Rina, clasping her stomach. Her face was contorted as she tried not to cry. She was walking towards the back of the apartment when suddenly she felt a peculiar sensation in the pit of her abdomen. She sank to the floor. At first she didn't know what had happened. Then she saw it and froze. The dead foetus had dropped out of her body.

Fear hit her like a bolt of lightening. 'Nita!' she screamed.

In an instant, Nita was by her side.

They both sat on the floor.

Rina was sobbing, 'Oh my God! Nita! That's my baby!'

Nita was speechless.

'Oh God! What am I going to do, Nita? Why didn't that man tell me this would happen. I thought they … I thought he … Oh my God, I don't know what I thought. I just didn't know this was going to happen. Nita. What am I going to do?'

Rina sobbed. Her body shook, violently. Nita hurried away and brought back the daily newspaper she had with her. Still sobbing, Rina gently lifted the foetus off the floor, placed it on the newspaper and brought it back to her bed.

It was a boy.

Weeping, she gazed in agony at every little part of his small form. She looked at his little head and face, membranous body, arms and legs, toes and fingers, formed but unseparated. In her traumatised mind, she kept thinking, *Perhaps if I put him back, he might live.*

Aeons later, Nita spoke, 'Rina, what are we going to do?'

'I don't know.'

'I think we'll have to bury it,' whispered Nita. She was also in shock.

There was no response from Rina. She sat in silence, staring at her dead baby. She had shut down emotionally.

CHAPTER THIRTEEN

'We have to bury it, Rina. It's three in the morning.' Nita's voice sounded desperate and urgent.

Rina trembled at the thought. But she knew it had to be done. Soon it would be daylight.

Nita walked through to the back of the apartment and returned with a broom. 'This is all I could find,' she said. 'I'll use the handle to dig a hole.' She opened the door very quietly and stepped into the darkness.

A wind was blowing outside. Rina shivered in the sudden chill that entered the room. Using Nita's newspaper, she carefully wrapped her foetus, layer after layer, and watched his little body disappearing into the parcel of newsprint. She felt dead inside.

Nita returned. 'I've dug a hole beside the Tamarind tree,' she whispered. 'Let's go.'

Rina walked out, holding the little parcel close to her chest. In the faint moonlight she saw that Nita had managed to dig a reasonably sized hole with the broom handle. Rina placed her precious bundle on the ground and knelt down beside it.

Labouring with her bare hands, she dug deeper into the soft earth. Very gently, she buried her baby, covered up the hole with soil, and arranged a huddle of stones and fallen leaves over his "grave."

No requiem, no flowers, no songs of farewell for my baby, she thought, only death and darkness, a wind blowing through the garden, and unbearable pain.

The well was nearby. The girls walked up to it in silence. Nita carefully and quietly plunged the rope and bucket in and drew out some water. They washed their hands and returned to the cottage.

Rina had no more pills to take for the searing pain that now engulfed her whole being.

A few days later Nita made some enquiries and found out how the abortion had been done. It was a kind of chemical douche, she explained to Rina, as best as she was able to fathom. Rina had then been sent home to await the horror of giving birth to a dead baby.

Nightmares plagued her for weeks. Rina would wake up sweating in the night, unable to get back to sleep. She could only confide in her friend.

'It's horrible, Nita. I keep dreaming that dogs have taken my baby from under the tree. In another dream I see him drowning in a pool and

I rush to rescue him. I lift him out of the water and place him on the edge of the pool.'

'Rina, stop it! You're torturing yourself,' said Nita. 'You've got to stop thinking about it all the time. Why don't you go and make your confession, I'm sure it'll make you feel a lot better,' counselled Nita.

Rina took her friend's advice. She went to a church a good distance away from her hometown.

The priest doesn't know me here, she thought. *I'll never have to face him again.*

She entered the confessional, eager to unburden her guilt, but so afraid to speak it out … to actually say what she had done.

'Forgive me Father, for I have sinned, grievously,' said the trembling eighteen-year old.

'What have you done, my child?' asked the unknown priest, through the meshed grill of the confessional.'

'I … I had … I fell pregnant and had an abortion.'

Silence from the priest!

She was agonised.

'Have you done this before?'

'No … Never!'

Silence again.

Every second was misery. She desperately wanted forgiveness.

'Do you know what you've done?' The priest asked. But it wasn't a question. 'You have murdered your first born-child.'

He continued with the rest of the prayers.

But Rina couldn't hear anything else.

She didn't hear the decree of penance, the pronouncement of absolution and the blessing.

The priest's verdict shouted in her head and found an echo in her heart. 'I'm a murderer! I've killed my first-born child!'

Rina rose from the confessional with her burden of guilt heavier than before.

Blinded by tears, she walked to a pew, knowing she deserved the death sentence she felt she was under. She knelt … sat … knelt again, prayed and recited the rosary, more distressed than she had hitherto been in her young and trauma-filled life.

Rina went home, unable to dispel the priest's accusation, which condemned her almost as much as her own aching heart.

CHAPTER THIRTEEN

Two months after her abortion, Rina's boyfriend Ivan, casually mentioned to her one Saturday evening that he was going to be 'playing a game of cricket with the boys tomorrow,' and wouldn't be able to visit her.

The next morning saw Rina on her way to the eleven o'clock Mass. She was running late. Hurrying with her brother Michael, she decided to take a shortcut through the garden of a private residence where one of the local girls lived. Rina knew her by sight. They walked the same streets to the bus stop every morning.

To her utter amazement and agony, Rina saw Ivan sitting on the front verandah with the girl. They were locked in an embrace, kissing each other passionately.

Ivan was the first to notice Rina. He pulled apart from the girl and they both looked at her.

Rina walked on with her head held high, neither looking again nor acknowledging that she had seen them. Numbed, she participated in the Mass through a blur of tears.

Not now, not again, and not after what I've just been through, she told herself, as she ended her three-year relationship with Ivan Schubert. It was another betrayal and one too many. Ivan had broken her heart enough with his many dalliances.

The first death was the searing loss of her first love. The second was the brutal extinction of a naïve young girl. But Rina Roberts died a thousand deaths over the part she played in ending the life of her baby. It tore her apart and fragmented her soul.

Six months later Rina was back in her father's house. Emma, who was now married, had pleaded with her father to allow her mother and siblings to come home.

Rina forced herself to shut the door on the painful memories of her teenage love, and the baby she had buried under a Tamarind tree in a stranger's backyard.

Helping her mother and looking after her family became the burning passion in her life.

And she took up singing again.

CHAPTER FOURTEEN

1965 – 1966

In the 1960s there was no television in Ceylon. Radio was the popular media. And each year local industry sponsored a prestigious radio song contest, "Stars of Ceylon." Winning it was every singer's dream.

The talent quest took a whole year for the rounds of auditioning, preliminaries, quarterfinals and semi-finals to be completed, and the Grand Finals were held at Colombo's exclusive Royal College.

In December 1965 both Rina and Esther were among the finalists in the "Stars of Ceylon Talent Quest." They had entered the competition as a duo, calling themselves "The Roberts Sisters," and Rina had also gained entry as a soloist. At each stage of the contest the girls had captivated Colombo's radio audiences with their lyrical voices and undeniable talents. Both entries made it to the Grand Finals.

Anita sat in the audience watching her two daughters on stage. Her heart swelled with pride as Esther and Rina sang "You've Got Me Under Your Spell Again," in perfect harmony.

The last item for the gala night was Rina's solo performance. The hushed crowd that filled the Royal College concert hall listened to the teenager singing Caterina Valente's "Kiss of Fire." It was a difficult song. Rina sang it flawlessly, accompanied by one of the city's best-known bands ... The Gerry Crake band.

The contest was judged solely on radio performance. The panel of judges, who didn't get to see any of the contestants during their performances, sat in a special chamber, listening to the eighteen finalists on radio.

CHAPTER FOURTEEN

At last the show was over and the judges emerged from their room.

A female solo singer won a well-deserved third place. The Roberts Sisters came second and the audience cheered exuberantly. Anita was beside herself with joy!

Finally, the Director of Broadcasting at Radio Ceylon ushered in the winner of the 1965 "Stars of Ceylon Talent Quest," naming her Rina, "Kiss of Fire" Roberts! The applause was deafening.

It was a singularly glorious highlight in Rina's life.

Backstage she was being congratulated by the judges and told of some of their comments. One accolade that particularly delighted Rina was made by a Diplomat, a Mrs Harrington from the American Embassy in Colombo. She had written, 'Most brilliant amateur performance I have ever heard! Could have won a similar contest in the States!'

Although three of Colombo's top-notch bands approached her for singing contracts, Rina declined, confiding in her mother that she wasn't ready to commit to a singing career just yet. But she performed on radio and at a few well-known dances around Colombo. And of course at every function she attended Rina was publicly feted and asked to sing.

Sadly, the joyful respite for Anita and her children was short lived. Two weeks into the New Year of 1966 there was another ugly fight between Ben and Anita, and again they had to leave their home in Merinda.

The only place Anita could find quickly was in a remote inland suburb. The owners of the house would have known this was a desperate woman who sought to rent their property within twenty-four hours. They demanded six months' rent as an unsecured bond and the money Rina and Esther had won in the talent quest was used to pay for it.

The day Anita and her children left their family home, a severe storm swept through Colombo. The seas roared and its fearsome breakers lashed Merinda's shoreline.

Anita had to move in a bullock cart for she had no money left to pay for any other means of transport. Her meagre belongings were covered over with cardboard and jute bags inside the leaking cart — a poor shelter from the driving rain.

Anita and her son Michael sat huddled inside the cart holding umbrellas over their heads. The rain splashed in through the thatched roof of the wagon, and the front and rear canvas closings were ripped and flapping wildly in the howling winds.

Anita felt disgraced and humiliated. In the country's class-conscious society this was not how people in her social standing moved house or travelled. She prayed fervently as the cart left Merinda. Never before had she been outdoors in a severe storm. The jagged streaks of lightning and loud clashes of thunder filled her with dread. She was petrified that the driver of the cart might have an accident in the blinding storm, or worse, that they would be hit by a lightning strike.

Rina, Esther and little May were drenched as they changed buses three times to reach their new home. Their umbrellas offered pitiful protection from the raging winds and rain. They had forgotten to get the keys from their mother and sat shivering on the damp cement steps, waiting for the cart to arrive.

The children were dismayed when they saw the house and its surroundings. The place was semi-rural and looked desolate. There was not a trace of the familiar suburban sights of Colombo.

Anita, Rina, and Esther were now working in the city and it took them hours to return home from work, while getting home from school was proving a nightmare for the children.

The day Rina learned that Michael and May had got lost, she wept. The postman had found them holding hands and crying as they walked along the road. Luckily Michael had their address scrawled on one of his schoolbooks, and the kind postman was able to lead them back home.

'We have to move from here, Mum,' Rina told her mother. 'We can't let this to happen to Michael and May again.'

Forfeiting their huge rental bond they left the premises hurriedly, three weeks after they had moved.

Anita managed to find a room to rent in one suburb and Rina and Esther rented a room in another. Thankfully, both locations were in the midst of Colombo's metropolitan district, but the separation was painful.

Soon after they moved, Rina visited her mother and young siblings to check on their accommodation. She was appalled to find them living in a shabby room at the back of an old house.

'What's with the cardboard, Mum?' she asked, pointing to the large board stuck on the rear wall, at ground level.

Anita moved the board to reveal a gaping hole in the wall. 'Rats come in through that opening during the night, Rina. I get up and shoo them

CHAPTER FOURTEEN

away, I'm afraid they might bite the children. This used to be a kitchen once, you see,' she explained. 'I've tried to cover up the hole with this piece of cardboard, but the rats still push through sometimes. Half the night I'm awake watching out for them.'

Rina was visibly shaken. 'Mum, I can't see you and the children living like this. Could you find us a small apartment to rent somewhere in Colombo? I'll ask my boss for a salary increase … They've promised me one and it's due now.'

And so Anita and her children moved again.

Their new home in the heart of Colombo comprised of two bedrooms, a little kitchen and a converted garage that served as a living and dining room. It was the best they had rented so far.

On their first night together in their new apartment they sat around a small table for dinner.

'Mum darling,' said Rina, putting an arm around her mother's shoulders. 'We are not going to be separated again, and we are never ever going back to Merinda. We can't put the children through this horror anymore.'

'I know, darling. I've made up my mind too. We've been reduced to living like gypsies,' said Anita. 'This time it's goodbye forever. But it hurts me that you've lost your home.' Her face crumpled.

The children clustered round their mother, comforting her. 'Don't cry, Mummy darling,' said the little ones, tearfully.

'MUM, our home is not in Merinda!' said Rina, firmly. Taking her mother's face in her hands, she kissed Anita and held her close. 'Wherever we are together, that's our home. Merinda was once beloved to us, Mum, but not anymore. It's become a place of torment, hatred and fear.'

'The evil Lydia has done is still there,' said Anita broodingly. 'I could feel it. She's probably buried more charms around the place, but I don't care anymore.' She was sick and weary of it all.

Rina rose from the table vowing to her mother, 'I'm never setting foot in that garden or house again, Mum.'

She walked over to the kitchen window and stared out at the semi-darkness, reflecting on all the heartbreak she had endured in her hometown.

Closing the window, Rina vowed to herself, 'Everything in Merinda is dead to me.'

Part Two
Rina's Story

PROLOGUE
1975

Graham Whittaker came out of the London Underground and faced the daylight of a cold autumn morning in Wood Green. He pulled up the collar of his padded overcoat, cosseting his neck against the blustery winds that blew down the High Street.

Graham worked nights at the British telephone exchange. He also had a part-time day job in Wood Green. On the three days a week that he balanced the accounts books at Blakey's Furniture Store, he ate a quick breakfast at the station tea-shop and walked down the High Street to Blakeys.

'Aaggh,' he said to himself with irritation, when he found his steps had led him away from the High Street and into Millet Grove where he lived. He had forgotten it was Friday. He worked at Blakeys on Mondays, Wednesdays and Fridays. Ah well, he thought, now that he was close to home he might as well have some coffee and toast and go in a bit late to work. Old Mr Blakey was fairly flexible with his young bookkeeper.

Graham was a lodger at No. 67, a modest, semi-terraced house in Millet Grove, Wood Green. The suburb was north on the Piccadilly line of London's underground rail network.

As he turned his key in the lock and pushed open the front door Graham felt something eerie. He was a man with considerable psychic ability, which he had developed through years of esoteric studies.

He felt the hairs on the back of his neck stand up and his first thought was, *A burglar.* 'Anybody home,' he hollered. He stood at the door, ready to bolt.

Silence greeted him.

He took a few steps into the hallway, leaving the front door wide open in case he had to flee ... He was no hero.

Moving cautiously through the ground floor, he checked the living room and the downstairs bedroom he shared with his Malaysian girlfriend, Peggy. She was at work of course.

Reaching the kitchen, Graham opened the rear door to give himself or the intruder, who he imagined was somewhere inside the house, another point of exit.

Okay, he thought, the ground floor was safe.

With some trepidation he ventured upstairs. On reaching the top landing Graham stood still for a few moments, more intensely aware of "the presence."

He was surprised to see the front bedroom door open. Nimahl Singram, the owner of the house and his girlfriend Rina Roberts occupied the large upstairs room facing the road, and when they were both out the door would be closed. Nimahl and Rina were from Ceylon. They had moved to London a few years ago, Graham had learned. Nimahl had his own company, a commodity-brokering firm near Victoria Station, and Rina worked as a temp secretary from time to time.

Graham liked Rina. He found her sensitive and artistic, and on a spiritual quest, just as he was. At times he thought she was like a lost kitten — restless, and not quite knowing where she belonged. He knew she was twenty-nine but she looked more like twenty, he thought. And quite good-looking too.

As he stood on the landing, somewhat unsure of his next move, a soft moaning sound came from the front bedroom. He quickly walked towards the open door and poked his head around it.

Rina was lying in bed, curled up and facing the doorway.

Embarrassed that he had intruded, Graham asked, 'Can I get you some coffee, Rina?'

She didn't reply.

Her half-opened eyes looked funny, he thought.

Moving further into the room he noticed several handwritten notes scattered on her bed. He picked one up and read it.

> *Mum darling, I'm sorry to do this to you, but I think you're okay now. I can't go on Mum. The pain is too much and there's no hope for me.*

He grabbed her shoulders. 'Wake, up, Rina! What have you done? Wake up!' She moaned again and her eyes opened more fully.

She recognised him. 'Gray ... Go away.' She had taken to calling him Gray.

He looked around and saw two small empty bottles on the ground. He grabbed them, put them in his pockets and reached for the telephone on her bedside cupboard. There was no dial tone. Glancing down he noticed the severed phone wire and a pair of scissors lying on the carpet.

'Go away Gray ... Please.' Her voice was faint.

'I can't Rina! I'm calling an ambulance.'

'Go away.'

Good, he thought, she was talking. Graham had done some volunteer emergency training.

He picked her up. She was light as a feather. Carrying her to the landing, he held her in the crook of his right arm, grabbed the banister rail with his left hand and dragged her down the stairs.

Her legs were buckling.

Still dragging her along, he moved swiftly through the hallway to the telephone in the dining room.

Using his free hand he lifted the receiver, dialled emergency and asked for an ambulance. She realised what he was doing and grappled with him to disconnect the line. He had to let her drop to the floor as he spoke to the operator.

In less than ten minutes an ambulance siren was screaming its way through to North Middlesex Hospital.

Graham sat in the back of the vehicle with Rina. He felt her pulse ... it was faint.

He wasn't a praying man but he prayed now. He had never seen anyone who'd taken a drug overdose. When Graham had handed over the two empty bottles he had picked up from Rina's bedroom to one of the ambulance men, the man read the labels and informed his colleague, 'She's OD'd on barbiturates.' He stuffed the two bottles into the pockets of his overcoat before they placed her on a stretcher and carried her out to the street.

As they wheeled Rina's unconscious body into the emergency room, Graham hurried to the phone booth and dialled his girlfriend, Peggy. She was shocked. 'I'll come over right away.'

Peggy arrived in twenty minutes. 'I've rung Rose,' she told Graham. 'She and Nimahl will be here soon.'

Rose Solomons, who had recently arrived in London from Ceylon, was Nimahl's secretary. She too lived at Number 67, Millet Grove. Rina, Rose and Peggy were roughly the same age and they had formed an easy bond of friendship.

A few minutes after Peggy arrived, Nimahl rushed in with Rose. Graham gave them the details of Rina's attempted suicide, mentioning that a doctor had already spoken to him to get some information about Rina.

The small group sat in silence, close to the room where Rina was being treated. Each time the doors opened they could see a cluster of medical personnel around her. A nurse hurried out and asked for the name and telephone number of Rina's doctor. Nimahl gave her the details.

Eventually someone emerged to speak to them. Dr Ron Sinclair informed the little group that they had managed to stabilize Rina. 'Someone up there is surely looking after her,' he said, as he looked at the empty plastic bottles in his hand.

He was the same doctor who had talked with Graham earlier. He now looked at Graham and said, 'Miss Roberts is very fortunate that you didn't go to your day job this morning, young man. You got to her in time … We were able to pump her stomach out.'

The doctor turned his attention to Nimahl. 'I take it you're Mr. Singram?'

'Yes, I am,' said Nimahl.

'I've spoken with her GP and he's given us some information about your young lady. Were you aware that she was on barbiturates?'

'No, I didn't know that, doctor. Rina has been suffering from depression for many years and Dr Price has been treating her. I thought she was only on Valium. Could I see her, please?'

'You certainly can, but she's unconscious. And she won't be awake for many hours yet.'

They followed the doctor as he led them into Ward 46.

Her bed was close to the nursing station. In a white hospital gown and with her long dark hair spread out on a pillow, she looked peaceful in repose. A cannula in her slender wrist was hooked up to a saline drip.

PART TWO PROLOGUE

They stood in silence at the foot of her bed, watching her for a few moments before they quietly filed out of the ward.

Nurse Wyndham paged Dr. Phil Isenberg, one of the Psychiatrists at North Middlesex Hospital. Rina Roberts had woken up, the nurse informed the doctor when he answered his pager.

He quickly gulped down his mid-morning cup of coffee and left the hospital canteen. Taking the lift to the fourth floor, he hurried along the corridors and into Ward 46.

Dr Isenberg had looked in on Rina several times since she was brought into his ward on Friday. It was Monday now.

She didn't acknowledge the doctor's greeting. Instead, she looked at him reproachfully. 'Why did you do this?' Her voice low and bitter. 'I wanted to die.'

'We know you did, Miss Roberts, but we want to help you.'

'You can't help me … Even God can't help me,' she said, and turned away.

Phil Isenberg walked around to the far side of her bed. He pulled up a chair and sat close to Rina, looking intently into her face. 'You're too young to die. You're only twenty-nine!'

'You don't know what you're saying. You don't know what I've been through. I've lived a hundred years, not twenty-nine, I'm tired of it all. The pain never stops.' Waves of despair swept over her as she thought of the never-ending saga of trouble and heartache she had lived through since she was nine. 'The dam is breaking,' she whispered. 'I've tried to hold it up for so long, but I can't anymore.' Sobs erupted.

The doctor summoned Nurse Wyndham over and spoke softly to her. Bending closer to his patient he told her, 'The nurse is going to give you something to make you feel a bit better. We are going to help you, Miss Roberts.'

He wasn't sure that she'd even heard him through her uncontrollable weeping.

The metaphor she had used wasn't lost on the doctor. *She needs to talk,* he thought, as he left the ward. *She's kept it all inside.*

Rina had been at North Middlesex hospital for six days when Dr Isenberg felt she was ready to talk. He arranged an initial meeting with her in one of the rooms outside Ward 46.

She walked in hesitantly, dressed in an orange, slightly faded sweater and a long, black woollen skirt. He took in her slender build. The medical reports said she wasn't eating much. She weighed only a hundred and five pounds. He looked at her face — pale, but still beautiful, he thought, and her eyes were liturgies of pain. Her dark hair was pulled back tightly.

'Have a seat, Rina, and tell me about yourself.'

Tell me about yourself. That's what Nimahl had said to her when they first met. She cast the recollection aside.

'What do you want me to tell you?' she asked the psychiatrist, as she lowered herself, gingerly, onto a brown vinyl chair.

'I'd like to know a bit about your family — your parents, your siblings — but more importantly speak to me of anything that comes to mind.'

He head was shaking with a marked tremor. Where could she begin? Her mind was struggling against this invasion. There were too many locked doors. Which one could she safely open?

She remained silent.

'When did you come to England, Rina?' Dr. Isenberg prodded.

'In 1972. I came to England to be with my ... to be with ... His name is Nimahl Singram and we've had a ... a relationship for some eight years.' She stopped.

'Would you like to talk about it?'

She didn't answer, but nodded.

The doctor waited.

Somewhat listlessly she began, 'I was twenty when I first met him, in Ceylon.' She trailed off and stared at the wall. *And I was full of hope,* she thought, remembering how it all began.

CHAPTER FIFTEEN

1967 – March

As she reached the end of her teen years all that her hometown Merinda once signified to Rina Roberts was shut away. The loss of her father's love and the years of terror, the abandonment, the rejection, the unending shame of it all, and the heartbreak of her teenage love affair and abortion were all locked away in places far removed from her realm of existence.

The awkward fledgling that had once been nervous and shy had blossomed into an attractive and purposeful young woman.

Anita Roberts often remarked that Rina had the same confident stance as her father. With an erect carriage and head held high she looked taller than her five foot five inches. Her dark, wavy hair was well below her shoulders. She had a golden tanned complexion, high cheekbones, a slightly aquiline nose, and lips that were full like her mother's. Only those who knew her well saw the laughter, sparkle or intensity in her dark brown eyes. They were usually inscrutable.

The Roberts family were now renting part of a rambling old house in an inland suburb, south of the city of Colombo. Rina and all her siblings lived with their mother, except Emma who was married. Much to her mother's delight, Rina had persuaded her younger sister Jean to move in with them. Jean, who had just turned fourteen, had been separated from the rest of her family, sporadically, for several years.

Rina's cousin Stella — her Aunt Vivien's daughter — was lodging with the Roberts family for the convenience of commuting to the city more easily. Stella was slightly taller than Rina and stunning in appearance. With elegant saris draping their slim and shapely figures the two young girls revelled in the admiring glances that came their way as they walked to the bus stop every morning.

The daily buses in which Rina and her cousin travelled to work were the old, red, London double-deckers. Their graveyard was Ceylon, but they were resurrected and put to good use, transporting thousands of daily commuters — at times precariously —along Colombo's main thoroughfares. Good-humoured passengers dismissed the constant threat of a footboard giving way under its burgeoning load, as it dipped down and screeched along the tarred roads whenever a bus approached a halt.

Rina had got herself a well-paying job as secretary to the General Manager of a French Engineering firm. Neyrgelex had a large, local field force, and French engineers working on its projects visited the island regularly. The company's small administrative office, with a Ceylonese General Manager was housed in a landmark building in "The Fort," commonly called Fort. It was the commercial hub of the island's capital city, Colombo.

Located on the southwestern shores of the island, Fort was a busy little metropolis, not comparable to international centres by any standards, but bustling enough for the tropical nation of ten million.

The major banks, the bulk of the mercantile sector, House of Parliament, hotels, shops, restaurants, the Governor-General's residence, and the general post office, were all situated in Fort, which was a walking distance from the country's chief port, the Colombo Harbour. A small body of water, called the Beira Lake, divided the commercial district from the House of Parliament.

Within weeks of starting her new job at the French company, Rina noticed quite a few good-looking guys also worked at the prestigious address, including some of Colombo's rich and elite. She often cast sidelong glances at them getting out of their Mercedes, sports cars and other impressive vehicles each morning.

Rina loved sports cars. Their sleek shapes captivated her and reminded her of butterflies. Beautiful looking, and could they fly! While she was growing up in Merinda, her coveted modes of transport were Harley Davidson motorcycles and sports cars. A cousin of hers, Will Roberts, was the proud owner of a Harley. Trained at the British Air Force base in Halton, England, Will was an aviation engineer in the Royal Ceylon

CHAPTER FIFTEEN

Air Force. He was also quite a daredevil! As a youngster, Rina's greatest thrill was when her dashing cousin took her for rides on the pillion of his shining black Harley. Her heart would pound as she clung to Will's shoulders, her young voice shouting over the roar of the engine, pleading with him to go faster. She was only twelve at the time, but had adored the magnificent Harleys. She still did. She had never ridden in a sports car yet, but she had hopes!

As part of her job, Rina worked a small two-line switchboard. One morning when she arrived at work she had hardly put her bag down when the phone rang. 'Good Morning, this is Neyrgelex,' she answered.

A deep, male voice, spoke. 'You looked very beautiful this morning. I was in the lift with you.'

Rina paused for a moment. *Someone's trying a joke* she thought and hung up.

Two days later, she heard the same voice again. 'Good morning, beautiful dreamer. You were right next to me in the lift today."

It occurred to Rina that the man might be mistaking her for someone else. 'Who do you want to speak to?' she asked.

'The lovely young girl who works at Neyrgelex and who's talking to me right now,' came the quick reply.

Rina smiled. The man's voice was incredibly alluring. 'Were you really in the lift with me?' she asked.

'Of course! I was right behind you. But as usual you walked in not looking at anyone and stood like a statue till you got off at the third floor.'

She laughed at his apt description. 'Where do you work?' she asked, her curiosity piqued.

'One floor above you, at Thornton Trading.'

The company was a well-known British commercial establishment. Rina was wondering if he was the good-looking guy she sometimes saw alighting from a low-slung Jaguar. His eyes often lingered on her.

She loved the car!

She had even asked the lift operator, Alfred, who its owner was. Alfred said it belonged to a guy named Harold de Alwis who worked at Thorntons.

'Do you drive the white sports Jag that's parked out at the front?'

'No ... Sorry to disappoint you,' said the mystery man. 'Do you like sports cars?'

'Who doesn't?' she answered breezily. 'Sorry, I have to go now, a call's coming through on the other line.'

She was disappointed. She had hoped her secret admirer was the man in the white Jag.

Rina's admirer called her again the following week. 'Hello, Rina.'

'How do you know my name?'

'It's not hard to discover the name of a good looking girl. And besides, I know more than your name,' he boasted.

'Really?' She was almost afraid to ask, 'like what?'

'Let me see now. How shall I begin? Rina Roberts, you're twenty years old. You were born in Merinda and attended St Lucia's Convent. You sing beautifully, and you won the "Stars of Ceylon Talent Quest" in 1965. How's that for a start?'

She laughed outright. 'Hey! How do you know all this about me? Who are you?' She couldn't stop laughing.

'I love the sound of your laughter, Rina,' he said, with a voice that entranced her. 'Seeing that you don't know who I am why don't we plan to meet?'

'Do you know Harold de Alwis?' she asked, thrilled and scared at the same time.

'Oh yes! He's a colleague of mine. Why? Do you know him?'

'Not really. I just know his name.'

'I see. Well how about I come down with Harold to the third floor today and meet you near the lifts ... Shall we say twelve thirty?'

Rina agreed, keen to see what he looked like.

At twelve thirty she walked down the corridor to the lift lobby. Her heart did a little leap. Harold de Alwis was better looking than she thought. She had only seen him in the car park ... from a distance. The sports car was beckoning.

Her gaze shifted to the man behind him. She stared, and couldn't stop staring. He was tall ... as tall as her father. That was her first heart-wrenching impression. But the words "good-looking" or "handsome" didn't quite fit.

This marvellous stranger who had been ringing her, and who was now standing before her, was a gorgeous, dark-skinned version of Robert Mitchum, one of her favourite movie stars. Even his hair looked the same, silver winged at the temples.

CHAPTER FIFTEEN

'Hello Rina, I'm Nimahl Singram,' said the stranger, reaching out for her hand. He held it for a few seconds before introducing her to the owner of the coveted sports car.

All thoughts of the Jag were forgotten. Rina couldn't take her eyes off Nimahl Singram. Backing away from him, she said, 'It's lovely to meet you, Nimahl, but I've got to go back to work.'

'So soon?' he asked, his eyes dancing with hers.

'Yes, I've got to … I … ' She felt flustered and looked away. 'My boss is waiting for an urgent letter to be typed.' The letter could have waited.

She rushed down the hallway and back to her office suite. As she turned the door handle she glanced down the corridor. He was watching her.

Going home that evening in one of the red double-decker buses, Rina sat upstairs and looked out of the window. In all of her twenty years she had never met a more handsome and overpowering man than Nimahl Singram. Her spirits soared as high as one of the kites she saw flying over Galle Face Green.

Galle Face Green was a pleasant oasis that hugged the shoreline immediately south of the capital city. In the evenings families would gather on the common, to socialise, stroll about or simply spend time relaxing near the ocean. Kite flying was a popular pastime on the spacious promenade, buoyantly fostered by the sea breezes that wafted in across the Indian Ocean.

Nimahl rang Rina the next day. 'Can I come down and see you during your lunch break, Rina, just for a little chat?'

Her heart fluttered. 'Sure, make it one o'clock.'

Neyrgelex had five employees, including Rina. The manager, who resided close to the city, lunched at home. The three other staff were mostly out and about at the middle of the day, so Rina was alone when Nimahl arrived.

There was an instant and electrifying chemistry between them.

Nimahl drew up a chair and sat facing Rina's desk. His presence dominated the small office.

Rina was wearing a crisp pink and white voile sari, teamed with a little white broderie anglaise blouse. Her dark hair was gathered back into a low chignon and tied with a white chiffon bow.

'I've been observing you for months,' said Nimahl leaning towards her. 'I love the way you walk, the way you dress, your reserved nature, and what you're doing for your family.'

'You know about my family?' she asked in astonishment. 'How do you know so much about me?'

'I've got my contacts in Merinda,' he replied. 'And I'm really sorry about what happened to your parents. Pretty awful, wasn't it?' His eyes were sympathetic.

She turned her face away, embarrassed at the tears that sprang without warning.

After a moment she returned his gaze and said, in a low voice. 'What happened to my family will always be a tragedy to me.'

He changed the subject abruptly and asked her about the projects the French company were engaged in, listening attentively as she spoke of what was happening in the hill-country, where one of the island's largest rivers had been harnessed for an ambitious hydroelectric project.

They carried on an abstract conversation for a few more minutes before he left.

Nimahl Singram rang Rina twice a day, morning and evening, and sometimes he visited her during her lunch breaks. After five weeks of this intense attention, he asked her for a date. 'Would you come out with me on Saturday night, Rina?'

'I'd love to ... where shall we go?'

'Nowhere in particular ... I just want to talk to you. How about I pick you up at seven? We can take a nice long drive somewhere.

Saturday night came around quickly and breathlessly for Rina.

She was waiting at the gate with Esther. Rina had confided in her younger sister, but said, 'Tell Mum that Angela and her boyfriend picked me up and that we're visiting friends.' Angela was an old classmate. Rina didn't want to tell her mother about Nimahl just yet.

As she waited for him, she realised she hadn't even asked him what car he drove.

She couldn't believe her eyes. A beautiful black sports Jag was approaching and Nimahl was at the wheel.

Esther disappeared as Rina stepped into the car.

Nimahl looked admiringly at Rina. 'You look lovely — naturally lovely. It's the way I like to see you.'

CHAPTER FIFTEEN

She was dressed very simply, in clothes she had worn as a teenager — a pastel-coloured, printed skirt and a light-blue blouse. Her dark hair hung loose, down past her shoulders.

'Thank you,' she said, as she tapped both hands on the dashboard, trying to contain her childlike glee. 'You didn't tell me you had a sports car. And a Jag! It's beautiful, like a big black eagle!'

He laughed, 'I wanted to surprise you knowing how you love sports cars.'

He reversed out of the small laneway and soon the vehicle was out on the main thoroughfare.

'Where are we going?' she asked, making an effort to be sedate while he carefully negotiated a steep and narrow descent onto the Galle Road.

'First I'm going to drive down south a bit to let you feel the power of this "big black eagle" as you call it, then we'll park somewhere and talk.'

Rina felt like the dizzy twelve-year old that once rode pillion on her cousin's black Harley. Nimahl revved up the Jag as much as he could. He took her south along the Galle Road and away from Colombo.

He's a brilliant driver, she thought, as she watched him weave in and out of the traffic.

She started singing, *Fly me to the moon and let me live among the stars, let me know what love is like on Jupiter or Mars ...*

'You sing like a bird,' he said.

'And your car flies like one,' she parried, laughing.

They went south for about a half hour before Nimahl headed back towards Colombo, and surprised her further by entering the deserted grounds of the domestic airport. He switched off the purring engine and in the next second was kissing her wildly.

Rina's heart pounded.

He pulled away, leaned across her and opened the car door. 'Let's step outside, darling.'

Darling!

They began walking. The vast grounds of the airport lay silent and still ... surrendered to ghostly shadows from the light of the waning moon.

'Tell me about yourself,' said Nimahl.

A strange request thought Rina; she didn't quite know what to say. She wasn't used to baring her soul, and spoke haltingly. But after a while, as he showed an interest in her stumbling speech she found it easier to talk to him. Mostly she spoke of her family, telling him that the greatest passion in her life was taking care of them.

'But what do you want for yourself, Rina?'

'For myself?' She pondered for a moment. 'I don't really know. All I want right now is to make sure my family is okay. My brother and sister need a few more years of schooling.' *And of course I want to get married and have children someday,* but she didn't tell him that. Those were the dreams of every young girl. Surely he'd know.

'You're going to be twenty-one in May, aren't you Rina?'

'Yes.'

'That's a lot to carry on young shoulders.'

'Ah, but I've got broad shoulders,' she quipped, laughing to lighten the topic.

'I've noticed,' he said softly, putting an arm around her.

'Nimahl, can I ask you something?'

'What is it, my love?'

My love!

Suddenly she felt safe. It was a glorious feeling. She hadn't experienced it since she was a child.

'How old are you?' she blurted. 'I'm just curious.'

'Twelve years and eight months older than you, little girl.'

They both laughed.

A week later Rina told her mother about Nimahl Singram. How she had met him, how wonderful he was and that he was coming home to meet her the next day.

Rina felt her world shaken, but unlike previous quakes that had ripped the ground from beneath her feet, these tremors were exhilarating.

Anita Roberts was polite to the tall and handsome stranger who had swept her daughter off her feet.

'You have a very lovely daughter, Mrs Roberts,' said Nimahl, charming as ever.

'She is,' said Anita, being very direct. She quietly observed Nimahl and thought he had the same strong and protective character as Rina's father.

CHAPTER FIFTEEN

When the time came for him to leave Rina hated to see him go. She persuaded him to stay a bit longer, and again a bit longer, till he laughed and pulled away from her embrace.

'Time you were in bed, Miss Roberts,' he said, glancing at his watch. It was past midnight. 'You're going to have a headache in the morning.'

Reluctantly, she let him go and tried to walk out to the garden with him. Despite her protests, he insisted that she go back inside the house and lock the doors, before he drove away in his black Citroen — his other car, he had informed her when she came out to greet him earlier in the evening and had asked, with disappointment, 'Did you get rid of the Jag?'

'Do you know anything about him, Rina?' asked her mother the following morning. 'I know you've fallen in love, darling. I can see that you're madly in love, but do you know anything about this man?'

'What's there to know, Mum?' asked Rina, with a disarming smile. 'We're in love!'

'Go easy, child,' cautioned her mother. 'You're young and very vulnerable and I don't want you getting hurt again. Besides, you know nothing about Nimahl. And you're forgetting that Sinhalese men, especially from his strata of society don't marry our Burgher girls.'

Rina knew there was a sizeable social gap between her and Nimahl. They moved in vastly different circles. She was a middle-class Burgher girl and he had an upper class Sinhalese background.

Although there was an open social interaction between the distinct ethnic groups in Ceylon at the time, they stayed pretty much within the confines of their own class and culture when it came to marriage. In the eyes of the conservative Sinhalese and Tamils, the Burghers were Westernised folk who loved to party and these aspects of their identity were viewed with a measure of disdain, although it was a well regarded fact that Burgher girls, with their mixed Asian and European ancestry, were, in general, considered pretty damned good looking and lent flavour and colour to the local scene.

And on the high rung of the beauty ladder it was a Burgher girl, the stunningly exotic Maureen Hingert, who won the place of runner up in 1955, in the highly acclaimed "Miss Universe" beauty pageant in America.

Although Anita's concerns were justifiable, they didn't bother her daughter. Cultural boundaries didn't exist for Rina. She felt her mixed lineage proved a happy contradiction to Kiplings's dictum: "East is East and West is West and never the twain shall meet."

With Dutch, Indian, Jewish, French and Sinhalese ancestors, Rina preferred to identify herself as a Ceylonese rather than a Burgher. Unlike most Burgher girls who garbed themselves in western dress, she wore saris, which was more the costume of Sinhalese and Tamil women in Ceylon. Rina found the graceful sari irresistible, and by the time she was twenty it became her preferred mode of dress.

Another feature of Rina's individuality was that she loved the Sinhala language, which again was rather uncommon among Burghers, for English was their mother tongue. But Rina found the national language highly evocative and the local idiom priceless.

She had a Sinhalese friend who patiently translated the lyrics of popular Sinhala songs for her. She loved their eloquence and poetry and lamented the fact that she had never mastered the language. Her knowledge of it was merely the vernacular jargon she had picked up as a child, through daily interaction with the servants in her father's home. And though Ben Roberts had paid handsomely for his three elder girls to be tutored in the local language, they had never quite grasped its intricate grammar and syntax.

Like her father before her, Rina hated the class structures prevailing in Ceylon. She could never forget, how in the good old days at Merinda they weren't allowed to use the term "beggar." Benjamin Roberts wouldn't hear of his family using such a denigrating word on those less fortunate in life. They had to call the three regular beggars that came to their home, (two old men, and a blind and very bow-legged woman), grandpa, the pensioner and the blind lady! Ben always referred to them as his visitors, and he arranged for his three visitors to come along to his home every Saturday for their weekly handouts, which included lunch. He would invite them to sit at the dining table, much to the horror of his wife and the servants. The bare-footed and raggedy beggars were embarrassed, but faced with such graciousness couldn't refuse, and conceded to sit on stools instead of chairs, and hold their plates in their laps rather than place them on the table.

Such preferential treatment was foreign to them, but as time progressed they grew more accepting of Ben's largesse, and promoted their plates from laps to the table. Ben would personally serve his guests, who looked forward to the nips of "arrack" he offered them in the same little glasses he used.

It was an unforgettable lesson Ben taught his children when the beggars eventually cleaned up, wore washed clothes and looked more presentable whenever they visited the Roberts' home.

With this fulsome background, and despite the enforced impoverishment of her adolescence, Rina Roberts was no conformist!

As Rina's romance with Nimahl blossomed, she told him about Ivan Schubert, and what had happened to her as a teenager — the pregnancy and abortion, minus the grim details. But she never talked to him of her father or her childhood in Merinda.

Nimahl visited Rina two or three times a week, and she lapped up his love and attention like a hungry kitten. He turned her twenty-first birthday into a magical evening when he arrived with a huge bouquet of twenty-one fragrant, dark-red roses.

And that evening he told her, 'Rina, I'd like to take you to Bangalore for a holiday, sometime in August. Will you come with me?'

'You know my answer is yes, darling,' she told him with customary candour.

A whole new world opened up for Rina when Nimahl took her away for weekends in the country. She had barely been out of Colombo before.

Their first trip away was memorable. Nimahl lost direction and they ended up in a vast rubber plantation.

Every wrong turn he took led them deeper into the "forest" and further in under the dense canopy of trees, which blocked out the sun, turning daylight into almost subterranean darkness.

There wasn't a sound for miles around, except the car and the creaking of the trees, and no sign of other moving life besides the slow dripping latex from the lacerated bark of the rubber trees. They were completely lost. Nimahl switched off the engine and they sat in the car, watching the sap from the trees filling into collection cups. And then they laughed, aloud and hilariously, and the "forest" echoed the sound of sheer joy.

Rina discovered a passion for rural bathing wells and Nimahl would indulge her. As they travelled along secluded country roads he would stop in little villages and ask for directions to the nearest bathing well.

These were mere springs dug up in the ground with no retaining walls around. Rina always brought along a length of rope, a small bucket and a *diyaredde* (a wrap around sarong women wore when they bathed outdoors). And Nimahl would bring his bathing shorts. Standing close to the edge of the ground level wells he would draw water from the shallow springs and pour it over her, while she would kneel, resting on her haunches and revelling in the fresh, cool, water. He called her his "water baby."

They shared idyllic times and their weekends away were unforgettable experiences for Rina. Nimahl treated her with the greatest tenderness — as if she were a priceless treasure. It was this profoundness in him that drew her irresistibly closer to this man she was beginning to adore.

By the end of July, Nimahl had made arrangements for their holiday to India. He was going to be travelling two days ahead of her on business, he said, but planned to meet her at the airport in Bangalore.

Rina was ecstatic. It was her first trip out of Ceylon and she was going to be with Nimahl for nine wonderful days. She couldn't wait!

A couple of days before he left for Bangalore, Nimahl said to Rina, 'Darling, you once mentioned to me that you were helping to pay off your mum's debts. I'd like to settle them all for you now, before we go to India.'

Rina was staggered. Since she first went out to work at the age of seventeen, she had been helping her mother repay the long-standing debts that had crippled Anita Roberts financially for many years. These weren't borrowings from a bank or finance company for there were no legitimate personal loan facilities in Ceylon at the time. Anita had borrowed the money — with exorbitant and compounding interest rates — from loan sharks who preyed on people in desperate situations. People like Anita Roberts ... an abandoned wife with six children, who was earning a basic wage and receiving only a pitiful monthly allowance from her husband, a meagre sum ordered by the Courts.

When Nimahl gave her the money to pay off her mother's debts, although she was embarrassed (she had protested, but he had insisted), Rina felt a huge burden lift off her.

Nimahl Singram became her knight in shining armour, rescuing the family she loved so dearly, and herself, from dire straits.

A very lofty pedestal snapped into place in a young woman's heart.

CHAPTER SIXTEEN

1967 – August

Rina looked around the airport terminal. Her heart leapt as she saw Nimahl's tall frame moving towards her.

He embraced her briefly, picked up her bags and led her through the concourse and out to one of the waiting taxis.

They snuggled up together in the backseat.

It wasn't long before the taxi was approaching the town centre. Rina and Nimahl were delighted to find Bangalore a very gentrified city, with beautiful parks and stylish homes.

It also housed the old British army cantonment, the driver informed his passengers when he learned they weren't locals.

Soon they arrived at their destination. A large, white, stately hotel set amidst stretches of lawn, sparkling fountains and well laid out gardens. The balconies had beautiful French styled, white, lacy balustrades.

In the mornings they went shopping or sightseeing, lunched in the numerous cafes in town and came back to their room to spend indulgent afternoons.

And in the evenings they dined out on fine Indian cuisine, returning to their hotel suite late at night — two lovers in love.

Nimahl lavished Rina with fine silk and delicate voile saris and he even got the little cropped sari blouses sewn for her by a tailor. He bought her a smart turquoise cardigan with black trim. Her first woollen garment! They weren't needed in the tropical heat of Colombo, but Bangalore was in a high altitude with a cool climate.

And of course he had to buy her a pair of sleek black gaberdine pants to go with it, another first.

When she got back to the hotel Rina paraded in front of the mirror, with her hands in the pockets of her new black pants, looking very chic in her turquoise cardigan.

Nimahl watched, with amusement. 'You're like a child dressing up for grown ups, darling,' he teased.

On their next shopping expedition he selected a pastel pink nightgown for her, with delicate embroidery. Merely taking it out of the box and the soft pink tissue paper it was wrapped in was a delight for Rina. She wore it that night. And while she sat at the dressing table brushing her long dark hair, Nimahl lay propped up in bed watching her, with admiration and desire in his eyes.

It was the fourth day of their holiday. After lunch Rina went out to the gardens of the hotel with a writing pad and pen. Nimahl was having an afternoon nap.

In her teens Rina had discovered she could write poetry. It was a cathartic gift. Sitting under a tree, after a few scribbles and jottings, she wrote her first poem for Nimahl.

> The wonder of this love!
> how can the universe not know two hearts have met
> lovers lifted high above the mundane gatherings of mortals,
> yet, no more than bodies made of clay
> but hearts flying swifter than the swallows turning back
> to springtime hopes.
> Where does this well rise up from dearest heart?
> How is it I have known you long ago,
> before this dream began.
> Why is it that your words
> soothe the jagged shores of my whole life —
> and your love
> brings me to a new world dawning,
> every morning
> with my waking thoughts of you.

When Rina returned to their room, she found Nimahl still asleep. She put the writing pad back on the desk.

A late afternoon on the fifth day of their holiday saw them relaxing on the balcony on a large cushioned couch. Entwined in each other's arms, they were absorbed in silent reflections, neither wanting to move.

CHAPTER SIXTEEN

Rina gazed out at the beautiful gardens. The sound of sparkling fountains cascading into pools was mesmerising. As the twilight folded into dusk, she stirred from the couch and stood up. Bending down to kiss Nimahl, she said, 'I'm going to have a shower and get ready, darling.'

They dined out every night. Rina revelled in the thrill of getting dressed in her new saris and adorning herself with tinkling glass bangles, bead necklaces and exotic earrings she had bought in the bazaars around Bangalore.

Rina came out of the bathroom after her shower and found Nimahl sitting on the bed with the writing pad in his hands. He was reading her poem. The look he gave her held such yearning. She came up to him and kissed him. 'What is it?'

'Is this how you feel about me?' he asked.

'Don't be surprised. That's only a glimpse, darling.'

Nimahl seemed astonished. 'You're a talented girl, Rina Roberts.' He read the poem again, placed the pad back on the desk and got to his feet. 'Get dressed while I have my shower, baby. I'm taking you to a new restaurant tonight. The manager here says it's the finest in Bangalore.'

That evening they feasted on Mogul cuisine. The rich North Indian food seduced Rina's palate and she succumbed to the wooing of its delicious sauces without the slightest resistance. So did Nimahl. The manager was right. The food was exquisite!

They returned to their haven of love.

Afterwards, Rina lay awake, replete and too deliriously happy to sleep. *If there's a paradise on earth, this is it,* she thought.

Drowsily, he reached for her. 'I love you, baby,' he whispered. It was his pet name for her and she loved it. He now addressed her as "baby" most of the time, seldom Rina, and occasionally he would call her his "princess." She couldn't recall a time when she was happier.

The setting sun cast long shadows across the manicured lawns of the hotel. Once again they were on the balcony, sprawled out on the comfortable couch.

Nimahl took Rina's hand in his. 'I have something to tell you, baby. It's the real reason I brought you here to Bangalore. I wanted to be with you for a few days before and after I revealed this to you.'

Suddenly she was nervous. She turned to look at him.

He held her hand tightly, but looked away, 'I'm married.'

Simply. No warning. A bullet was fired through her heart.

She sat upright and perfectly still. 'Married!' she said. 'You're married!'

'Yes.' He turned to look at her, his eyes miserable.

She sat silently. *Find out more about him.* Her mother's warning rang in her ears.

'And where's your wife?'

'She's at home with the children.'

'Children! How many?' She was emotionless — a policeman questioning a criminal.

'Two: a girl and a boy.'

'How old are they?' Persistent.

'The girl is four and the boy is two.'

'How long have you been married?' Probing.

'Seven years.'

End of questioning.

She took her hand away from his, walked quickly along the balcony and ran down the stairs leading to the garden.

He followed her and caught up with her, led her to a seat and kissed her tears away, almost drinking them off her face. 'I love you, baby, I know what I've done is wrong, but I love you.' He covered her face with kisses. 'I can't give you up ... Don't walk away from me, Rina. Please!'

She heard the sound of his faltering voice, but he couldn't hear the breaking of her heart, she thought. He couldn't see the smashing of her dreams, and wouldn't know how savagely he had crushed the hopes she had dared to hope, after years of despair.

She remembered her father's adultery with a family friend, and the betrayal her mother had discovered when Rina was nine. Now she faced her own burdened thoughts of Nimahl's wife. Her soul groaned at the weight of her love for a man who was the husband of another woman.

How brief was my joy — five months? Perhaps I can write a poem and call it "Five Months in Paradise," she thought, among the other turbulent thoughts swimming in her head.

Her mind kept going back over the past five months, recalling the now obvious signs she hadn't even considered. She had been so naïve! He never took her to a café in Colombo or a movie or a restaurant.

CHAPTER SIXTEEN

He had only taken her for long drives, trips away, or to the beach on moonlit nights, where they would be hidden under palm trees or under the shelter of the large rocks. She should have guessed. But her heart was aching to be loved, and she innocently believed that he didn't go out with her to crowded places because he wanted to be alone with her. It had even made her think — for the first time in her life — that she was special.

Her mother's concerns now seemed prophetic. Anita Roberts had cautioned her daughter. But Rina was a sensitive romantic looking for her dream.

When she was fifteen, and impressionable, she had read Pearl Bucks' book "Portrait of a Marriage." It had affected her deeply. A happy marriage was all she wanted from life she had decided at that nubile age, confident that one day her dream would come true. She told herself she would nurture love, make it grow and blossom. She would do all she could and go through every sacrifice to make her marriage something beautiful, to erase the scars of her childhood. Her heart had been set on her dream. She would have her portrait of a marriage some day. And so she waited in hope, to plumb the depths and find the heights of love.

Again, her mother's accusing words to her father screamed in her ears, 'You're sleeping with that whore.'

Whore!

A word she had heard from her mother's lips when she was nine, ten, eleven ... *Was that what I've become now?* she asked herself with anguish. *If you slept with another woman's husband were you a whore?*

'What's her name?'

'Anoma.'

'And the children's names?' The policeman again.

'My eldest is a girl. Her name is Dhilani and my son's name is Sirimal. We call him Siri.'

WE! She felt the full impact of that collective noun and the first, absurd pangs of jealousy that followed. *He has a wife. I can never be his wife. They are WE and I'm just me. Insignificant Rina Roberts, undeserving of being mentioned. He has a wife who is Mrs Singram. I will never be Rina Singram.*

Her newly ascendant soul was relegated back to the dark caves of her childhood, her heart rewritten in the shadows of the night. *You're a nobody, and you always will be,* were the words silently carved with a lance.

They went out as usual for their evening meal, but hardly spoke. They were both confronted with a new and alarming topic of conversation, one they had to conceal in public, and tonight every other subject seemed ludicrous.

They went back to their room and instantly turned to each other, bridging the awkward gulf that had separated them at the dinner table … crying, comforting, kissing, loving, passionate, tender, arms around each other, drifting off to sleep.

Later in the night, Rina awoke to find he wasn't beside her. In the partial darkness she looked through the open door and saw him on the balcony. She lay in bed and watched him.

For several moments he stood, unmoving, leaning forward against the metal railing and staring out into the faintly illuminated garden. Smoothing back his hair, he held his head with both hands and looked up at the night sky.

Her heart yearned towards him. She was familiar with signs of despair. She rose from her bed and threw a robe around her, an opulent, sapphire-blue silk robe he had bought her. 'Fit for my princess,' he had declared, when they returned from their shopping spree. After her shower that night he covered her slim body with the shimmering silk and carried her off to bed.

She walked out to the balcony, barefoot and silent, gathering the voluminous silk around her.

The night was cool. He started when she touched him. Embracing her, he led her to a seat. 'I have never loved anyone like I love you, my angel,' he said, kneeling before her. 'I cannot live without you.'

She put both her arms around him, clasping his head to her breast. She held him fiercely and believed him utterly, for he was only echoing the words in her own heart, as yet unspoken.

He glanced down at her bare feet. 'No slippers? You'll catch cold,' he chided, gently. Embracing her, he led her back into the room.

Anita Roberts was quiet in her displeasure when her daughter returned from India. She hadn't approved of Rina's trip, but by now she was used to her very independent daughter doing pretty much as she pleased.

CHAPTER SIXTEEN

Anita was now fifty-one and ailing, a mere shadow of the younger and vibrant Anita Roberts that Rina sometimes remembered. Encouraged by her daughter, Anita had gradually handed over many responsibilities to Rina. The family finances, disciplining the children and most of the household affairs were now her daughter's domain.

Rina was also the main "parent" in the house, and over-protective of her siblings. She felt her own life was the assault line. If they were spared she could take all the hits, she thought, and frequently prayed that way.

Rina told her mother about Nimahl being married.

'Give him up, darling,' urged Anita. 'Don't do to another woman what Grace did to me.'

'MUM!' Rina recoiled, as if stung. 'How can you say that to me?' How can you compare me to that bitch?'

Her mother hugged her. 'I'm sorry, darling.' She kissed Rina's cheek. 'Forgive me. I shouldn't have said that.'

Rina knew the story well. How Lydia Wilmet, a friend of her mother's had engaged in deadly sorcery to lure her father away from his wife and children.

'Mum, I haven't charmed Nimahl,' Rina pleaded. 'I didn't pursue him. He pursued me. He should have known better. He's the one who's married. But I love him, Mum! I love him with all my heart.'

'I don't want a daughter of mine to be the cause of a marriage breaking up, Rina,' said her mother. 'Forget him, child. If you really want to, you can.'

But she didn't want to.

Rina didn't dare tell her mother of the conversations that took place between her and Nimahl during the last two days of their holiday in Bangalore.

She had asked him never to leave his wife and children. She told him she never wanted to see his marriage fall apart. Having said that to him somehow lessened her guilt.

He said he would take care of her and help her look after her family. And as soon as they returned to Colombo, he said he would buy her a car and teach her to drive. 'I'll see to it that you're well looked after, baby,' he promised.

They took separate flights coming back to Colombo. On the plane Rina reflected on her pledge. At twenty-one she had committed herself to becoming the mistress of a married man. For life, she thought, expansively. Was any marriage happy? Rina wondered, with a sense of aching sadness.

Nimahl kept his word. He raised Rina's standard of living back to what it was when she was a child. And soon Rina was driving around in a Black Ford.

Her old school friends were surprised when she stopped working. She cringed the first time she had to speak the lie. 'I'm married to a planter,' she told them, blithely. But she couldn't go upcountry to live with her husband on his tea plantation, she explained, because she was helping to parent her family. And for that she needed to be in Colombo, didn't she? Her friends knew this was true and saw no cause to disbelieve her.

Within a few months the deception became reality. Rina hated the charade and gradually dropped out from her circle of friends. Only one or two of them ever met Nimahl, and even then she introduced him under a fictitious name. To everyone other than her immediate family he was Sam Ranasinghe.

Whatever she did she did completely, and so, to give credence to her masquerade Rina bought herself a wedding band and had it engraved: *RR&SR 26.12.67*. Nimahl Singram, alias Sam Ranasinghe became Rina Roberts' phantom husband.

Nimahl Singram was a director of Thorntons. He belonged to and moved in the upper echelons of Colombo's elite society. None of his associates, acquaintances, family or friends knew of the secret life he shared with Rina Roberts.

One of the first things Nimahl bought Rina after he got her the car was a beautiful, German Shepherd pup.

They both loved Bruno, but Rina was mad about her brown-eyed bundle of fur. By the time he was fully grown, Bruno was a friend. When he heard Rina cry at night he would walk up to her bed and nuzzle her face through the mosquito net.

Rina's tears would flow well into the night. The nights Nimahl promised he would come, and couldn't. The nights she would prepare a special meal for him and he wasn't able to get away. On other nights he would turn up unexpectedly, delighting her with his passion and love,

CHAPTER SIXTEEN

obliterating the silent pain she never confessed to anyone; not to her mother, not to her now absent friends, and certainly not to her siblings. She couldn't, for this was the path she had chosen.

She lived a shadowy and unreal life, hungering to hear the low hum of his car driving up the pathway to her house, and the sound of Bruno barking, racing to welcome his master, before her own eager eyes and lips said hello.

CHAPTER SEVENTEEN

1969 – February

'You're going to love the house, baby. It's huge! Eight rooms, four bathrooms and two large kitchens.' Nimahl seemed excited. He was driving Rina to the hill-country to show her a house he was planning to buy in Bandarawela.

'How would you like to live upcountry?' he had asked her the week before. They had been together for two years.

'I don't know, darling,' she answered, 'I've never given it any thought.' But the idea did appeal. The few times she had travelled with Nimahl to the beautiful hill-country of Ceylon, Rina had loved the scenic drives along roads that twisted and curved as they climbed, treacherously sometimes, up to eight thousand feet above sea level at the highest altitude.

Rina had discussed the possible move with her mother and siblings, and they were all in favour of it.

Bandarawela was a well-known town, nestled among mist-clad mountains. The district had a cool climate and was one of the many upcountry regions that were home to Ceylon's famed, emerald-green acres of tea.

He was right. She did love the house. Sun-drenched and painted white, it sat proudly atop a high hill overlooking the sleepy town. The driveway was tarred and ascended up a steep incline that took in a hairpin bend at the top.

As they got out of the car Nimahl pointed to a cottage sitting higher up the slopes. 'Hector, the owner, lives up there and I've got to get the keys off him,' he told Rina.

CHAPTER SEVENTEEN

She watched him leap over a wire fence and walk briskly up a narrow dirt road.

It was late afternoon and the sun had started its downward descent over the mountain ranges. As she waited for Nimahl, Rina limbered up with a few bends and stretches, taking deep breaths in the invigorating air. Glancing around the property she noted the vast, but somewhat neglected garden that surrounded the huge white house, before the grounds sloped down a terraced hillside to the road below.

Nimahl returned and the two of them walked around to the front of the house, their feet crunching along the broad gravelled footpath. 'Apparently it was built by the English as a school boarding house, back in the 1920s,' Nimahl informed Rina. 'There are two identical wings with four bedrooms and two bathrooms on either side,' he added, as he opened the front doors.

Together they stepped onto a long verandah, encased with glass windows down to waist level, affording magnificent mountain views.

From the verandah, two sets of doors led into an enormous combined living and dining room. The previous owners had left some furniture: an old Chesterfield lounge suite, several occasional chairs and a circular card table — its green felt top, faded and threadbare — scarcely filled the room. Rina walked around admiring the lovely old pictures on the walls. She could sense the colonial grandeur the place must have had once.

'Hector's servant has got this room ready for us,' said Nimahl, leading Rina to the front bedroom on the south wing. They were going to be staying for the weekend.

The room had a westerly aspect and was filled with afternoon light.

The magnificent four-poster bed looked inviting with its fresh white sheets and pillows. Above it, a large mosquito net was bundled up and tied midway from the ceiling. The other furniture in the room —a large dressing table and wardrobe, though old — was in excellent condition.

Rina walked into the adjoining bathroom and freshened up. Nimahl did the same.

'That feels better,' she said, sitting on the bed and patting her face dry with a towel. Their journey from Colombo had taken nearly ten hours and she felt a bit tired. Giving into an impulse Rina lay down on the bed with her arms outstretched and heaved a relaxing sigh.

Nimahl stood in the middle of the room, watching her, 'Better get up from there, baby, or we're not going to see the rest of the property before the sun goes down.'

Rina was on her feet in a flash. Nimahl hugged her close and kissed her, edging her back towards the bed. 'Later, sweetheart,' she promised, with a beguiling smile. 'Let's have a look at the gardens first.'

Arms around each other, they walked through to the rear of the house. A large plateau loomed up above them and a set of steps had been cut into the side of the broad hill.

They climbed it.

A breathtaking scene awaited them at the summit. The sun had moved further down towards the west and the distant mountain ridges were edged with gold. The surrounding hills were shrouded in a blue mist rising from the gum trees ... a familiar feature of the region.

'I'm going to call it *Blue Haven*,' said Rina.

'*Blue Haven* it'll be then,' responded Nimahl, promptly.

The plateau had a sunny open vista and they walked the length and breadth of it. The land had been cleared for cultivation, there were signs of past crops.

'I'm going to grow potatoes up here,' Nimahl said suddenly, as if inspired by the fresh mountain air.

Rina laughed. 'You, a farmer?'

'Why not, baby? You'd be surprised at what I can do if I put my hand to it.'

She took both his hands in hers and kissed them. 'I know you're a very smart man, Nimahl Singram, but somehow I can't see these hands digging the earth and planting potatoes.'

'You'll see,' he said, with an air of confidence.

They descended the hill and looked around the back of the property.

A little garden lay nestled in the curve of the U-shaped back verandah and in the middle of the garden was a spreading cherimoya tree, laden with fruit. Rina picked one off a bough and opened it up, savouring its soft, sweet pulp.

Nimahl was seated on the wall of the verandah, observing her.

She approached him with a piece of fruit. 'This is sun-ripened and absolutely delicious, darling. Try it,' she tempted.

CHAPTER SEVENTEEN

He looked at her, with the look that always melted her. 'I'd rather have you.'

She flung the cherimoya away and embraced him passionately. Lingering kisses slowed their short journey to the bedroom

The doors of the house were wide open, but they were too much in love to care. They tumbled into the large four-poster bed, arms still locked around each other.

'How often will you come up to see me?' she asked him much later. They were lying cosily under the covers.

'As often as I can, my darling,' he mumbled, kissing her bare back. 'You know I can't stay away from these beautiful shoulders.'

Within a few weeks of inspecting the property, Rina moved upcountry with her family. Before they left Colombo she scoured the second-hand furniture shops and managed to find just what she was looking for to complement the existing furniture at *Blue Haven*. Among the pieces she prized were a large oval dining table with carved legs, and a very grand-looking European chiffonier. The mahogany-stained pieces looked splendid in the stately home.

Rina invited her cousin Stella, who was in-between jobs, to move up to the hill-country with them for a while. Stella's boyfriend, Mahen, was serving in the rank of Major in the Ceylon army and he was temporarily stationed at the military camp in the adjoining town.

Mahen had been trained at Sandhurst in England. He was a fine officer and a gentleman. He was also a charming, fun-loving man and the Roberts family took to him very quickly. He and Nimahl established a great camaraderie and Mahen was the only outsider in Rina's circle who knew Nimahl's real identity. Whenever Mahen was around he would initiate games on the long verandahs in the evenings. The whole family would join in, even Nimahl on the occasions he was with them.

Finding a school for Rina's brother Michael, posed a problem, but May was soon attending the local Catholic convent. Rina was extremely fond of her two young siblings. She particularly treasured May who had never experienced the good times, when her father's home was a place of love and abundance. 'At least us older ones enjoyed life at Merinda for some years, Mum,' Rina would tell her mother, 'but Michael and May have been so badly deprived.'

They had idyllic times at *Blue Haven*. There was singing, fun and laughter, and for Rina it was like the grand old days of Merinda. That once happy atmosphere, which had been the centre of her life as a child, was her true north. The word Merinda had changed meaning for the Roberts family now. No longer did it refer to their former hometown. Whenever they spoke of Merinda it was synonymous with their family home.

Nimahl hired two servants for Rina, Thiyagarajah and Charlotte, a middle-aged husband and wife team who had looked after the house for the previous owners. They proved invaluable in helping Rina maintain the large house and garden

Much to her delight Rina discovered she had a flair for gardening. She was energetic and unafraid of hard work. With a hat on her head, a pitchfork in her hand and some help from the servants she soon restored the neglected grounds, and planted cool climate flowering plants, vastly different to the exotic tropical foliage of Colombo's gardens. She grew dahlias, carnations, asters, marigolds and a colourful array of perennials to decorate her garden, and decorate it she did, very beautifully.

Most days her mother and the servants would repeatedly summon her in for lunch, but Rina ignored their calls, working tirelessly in her garden until the sun turned gold and disappeared over the mountains. She also became the "man about the house," climbing ladders, fixing fuses and doing all sorts of odd jobs capably and efficiently.

True to his word Nimahl got his potatoes off the land. But it was Thiyagarajah that did all the hard work, directed by his master, of course.

It was a glorious sunny day when they climbed up the plateau to celebrate their first crop. Thiyagarajah had decided this was the day to dig them out. After a little shallow and careful hoeing, the wiry old servant gathered a few earth encrusted potatoes into a wicker container and brought them over to Nimahl. Dropping the basket at his master's feet, Thiyagarajah beamed, 'Here you are, sir. Your first harvest!'

'Isn't this wonderful,' said Nimahl. Squatting down on his haunches, he handled the tubers lovingly and admiringly, as if he had never seen one before.

CHAPTER SEVENTEEN

Watching his childlike pleasure Rina knew instinctively that he too had discovered the almost mystical thrill of cultivating the earth and seeing it yield something, even if it was just a humble potato.

In the poignant little cameo she was witnessing Rina felt she had caught sight of the child within this tall handsome man she loved so dearly.

'We might be farmers yet, darling,' she told him as she knelt down on the dirt beside him.

'I wouldn't mind,' he said, looking around as if seeing the good brown earth for the first time. 'I wouldn't mind at all.'

After Nimahl had returned to the city Rina took her journal out to record their little "potato harvest."

> *I wish I could have seen him when he was a little boy and while he was growing up. There's something so appealing about the very core of him, so rarely seen. But I saw it up there on the plateau last Saturday. How innocent and childlike he looked.*
>
> *Dear God, what wouldn't I give to live out the rest of our lives together. I know there's no one else with whom I could have my 'portrait of a marriage'. When I'm with him the world disappears and it's only us. How precious are the days that he's with me. I miss him terribly the moment he leaves. I never go out to wave goodbye. When I hear the sound of his car going down the driveway it feels as if my heart is being emptied out.*

Living in the hill-country was a time of self-discovery for Rina. She found she had a sense of adventure and loved going out with her family to explore the surrounding countryside, while her mother stayed home with the servants.

Stella's boyfriend, Mahen, always accompanied the Roberts clan on their excursions. Since he was familiar with the district they gave him the task of selecting their picnic area. After hours of tramping around the hills and dales they would assemble at the bottom of a wide ravine, a spot Mahen favoured, near one of the many streams and waterways that traversed the mountainous region. A suspension bridge connected one end of the ravine with the other, and its thick cable ropes stretched over a fast-flowing stream that coursed through the middle of the gorge. The walkway was made up of well-tethered, sturdy planks.

Rina's young brother Michael, and Mahen, took perverse delight in gently swinging the cables whenever the girls precariously inched their way across the bridge, rending the serene mountain air with their screams.

On one such crossing Rina's German Shepherd, Bruno, fell through. Naturally, Mahen led the rescue operation. Like the well-trained army officer that he was he gave orders, calmly, to his "foot-soldier" Michael. First to get five panic-stricken females off the bridge, and then to recover the dog, whose furious barking could only be heard. Bruno had disappeared into the lush vegetation below. Luckily he had fallen at the entrance of the gully, well before the bridge crossed over the rapid stream and rocks below.

But there was one thing they all hated in the mountains. Rina loathed them. Most were only small, about an inch long, but they were more fearful to her than snakes. She lamented the fact that stepping on moist grass, particularly in areas near waterfalls or mountain streams — alluring habitats for her — would invite the disgusting creatures to clamber onto any exposed flesh. Their sinister advances were never perceived until they drew blood, and then, for Rina, all hell broke loose.

Whenever the Roberts family ventured outdoors, particularly on their mountain excursions, Rina made sure they carried lots of salt with them. Leeches could only be dislodged with cigarette ash or salt. Hill-country folk who worked outdoors habitually applied a thick coating of soap on legs and feet to deter the disgusting creatures from clambering onto their limbs. The very thought of them gave Rina the shivers!

She could never forget the time, during one of their trips to the hill-country, when she and Nimahl had stopped at the Belihuloya Hotel for an afternoon cup of tea.

'Come and have a look at the rock pool,' he invited her.

Rina was reluctant to go knowing leeches would be lurking in the wet grass, but Nimahl was so eager to show her the water feature she followed him, gingerly, gathering in her blue voile sari so it wouldn't accidentally brush against the plants and pick up any unwelcome guests.

When she did see the pool she wasn't all that enamoured with it due to her pressing anxiety over leeches. She couldn't wait to get back to the

CHAPTER SEVENTEEN

open verandahs at the front of the hotel, which bordered a safely paved courtyard! All she wanted was to relax with a cup of tea and take in the beautiful surroundings of the elegant, upcountry retreat.

They were sitting on the sprawling verandah and sipping cups of delicious high-grown tea when Rina felt an itch on her right leg. She reached down to scratch it, and through her voile sari and slip felt a huge rubbery bump on her mid-calf.

She screamed blue murder

The waiters came rushing over.

Rina stretched out her leg and raised her blue satin slip and sari up to her knee. 'Get it off me, get if off me,' she shouted hysterically in Sinhalese, oblivious to the fact that strange men were looking at her bare limb.

A waiter grabbed a saltshaker and tipped its contents over the large black leech clinging to Rina's right calf. After one glance at her leg she averted her face. She had never seen such a huge leech.

In seconds the creature disgorged itself and fell to the floor. Rina made whimpering noises as she looked at it with disgust.

The manager had now arrived on the scene. 'It's only a little leech,' he said, peering at the floor.

Nimahl was trying to hide his amusement.

'Little?' Rina cried out indignantly, pointing to the blubbery horror. 'Look at the size of it!'

A waiter quickly swept it away and out of sight.

But what Rina absolutely adored in the hill-country were the waterfalls.

Discovering them on weekends was another favourite pastime for the Roberts clan. Again, Mahen was their guide. Quite a few waterfalls were hidden and only accessible by trekking along narrow dirt roads on foot for a few miles.

From the first time she caught sight of one Rina fell in love with the cascading waters. Some were like gentle, gossamer bridal veils, meandering down the face of moss-covered rocks. Others were wild, uncontrollable cataracts that roared over towering boulders, drenching the surrounding vegetation with their surging sprays.

The Diyaluma waterfall was a sight to behold. They had travelled many miles to see it. Rina was captivated as she gazed up at the thundering torrent of water. It's like an ardent lover, she thought, urgently rushing to meet the waiting arms of the river downstream, which gathered in her swirling waters, never tiring of the unceasing passion that moved towards it endlessly.

As soon as she got home Rina wrote to Nimahl about it.

> When I saw the Diyaluma waterfall today, I was enraptured. I'm longing to see it again someday with you beside me, darling. I feel as if I am that tempestuous waterfall, always reaching towards you in body, soul and spirit, and you are the river gathering me into your arms. Tell me, my dearest beloved, has anybody ever loved like this? ...

They wrote each other long and passionate letters. Rina sent hers to his office address. At *Blue Haven* when the postman arrived with mail from Nimahl, Rina would hurry to her room, sit on her bed and read his lengthy and captivating letters.

Her letters to him were equally enchanting, he told her. There was one he said he would always treasure.

> My darling Nimahl,
>
> It's a pleasant evening here at Blue Haven, and I'm sitting on the steps of the verandah, longing for you. A half-moon is rising, and the trees are silhouetted against a faint pink glow, still lingering in the western sky. The air is sweet, my love, with the smell of jasmines and the scent from the lemon verbena tree. The red lilies on the terraces are now in full bloom. I wish you could see them. I discovered on the weekend that the slender young pine tree we staked to the metal post has broken loose and lost its moorings. Remember how we anchored it together? It's now tottering, like the "Leaning Tower of Pisa," looking slightly lost, as I am without you ...

CHAPTER EIGHTEEN

1969 – October

The most significant thing Rina discovered about herself while living in the mountains was that she was, after all, a city dweller. Eight months after she had moved upcountry, she found she was missing the hustle and bustle of suburban life in Colombo.

The hard task of restoring the gardens at *Blue Haven* had been completed and time was hanging on her hands. There was nothing much else to do. There were no decent cinemas, no beaches for recreation, no friends or relatives to visit and not even the remotest possibility of finding a job.

The days dragged on rather listlessly, but the major cause of Rina's despondence was the infrequency of Nimahl's visits. Down in the city he had been with her at least five times a week. Now she only saw him one weekend in a month.

Although she treasured the long and passionate letters he wrote her, unspoken doubts started to niggle. She didn't talk to anyone about it, not even to Stella in whom she usually confided, but Rina found herself questioning Nimahl's motives for wanting her to live upcountry. She knew his wife had given birth to a third child and she wondered if that was the reason he had moved her out of Colombo, so that he could devote more time to his family, and keep her in his life as well, but somewhere out there. The thought hurt.

She was sure she heard her mother discussing it with Stella one day, but they stopped their conversation when she approached, and she was too embarrassed to bring it up.

She decided to raise the question with Nimahl on his next trip.

Seated on the edge of her bed, Rina watched Nimahl search for something in his bag. He had arrived the night before. It was now Saturday afternoon.

'Darling, why did you want me to move upcountry? I never thought to ask you before.'

'Don't you like it here, baby?'

'I miss you,' she said, noticing he hadn't answered. 'I only get to see you one weekend in a month. I keep wondering whether you wanted me out of Colombo for some reason?'

He straightened up and frowned at her. 'Rina, that's ridiculous.' He only called her Rina when he was annoyed.

'Tell me why, then?' she persisted.

'There was no particular reason. I thought you might like a change. You've lived in Colombo all your life.'

'But didn't you think of the distance there'd be between us? Or is that what you wanted?'

'Rina, you're forgetting something. I love you. You know that. Why would I want you out of the way? You're being very irrational.'

That hit a nerve.

'You're perfectly right,' she said. 'I am irrational. I'm twenty-three and the mistress of a married man who's living in Colombo with his wife and *three* children,' she said, pointedly, 'while I have been relegated to no-man's land. That's certainly not how a rational woman would choose to live now, is it?'

He looked at her sharply. 'You're trying to pick a fight with me, Rina, and I'm not having it. I'm leaving.'

'You're leaving because you haven't got the courage to answer my question,' she shot back.

He didn't say another word. He gathered his few toiletries from the bathroom, threw them into his overnight bag and walked out of the room. In a few minutes Rina heard him drive away.

'Rina, where are you?'

'In here, Mum.' She was still sitting on her bed, locked in her misery.

Anita entered the room. 'Why did Nimahl take off so suddenly? And with such an angry look on his face. What happened?'

'Don't ask, Mum, please.' Tears were close, but Rina restrained herself. She never cried in front of her family.

He'll come back, she thought, it's only Saturday afternoon.

CHAPTER EIGHTEEN

Monday morning came around and he hadn't even called her. She went through the day feeling desperate. By Tuesday, lunchtime, he still hadn't rung. His silence enraged her all the more. For although she could write letters to him at his office she could never ring him. Such were the boundaries set for his hidden mistress. By Tuesday afternoon the turmoil inside her was unbearable.

She rushed out to her car, reversed it out of the garage, ready to take off. Where? She didn't know. She just had to do something, to get away and release the enormous tension she was under.

Stella was in the garden. 'Are you going into town?' she called out.

'Yes, I need to get some stuff,' Rina hollered back.

'Wait! I'll come with you.' Stella hurried to the car. 'Where's your handbag?' she asked as she got in.

'Blast! I forgot. I'll go and get it.'

Rina was back in less than a minute, thinking, *Damn ... I'll have to ditch her somewhere.*

She drove into the town's main street and parked. Pointing to one of the grocery stores, Rina said to her cousin, 'Could you go over there and get us some bread and sugar, Stella, I'm going over to the fruit stall.' She gave Stella some money and waited till she was out of sight.

Rina started up the car and was about to reverse when a tap on the window of the passenger seat halted her. She groaned inwardly as she leaned over and opened the door for her sister, May.

'Hi, Rina,' said the happy schoolgirl, who was on her way home from school. 'I don't have to walk home now, I can get a ride with you.' She waved goodbye to her friends.

Rina flinched at the thought of duping her sister. She spoke quickly. 'May, do me a favour, Stella's gone to buy some bread and sugar from over there.' She pointed out the store again. 'Can you go and ask her to get us some tea-leaves as well?'

'Sure,' said May and dropped her schoolbooks onto the seat. She skipped out of sight.

Rina reversed and took off hurriedly.

The tears she had held back for four days gushed forth. Heading west, she drove quickly through the almost flat terrain of the next town. After that the landscape changed dramatically.

From an altitude of six thousand feet above sea level, the road spiralled down towards the low country in swift and continuous turns, some of them hairpin bends. Manoeuvring the treacherously winding road was no easy task and this was the first time Rina was making the hazardous journey alone. Blinded by tears, she kept turning the steering wheel sharply and constantly, from left to right, while negotiating the steep descents. She didn't know what she was doing or where she was going. The built up tension, hurt and anger erupted in hysterical sobs.

She hadn't gone very far when a preposterous idea took hold of her. *Just drive off the road.*

I'll do it fast, she told herself, *right at the very next hairpin bend, I won't turn, I'll fly straight off the mountain.* The thought of plunging her car thousands of feet down a ravine brought a macabre relief to her raging emotions.

As she negotiated the next small curve in the road Rina was forced to brake hard and stop. The traffic had stalled. Struggling to control her tears, she cursed furiously as she sat behind a small van. How far, how near to the next hairpin bend, she wondered feverishly.

She became aware of a commotion on the road up ahead. Craning her neck to see what was happening, she discovered a lorry coming up the mountains had awkwardly manoeuvred the hairpin bend lying immediately ahead of her! Motorists travelling in both directions were held up as the driver tried to correct the fault.

Vehicles banked up behind Rina and she was hemmed in completely. Her car was idling for a while before she realised she'd better turn it off. Her Ford Prefect was notorious for overheating.

As she waited, Rina glanced down at May's schoolbooks and a surge of affection for her sister overwhelmed her. She kept seeing May's happy face at the window of her car; the angelic smile, and the blue-ribboned plaits swinging as the child had run off to the store.

In a little while the traffic began to clear, very slowly, and Rina kept inching forward behind the single lane of vehicles. Suddenly her car started jerking and spluttering. She quickly brought it down a gear. Motorists behind her tooted their horns impatiently as the car bucked and stalled a few times.

With a good measure of panic, Rina's full attention was absorbed in getting the wretched vehicle to behave. In the mirror she noticed the string of vehicles following.

CHAPTER EIGHTEEN

Distracted by the problem with the car, Rina's frame of mind was subdued, and gradually the hysteria left her. Thoughts of May had been a strong and sobering influence too.

But the car was now totally unmanageable. She had to get it to a garage. She knew there was one at the start of the low country looming up ahead.

The car spluttered so badly that for the last half a mile or so she had to let it crawl along in first gear to reach the repair shop.

It was five thirty in the evening when Rina left the garage at Pelmadulla. Her sanity had returned. She decided she wouldn't even attempt to go back to *Blue Haven* this late for night fell swiftly in the hill-country. She didn't want to negotiate those twisting roads in the dark; many mountain passes were usually blanketed in thick fog at night.

Besides, she wanted to see Nimahl. She had to talk to him.

Her driving was smooth and the car hummed pleasantly as she sped towards Colombo.

Four hours later Rina breathed a sigh of relief as she reached the outskirts of the city, heartened by the sights and sounds that greeted her.

She decided to go to the house of an old family friend, Roland Cotterling, who lived in one of Colombo's central suburbs. He was a retired teacher and a widower, and well known to the Roberts family.

It was nearly ten pm when Rina arrived on his doorstep, relieved to find the lights still on.

'Rina! This is a pleasant surprise. Come in, come in,' said Roland as he answered the tap on his door. 'I thought you were all living upcountry, my dear.'

'We are, Roland. I just came down to Colombo to attend to something, but ran into a bit of a problem. Could I use your telephone?' She didn't want to tell him anything and he, being impeccably polite, didn't ask.

'Of course. Come inside and I'll make us some tea.'

Rina phoned Mahen. He was now back on duty at the army headquarters in Panagoda, outside Colombo.

'Oh my God, Rina! Where are you? Everyone's worried sick,' said Mahen.

'I'm at a friend's place in Colpetty.'

'Nimahl is like a madman!' said Mahen. 'I rang him as soon as Stella called me. Give me your address and phone number, Rina, and I'll ring you right back. Now stay there and don't move.' Mahen laughed to lighten his command.

'Nimahl will be there in ten minutes,' informed Mahen, when he called her back. 'Are you all right, Rina?'

'I'm okay, Mahen.'

'You know Nimahl and I rang all the police stations from here to *Blue Haven*, checking whether there'd been an accident. When we found that nothing had been reported, Nimahl wanted to get a roadblock set up to stop you, but I told him that would embarrass you too much. I tell you,' said Mahen, laughing with relief, 'you deserve a spanking.'

As soon as Mahen rang off, Rina telephoned home.

Anita Roberts was justifiably upset. 'Are you trying to kill your mother, Rina? You've given us all a horrible fright.'

Rina was mortified. 'I'm sorry, Mum. I really am. I don't know what happened.'

'What do you mean you don't know what happened? What the hell are you doing?' It was a rare display of anger from her mother. 'We've been frantic with worry. Stella and May waited in town for ages before they walked home. Stella was so upset. She thought you were going to commit suicide! Why did you take off like that?'

'Is May all right?' Rina asked her mother.

'Yes, she is. She's about the only one who is. "Mum, don't worry," she said to me, "when Rina sees my books in the car she won't do anything silly."' Anita's voice softened, 'Where are you, Rina?'

'I'm in Colombo, at Roland's place. Don't worry, Mum, please. I'll be back at *Blue Haven* as soon as possible ... I have to go now.'

She hurried to the bathroom to stifle her rising sobs, aghast at how close she had come to shattering May's supreme confidence in her.

In a few minutes she came out and joined Roland in the living room, drinking tea and exchanging pleasantries with him, making out that life was just a breeze, an art she had mastered well throughout her young life. Soon there was a knock on the door. Rina had mentioned to Roland that her *husband* would be picking her up.

'Leave your car here, baby we'll get it later.' The voice was gentle. Taking her by the hand like an errant child, he said, 'Come with me.'

'I've never been so worried in my life,' he told her, as she climbed into his car.

CHAPTER EIGHTEEN

She didn't respond.

He took her to a late night café. 'You must be hungry.'

'I can't eat anything.'

'We'll have two lemonades,' said Nimahl to the approaching waiter, who took their order and disappeared.

'Okay, baby ... so what was all that about?'

She felt like a schoolgirl before the Principal. She didn't know how to begin. 'I don't know,' she said, sullenly. 'You should have rung me.'

'Yes, I admit that's my fault, I should have rung you. But why did you take off like that, scaring the hell out of everyone?'

'I was upset. I didn't really know what I was doing.'

'You didn't know what you were doing?' The question was asked with a measure of controlled anger.

Rina's heart sank. She wanted to tell him so much, but could she tell him anything? She looked briefly at the waiter as he set down the drinks. He smiled at her. She smiled back rather weakly.

Nimahl glared at the young boy and waited till he was out of earshot. 'You take off from *Blue Haven*, fobbing off your sister and Stella. You leave them stranded in the middle of town and make a damned dangerous journey down the mountains alone, and now you're telling me you didn't know what you were doing?'

'Stop it! Please!' she pleaded, miserably. 'I was very upset.' She felt barriers tumbling into place. Tongue tied and unable to communicate, she couldn't tell him how she had been feeling; couldn't talk to him about her despair, her misery, her restlessness, and her future that seemed so hopeless; about the marriage she could never have with him, how angry she had been that she couldn't ring him; how much she loved him; how much she missed him. She looked at him and knew instinctively that he'd never understand what had driven her to take off like a captive bird, yearning for the forests and freedom.

For the first time she saw the real distance between them, and it wasn't geographical.

'If you're trying to force my hand and get me to leave my family, it won't work, Rina. I'm not leaving my wife.' Nimahl banged his fist on the table. 'At least not now.'

With the words he spoke and the sound of his fist on the wooden table, her flawed paradise disappeared, like shifting plates in an earthquake. They moved, dominions away, to the lowest region of Hades.

Rina looked at Nimahl and wondered if he could read her eyes and see the death she felt. 'I never ever wanted you to leave your wife, Nimahl,' she said in a pained voice. 'Never ever. I've never asked you to leave your family. There's no need for you to tell me this.' The masks were on, for the first time with him, and she could feel doors closing in her heart.

Immediately contrite, he said, 'I'm sorry, baby. I'm really sorry I said that ... I was angry.'

He reached out a hand to hers, lying on the table. She withdrew hers, surprised at the absence of emotion.

The look on her face told him she had closed off. 'What am I going to do with you, child?' he asked, with a sigh of exasperation.

'I'm not a child. Please don't call me one,' said the wounded child. 'And you can always leave me, Nimahl. Leave me!' she said with a raised voice. 'I can get along without you. I did so before and I can do so again.'

Pitiful bravado. They both knew it. They finished their drinks in silence.

'Come on,' the voice was gentle again. 'I'm taking you to your Aunty Vivien's.'

Once outside, he embraced her.

She was still withdrawn. 'What about my car?' she asked, as she got into his.

'You're not in a fit state to drive any more tonight,' he replied, glancing at her.

If he was expecting a response or protest, she gave none. Instead she sat calm and controlled beside him as he started up the car.

'I'll get it picked up and sent to Aunty Vivien's tomorrow morning and I'll come over in the evening. We'll talk then.'

It was another month before Rina and her family returned to Colombo. Nimahl decided to keep *Blue Haven* and run it as a holiday home, with the help of his two servants, Thiyagarajah and Charlotte, of course.

Rina's family, as well as Stella and Mahen, spoke about her "solo flight" occasionally, which was what they had dubbed her "running away from the mountains," as they put it. After it was all over, Rina was embarrassed by what she had done, and so they joked about it a few times to redeem the incident for the girl they all cared about.

CHAPTER NINETEEN

1970 – April

The breeze wafting in through the open doors and windows dispersed the pleasant smell of Pynol, freshening the air inside. Rina had just finished washing down the cement floors in the house, cleaning and disinfecting them as she did every Saturday.

'That's nice and spotless again,' said her mother encouragingly, as she stepped on the rags Rina had laid down for a footpath until the floors dried.

'Till tomorrow!' said her daughter.

Anita observed the look of tiredness. 'Why don't you have a little lie-down, darling?'

'I'm just about to, Mum,' said Rina, heading towards her room.

She was surprised at how weary she felt. Sitting on her bed, she took a couple of slow, deep breaths before giving in to the impulse to rest her head on the pillow.

A tap on the front door disturbed her light sleep. *Better get up and answer that,* she thought. In the very next second, terror engulfed her. She couldn't move a muscle. Not a foot, or a leg, or a hand, or an arm.

Panic coursed through her body. She tried to shout, to call for help, but she couldn't even open her mouth. She heard Stella greeting Mahen at the front door, so she knew she could hear. And she was able to think, her mind was clear. But no matter how hard she tried, she couldn't move.

This must be a stroke, she thought.

Fear gripped her. No one would know she was lying paralysed on her bed. On her strict instructions nobody ever disturbed her when she was asleep. *Dear God, how long before someone finds me?*

She was trying to remember all she had read about heart attacks and strokes. Time was important, she knew.

Her dressing table, with a full-length mirror, stood next to her bed. She could see her hairbrush. *If I can grab that I can make a sound with it,* she thought. Focusing all her resolve she made an attempt to raise her right arm. Miracle! It moved. But there it sat like a dead weight on the dressing table.

Stella was now chatting to Mahen in the lounge.

After making more of an effort to move her arm Rina found it had gained some strength. She made a grab for the brush and brought it down heavily on the dressing table, and did so again, and again, and more slowly as her arm tired out.

Please God, let somebody find me, soon. I'm so scared. Ma ... Mum!

'Stella,' Mahen's voice reached her ears, 'there's an odd sound coming from that first room. Can you check it, please?'

Stella's footsteps ... the curtain moved. Relief!

Rina felt tears trickling past her ears, down her neck and into her hair, but she couldn't move her head.

'Rina are you okay?'

There was no response.

Stella moved closer — saw the open eyes and the tears. 'Oh my God! Mahen!' she yelled.

A few quick strides and Mahen was in the room.

'She can't talk, Mahen! She can't move. Look at her!'

'Rina, can you hear me?' asked Mahen.

Not a sound issued from Rina.

'Oh my God, what are we going to do?' Stella's voice was high-pitched.

'Calm down, Stella. Rina can you hear me?' Mahen asked again.

Yes, I can, she was screaming inside, but her jaws were locked.

'I'd better get Aunty Anita,' said Stella, running out of the room.

'Keep the children away,' Mahen called after her.

Anita came rushing up to her daughter's bed. 'Rina, darling! Rina!' She looked at Stella and Mahen. 'What's happening?'

Mahen placed a firm hand on Anita's shoulder. 'Don't panic, Aunty, Please! We're taking her to the doctor's. Help me, Stella.'

Anita raised both hands to her mouth as she saw her daughter being carried out to Mahen's car.

CHAPTER NINETEEN

On the way to the doctor's surgery, Rina regained movement as well as her speech. But she felt exhausted.

Within a few days Nimahl managed to get Rina an appointment with one of the city's finest neurosurgeons, recommended by her doctor. Meanwhile she had two further episodes of the strange attacks.

The specialist was thorough. Anita sat with her daughter while he questioned, probed and examined. He sent Rina for X-rays and blood tests. A week later, on her follow-up visit, the neurosurgeon informed Rina, much to her relief, that there was nothing wrong with her physically.

'I'm convinced these seizures are some kind of anxiety attacks, Miss Roberts and I'm referring you to a psychiatrist,' said the specialist. 'Please see him as soon as you can.'

But Rina couldn't get an appointment for nearly a fortnight. And despite her constant assurances to her mother that there was no cause for concern, Anita was stricken by what was happening to her daughter.

The psychiatrist's practice was situated in a large bungalow in one of Colombo's elite and very leafy suburbs. Rina sat in his consulting room while he was writing up notes, following a preliminary discussion he had had with her. Nimahl was also in the room.

Through an open window Rina glanced out into the garden. *It looks like a small rain forest*, she thought, as she gazed up at the dappled sunlight, dancing with the flickering leaves of the camphor laurels. A strange and sad yearning stirred within her. This was the first time she was experiencing an indefinable, deep ache in her heart.

She sighed heavily and turned her attention back to the room to find the psychiatrist observing her intently.

'Are you living a normal life for a young girl your age?' He asked, and glanced momentarily at Nimahl. Rina had introduced him to the doctor as her fiancé.

'Yes,' she said quickly, knowing how untrue it must sound even to Nimahl's ears.

The psychiatrist diagnosed her seizures as a type of fugue state, brought on by prolonged anxiety. He wrote out a prescription for Valium, 'to help relieve any stress you might be experiencing. But I'd like to see you every fortnight, Miss Roberts, just by yourself. We've got to find out what's causing you such anxiety.'

On the way home Nimahl bought Rina the Valium. 'Don't let these become a habit, baby,' he cautioned. 'Take it only when you're feeling stressed.'

But that night Rina took five milligrams and enjoyed the feeling of relaxation. She mused as she lay in bed. *Fugue state! Sounds like a dirge composed by a melancholy Mozart. I'm melancholy too. How can I tell the psychiatrist what's really bothering me? How can I tell him that I'm living a lie and I hate it, but that I love this man so much that I can't see a future for me without him, and there isn't one for me with him, either.*

For the rest of the year life went on in a desultory fashion for Rina. At twenty-four she found herself moving between moments of joy, when Nimahl was with her, to states of unease and anxiety where her thoughts persistently dragged her down.

Writing poetry gave her some respite and she took Valium to fall asleep at night, but she was baffled at what was happening to her, not knowing then that she had entered the dark, confining world of depression.

'Mea Culpa, Mea Culpa, Mea Maxima Culpa,' she would confess to her dog Bruno, repeating with irony the lines she had memorised from the Latin Mass Book when she was a child. Sitting on the floor of her bedroom she would hug the German Shepherd and translate the confession. 'Through my fault, through my fault, through my most grievous fault,' she would strike her chest and tell him in mock solemnity. Bruno would look at her rather quizzically, unsure of this new command. Head tilted, he would offer a paw as if to assure her of his very faithful support through whatever it was that was troubling her.

Rina's peculiar dreams began a couple of months later.

She had just settled into the spacious four bed-roomed house Nimahl had bought for her to live in, at Nawala, just outside Colombo's metropolitan precinct.

At first she didn't talk to anyone about the dreams, but only recorded them in her journal.

> *The first time I had these strange dreams was about a month ago. I found I was in an upstairs section of a house, in a sort of dingy old attic, and I'm looking out between the slivers of torn*

and dusty curtains. I can see soldiers on the street outside and they've surrounded the house. I know there's danger around and they mustn't find me; I have to hide up here. I can hear their marching boots and I'm terrified they might look up and see me.

I've had other variations to this dream. The attic has now become the upstairs floor of our home in Merinda — and that's funny, because dad never did build that second floor he planned. But in my dream, that's where I am. And I find there's no door into or out of the place, and I don't even know how I got up there. I'm trapped! But what really distresses me is the fact that no one knows of the existence of this upper floor, and so the value of the house isn't fully realised. That seems to fill me with agonising despair.

In another version I find myself going around lamenting over the furniture that's neglected and unkempt, carelessly bunched up together and covered with old, dirty dustsheets. In another I see the walls full of cobwebs and there are many dark rooms, half-closed. But I'm too scared to go into any of them and as always, in these dreams, I find I am alone and I can't get out of this second floor.

Eventually Rina mentioned the recurring dreams to her mother, but Anita was stumped. Usually she was quite good at figuring out the meanings of dreams, but these she couldn't interpret.

During this period Rina had other significant dreams too. She told Stella about one in particular.

It was a weekday evening and both cousins were sitting in the lounge-room, reading. It was the monsoon season and the rain was a roaring downpour outside.

'I had a strange dream last night, Stella.'

'What about?' asked Stella, promptly putting her book down and looking across the room at Rina.

'I'm not exactly sure. There were roads and some water — let me tell you about it.'

Stella moved to a closer chair so she could hear her cousin over the din of the storm.

'In my dream,' Rina began, 'I was walking along this broad, tree-lined avenue when I noticed some of my old school friends splashing about and having fun in a pool nearby. They called out to me, "Come on, Rina, jump in. The water's lovely, come and join us." I shouted to them, "I can't stop, I have to keep going," and I walked on. I came to an intersection and hesitated for a bit, but decided to veer to the left. As I walked along this road I found there were no trees around, not even one, and the sun was beating fiercely on my head. No one else was on the road except me. And there I was, this solitary figure walking in the hot noonday sun. Up ahead I could see the road was coming to an end and beyond that were marshlands, but I still kept going. And then I saw this house under construction and the builders were watching me. As I drew close to the house, and to my utter shame, I found I had no clothes on. The workmen started jeering. I ran as fast as I could, using my hands to try and cover my body, and as I came to the end of the road I jumped into the marshes.' Rina stopped abruptly.

'Was that the end of it?' asked Stella.

'No. I woke up when I felt myself slowly sinking into the muddy waters.'

Stella had been listening intently. Her forehead creased in a frown. 'Goodness, Rina. It's very symbolic, don't you think? You're not living the lifestyle of your friends, so in a sense you haven't joined them ... that's the meaning of the pool. And you've taken another road, quite different to the pleasant tree-lined avenue that they're on. Can you see it?'

'I do,' said Rina, nodding her head. 'And I think the sun beating fiercely down on me means I'm going to be scorched by troubles.'

'That's right, and then you find you're alone on that road.' Stella sighed, and looked sadly at her cousin. 'Very few girls would have chosen this path you're on, Rina. I certainly wouldn't have. But I don't like the muddy waters bit and you being naked and all that.'

'Nor do I,' Rina said despondently. She stared at the closed window. The rain was lashing against the glass panes. 'God only knows what's lying up ahead for me.'

'Don't think of it that way, Rina. This dream could be a warning. Perhaps it's telling you to get off this road, and showing you the disaster up ahead if you don't.'

Rina looked at her cousin and raised her eyebrows. 'Stella darling, you and I both know I won't be able to avoid disaster no matter which road I take now.'

CHAPTER NINETEEN

A sad day arrived for Rina when she had to farewell her cousin. Stella had lived with the Roberts family for several years while she worked in the city. Now she had found employment as a receptionist in one of the many beachside hotels springing up on the island, and she had to move closer to its location. Tourism was fast developing into a very lucrative industry in Ceylon.

Rina's household had shrunk almost overnight. Her younger sister Jean had married and moved away. Esther had already migrated to Australia with her husband. Now there was only Rina, her mother Anita, and her siblings Michael and May, who were still at school

'I'm getting concerned about these dreams of yours, Rina. What was it this time?' asked Anita.

They were having breakfast and Rina had just mentioned to her mother that she'd had another recurring dream the previous night.

'I was in that upstairs place again, Mum, and I was washing the walls even though they looked clean. But the more I washed them a red stain kept spreading and it ended up looking horrible, like blood-stained walls.'

'These dreams of yours are baffling me, child,' said her mother. 'You know Papa used to say if you had recurring dreams your soul is trying to tell you something?'

'Really? I wonder what my poor soul is trying to tell me,' said Rina, with a grimace. 'I wish I could understand these wretched dreams.'

'I think I'll have to visit an old neighbour of mine,' announced Anita.

'Not Lydia Wilmet!' said Rina.

They both laughed, surprised that they could.

'Heaven forbid!' exclaimed Anita, rolling her eyes. 'No, I'm going to visit Lorna Johnson. She used to be a matron at a private hospital and I remember how interested she was in psychology, when nobody else was. She was forever reading books and trying to tell me stuff. It was Greek to me! But I recall her saying that meaningful dreams have significance, and your dreams are certainly meaningful. Who knows, she might have some answers for you, Rina.'

'Mrs Johnson is smart,' announced Anita to her daughter, a few days later. She had just returned from visiting her former neighbour.

'Tell me, tell me, I'm dying to know,' said Rina, eagerly.

She led her mother into the living room. 'Sit, Mum, please, and tell me what she said.'

'Let me get changed first, child.'

'Mum, mum ... Please! Tell me first. It won't take long.'

'Oh all right,' Anita conceded, seeing how impatient her daughter was. She settled into a chair. 'This is what Lorna said. The upstairs floor that you keep dreaming about is you — your inner self. And it's more than just your mind. It's the deepest part of you. You've closed yourself off to things that have affected you emotionally, and you don't know how to open them up and deal with them. That's why there's no door, she said. But this repression is now affecting your life, so the dreams are recurring. And you know the one about the bloodstained walls? She says that although externally you seem fine, there's a lot of wounding inside that's messing you up. It's as if you're bleeding inside.'

'Is that all she said?' asked Rina, looking at her mother with disappointment.

'Concerning the dreams, yes, but she also said you should seriously consider seeing that psychiatrist. She feels you're a very troubled young girl. That's what the dreams are signifying.'

For many days Rina thought of what her mother's friend had said, but the explanations seemed vague and didn't clarify anything for her. And as for seeing the psychiatrist, that was impossible. How she could divulge the secret life she was living. So that proved a dead end.

The house was quiet except for Bruno sighing on the floor near her bed. The gentle whirring of the ceiling fan overhead was soothing, and the large, voluminous mosquito net seemed like a protective mist around Rina and her mother.

Whenever she felt particularly anxious or disturbed, Rina would ask Anita to sleep in her room with her. Besides the strange dreams, some scary nightmares plagued Rina now.

'Mum, are you awake?'

'Yes, but you disturbed my thoughts.'

'Sorry ... What were you thinking?'

'I was remembering how much my father adored you when you were a baby.'

'I love hearing about him, I only wish I could remember him.'

CHAPTER NINETEEN

'You were only five when he died, darling. You wouldn't be able to remember him much.'

'You know I talk to Papa sometimes, Mum, because I know how much he loves me. You've told me that. Whenever I'm really upset and sad I talk to him.' She didn't tell her mother they were tear-driven, passionate appeals for supernatural help, late at night in her bedroom when she felt she was drowning in despair.

'I'm glad you tell someone.'

'Mum?'

'Yes?'

'I had a strange dream last night.'

'Oh, child,' Anita groaned in the semi-darkness. 'Not another one of those wretched dreams.'

'No, no! This was a new one, and completely different. I dreamt I was in the front garden in Merinda. Remember how horrible it looked when we went back after a few years?' Rina reminded her mother.

'Yes. Poor Danny,' sighed Anita. 'All his hard work ruined.'

Dad's too, Rina thought, but didn't say. 'In my dream, I was out there in the garden looking at the overgrown brambles, when suddenly on an impulse I rushed towards them and started lifting them up. I was surprised to find how weighty they were. And as I raised them up, the thorns scratched me badly and my arms were bruised and bleeding. But I got a real shock, Mum. Underneath all that horrible mess the beautiful miniature roses were still flourishing. Remember how I used to call them my trinket roses? Well there they were, still beautiful and untouched by the thorny brambles, but totally hidden from view.'

Anita was quiet for a few moments. 'That's you, darling,' she said, unhesitatingly. 'You are the trinket roses. And you know what I think? This dream tells me that your heart and spirit will always blossom, no matter how much life bruises you, child. But few will see that hidden part of you. They'll only see the brambles and the mess.'

Rina reflected on her mother's interpretation of the dream. It made sense. Leaning over, she kissed Anita on the forehead. 'I'll be like you then, Mum,' she said softly, comforted by the thought.

'God bless you, darling. Goodnight. Sleep well.'

'Goodnight, Mum. God bless!' She hadn't said them in a long time, her childhood goodnights. Old memories stirred and she remembered the last of their nightly prayers, when she, Emma and Esther were children, before the "Troubles" began. Kneeling beside their beds, with their little hands clasped together, they would recite the closing prayer taught by their mother. 'God Bless daddy, mummy, brother, sisters, aunties, uncles, cousins, teachers and friends. God bless me and make me a good child. Goodnight Jesus.'

Rina mumbled the prayer as she drifted off to sleep.

CHAPTER TWENTY

1970 – June

The sound was unmistakable. Stepping outside the bathroom, Anita halted in the dark, listening. She walked down the corridor and tapped on the door of her daughter's bedroom. 'Rina, are you all right?' There was no response, and though it was instantly muffled, Anita could still hear the sound of weeping.

She opened the door and walked in. Switching on the light, she approached the bed where her daughter lay huddled. 'Rina?' she whispered, enquiringly, moving the mosquito net aside. Her heart ached as she saw the flushed and tear-stained face.

Unable to contain her distress, Rina allowed herself the rare luxury of being comforted by her mother.

Anita held her daughter in her arms and hushed her, smoothing the strands of hair away from her face, and wiping the tears with her bare hands. 'Look at yourself, child! How can you go on like this? You're living in a tomb. You've stopped seeing your friends, you don't have a social life, you've given up your singing, and you've cut yourself off from everything that mattered to you once.'

For the first time Anita revealed how disgruntled she was over her daughter's life. 'You're a gifted girl, Rina, but all your talent, your intelligence, your beauty is wasted. And you're only twenty-four! Is it worth it?' She stroked her daughter's head and pleaded, 'Why don't you end this misery, darling?'

As her mother spoke, Rina grew calm. She sat cross-legged in the middle of her bed and told Anita of the plans she had made, the reason she had been crying. She was going to leave Nimahl.

'I've spoken to Mr Nathan, Mum, and I've told him everything. I asked him to arrange a job for me at Neyrgelex and he rang today to tell me that it's all fixed up. I've got a job in Paris!'

'Paris?' Anita voice was almost a shout. 'Why Paris, darling? Can't you work at Neyrgelex here?'

'I can, Mum, but I don't want to stay here. I have to go someplace where I'll never see Nimahl. I'll weaken if I'm here, and I'll be back to all this again.'

'Oh God!' Anita groaned. 'I've had such fears for you from the start, Rina. I wish you had listened to me. I told you it would never work. Not only have you given this man your heart, you've given him your whole life,' complained her mother. 'So when will all this be happening?'

'Soon. In a couple of weeks Nimahl and his wife are going to London for a holiday, and that's when I plan to leave.'

'Does his wife know about you?'

'No.'

'Thank God,' said Anita, shuddering. 'Go then, Rina. Go to Paris and start a new life. We'll manage here somehow. Hopefully it'll only be a couple of years before we're all in Sydney.'

The Roberts family were planning to migrate to Australia. Rina's younger sister Esther was getting ready to sponsor them from Sydney.

Over the previous few months Nimahl had gotten a bit bolder about being seen in public with Rina, and occasionally they would go to the late night movies.

Before his trip to London Nimahl spent a weekend with Rina and on the Saturday night he took her to see the film "Dr. Zhivago." They were both gripped by the pathos of the story. Lara's parting from the Russian doctor was painful to Rina. She was driven to tears when Dr Zhivago caught sight of his beloved Lara, many years later when they were both much older. She, in a bus, but never seeing him; he, clutching his heart as he collapsed on the street after his desperate bid to catch up with the moving bus had failed, and she had disappeared from his sight.

Later that night they discussed the movie as they prepared for bed.

Rina's most frequent meeting place with the man she loved was in her bedroom, and she had done her best to make it a haven for him.

The front section of the house was Rina's domain. Nimahl had converted two rooms into one large bedroom for her. The room had

CHAPTER TWENTY

three sets of windows. One overlooked a secluded front courtyard, and the other two opened out onto the side of the house, which was bordered by an abundance of tropical foliage plants. A perimeter brick fence encircling the whole property stood just behind the shrubs, making the bedroom private and picturesque. The floor was black cement, and always polished to a high gloss. The walls were painted light yellow, with lilac cornices.

An assorted collection of cushions and bolsters lay scattered on Rina's large bed, and her throwovers and matching pillowcases were always lilac, her favourite colour.

She often arranged bowls of white frangipani and jasmine blossoms on her dressing table, which delicately perfumed the room. Her whole bedroom had a soothing atmosphere and she loved it.

They both did.

Rina switched off the overhead lights and drew back the curtains at the front window. Moonlight flooded the room.

Nimahl sat on the stool by her dressing table, watching her expertly unwind the sari draped around her slim body. It was a vibrant sapphire-blue and emerald-green shot-silk. One of his favourites. He had bought it for her in Bangalore in 1967 and he loved seeing her in it. The luminous silk glowed with every move she made.

Rina was standing alongside her bed, clad in her long, satin slip and a little fitted top. Carefully she folded the billowing silk sari shimmering in the moonlight.

Nimahl came up from behind and embraced her. Covering the nape of her neck, back and shoulders with kisses, he whispered, 'You looked beautiful tonight. I was so proud to walk beside you. You were like a princess — my princess.'

She stood quietly for a few moments, delighting in his embrace, before she turned around and clasped her hands behind his neck. Looking up at him with wistful eyes, she asked, 'What will you do if we have to part like Dr Zhivago and Lara?'

'We will never be separated, baby. Never, ever! It's unthinkable. You and I will be together for the rest of our lives. I can't live without you.'

She put away her folded sari, unpinned her dark hair and shooed Bruno out. She closed the doors, shutting everything out.

Later in the dark, he comforted her, 'I'm only going for two weeks, darling. Why are you crying so much?'

At the airport terminal, Rina lingered, kissing May, Michael and her mother many times over. 'Just wait for my phone call from Paris, Mum, then move with Michael and May to Aunty Vivien's.' Rina had made all the necessary arrangements to relocate her family, and for the servants and her dog to be taken care of until Nimahl returned from London.

She walked bravely away, blowing kisses to them till she was out of sight. Despite her sadness, hope was unfurling like a banner.

Soon she was airborne, focusing only on the chance she now had to bury her mistakes and make a fresh start. She didn't allow herself to think of Nimahl.

Her first stopover was an overnight stay in Bombay. She was in Rome the next night, and the following day saw her on the last leg of her journey to Paris.

It was late evening when her plane touched down at Orly airport.

Charles Nathan, Rina's former boss at Neyrgelex in Colombo, had made plans for Remy, one of the company's engineers, to meet Rina. Remy was half Ceylonese and half French, and he shuttled between Paris and Colombo. He had homes in both cities and was the superintendent of the French company in Ceylon. He knew Rina well.

Remy welcomed her to Paris, greeting her warmly with kisses on both cheeks.

'I've arranged for you to start working within a week,' he told her as he drove her to the small Parisienne pensione he had booked her into. 'This will only be for a few days, Miss Roberts, until we fix you up with something close to the office.'

Remy helped put her luggage in her room and waited downstairs while she freshened up. He was taking her out to dinner.

Looking around the elegant little restaurant Rina found it hard to absorb all that was happening to her. It was too surreal.

'Charles has told me about your situation, Miss Roberts,' said Remy, over dinner.

Rina was grateful he didn't mention Nimahl. She knew Charles had given him the reason why she wanted to get away from Ceylon. Both Remy and Charles knew Nimahl well. They moved in the same social circles in Colombo.

'So you want to work here for a couple of years?' Remy asked.

'I do, sir.'

CHAPTER TWENTY

'I know how efficient you are, Miss Roberts, and I'm sure you'll soon pick up the language. I can't see you having any problems.'

Rina had attended the Alliance Francaise in Colombo for some months and had learned a bit of French. She decided to surprise Remy 'Je vous gagne, beaucoup de l'argent.'

He laughed. 'Bon! With your fine knowledge of English, Mademoiselle, and your superb secretarial skills, you'll soon be earning a very handsome wage,' he assured her. 'But keep developing your French, it's most important.' He leaned towards her and whispered, 'You know they don't like speaking English.'

'I know,' she whispered back. 'Mr Nathan told me.'

It was ten-thirty when Rina got back to her hotel room. After a quick shower she put on her nightgown and tucked herself into bed. Unaccustomed to wine, the two glasses she had sipped over dinner was an effective tranquilliser.

A knock on her door startled her. Groping around in the dark it took her a few seconds to locate the bedside lamp.

In her soft, white cheesecloth nightshirt she had bought in Bombay, and with her tousled dark hair covering half her face, she sleepily answered the door.

It was the manager of the pensione, the old lady who had welcomed her just a few hours before. 'Your husband is here, Madame!' she said in perfect English.

Rina was shocked into wakefulness.

Nimahl walked into her room and closed the door. He dropped a small travelling bag on the floor and grabbed her in his arms. 'What are you trying to do to me, baby?' His voice had a desperate edge to it.

Rina was aghast. Disengaging herself from his embrace she walked over to the wall and switched on the overhead lights. 'My God, Nimahl!' she exclaimed, 'How did you find me?' She moved over to the bed and sat down.

'I can't believe you've done this, Rina! I phoned home last night and was shocked when Mum said you'd left to take up a job in Paris. I couldn't believe it! I spoke to Charles a couple of times and got him to phone Remy to tell him I was on my way here from London. And I called Remy just now from the airport to find out where you were. What the hell are you doing, girl? This is crazy!'

Rina groaned inwardly. She felt like a runaway ass that had been caught and tethered again. She got up off the bed and paced the room. 'I can't live like this anymore, Nimahl,' she pleaded. 'Every young woman wants to get married and have a family. There's no hope of that for me with you. And I don't want to break up your marriage. Please — go back to your wife and let me start a new life for myself here in Paris.'

Nimahl sat down on a small cushioned chair. 'That's out of the question, Rina. You don't know what you're doing,' he said, angrily. 'You can't look after yourself. You opened that door just now without even asking who was there?'

It was a pitiful argument.

'I was half asleep,' she shot back, peevishly.

'You can't live and work here alone. I won't allow it. And I can't give you up.' His voice softened. 'You know you can't either. You know you love me.'

'Did I ever say I didn't?' she said, wearily. 'But I can't live like this forever, Nimahl. I don't want to be hidden anymore. I want to go out, to be free, to live!' Her voice was passionate, arms gesticulating. 'I'm not living now. I feel crushed and I'm only twenty-four. Please! Can't you see what's happening to me?'

'Just give me a few more years, darling.' It was his turn to plead. 'I will come to you. We will have a future together. We will get married! I promise.'

'That can never be,' said Rina and climbed back into bed. She knew it was useless to argue with him.

She lay there, unable to think clearly. In the deepest place of her heart there was a strange rejoicing that he had come looking for her, but hope of starting a new life away from him had now vanished.

She felt defeated and confused by her conflicting emotions. She lay on her side and silently watched him unpack a few things before he headed off to the bathroom.

Nimahl returned from his shower and turned out the overhead lights, leaving only the dim bedside lamp on. Throwing his towel over a chair, he slid into bed beside Rina.

It was a night unlike any she had ever known. She felt he was claiming her in some way, poignantly impressing upon her, over and over again, that she was indelibly his.

CHAPTER TWENTY

'I thought I'd die tonight if I couldn't find you,' he whispered. 'You can't leave me, my angel. You'll always be mine.'

While their silhouettes threw shadows on the wall, she allowed him to claim her completely, many times over. With yearnings and whispers, she let him know she was totally his, from the crown of her head and her long dark hair to the soles of her feet.

Through moments mingled with tears and passion, she looked at him and wondered. *How did I ever think I could live without him? How could I ever erase him from my heart, my body, my soul. He's embedded in every part of me.*

The light of dawn was spreading across Paris as she lay spent beside him. Drifting off to sleep, he still held her close to his body.

Her tears fell silently onto the ruffled sheets. She remembered a brief line she had read somewhere, "post coitum triste omni est." But her sorrow was for something else; a futile lament that always seized her at the most profound moment of their intimacy. *This is the man I love and he can never be mine.*

Later in the day Rina phoned Remy, embarrassed to tell him that for now it didn't look like she'd be earning wages in France! He said he understood, Charles had telephoned him the night before and explained everything. Remy wished her the best of luck.

Nimahl was boyish in his exuberance of having reclaimed Rina. And she treasured the freedom she had to hold hands with him and walk about the streets of Paris. She felt invigorated — like a teenager in love. *Look at me, everybody*, she wanted to shout. *Look at us! Here we are and I'm not hiding. Not here in Paris, I'm not.* She refused to think of the impossible promises he had made the night before.

Rina and Nimahl spent five days in Paris.

They walked along the banks of the River Seine and took a cruise along the famous waterway. Rina was fascinated with the open markets that sold artwork, antiques, gypsy jewellery and a myriad of other tantalising wares. Nimahl bought her a beautiful, handmade, black bead necklace from a gypsy stall. She adored the necklace.

They strolled down the broad, tree-lined Champs Elysees, climbed the Eiffel Tower, ate ice cream cones while strolling through the parks and did all the other usual tourist things. It was the summer of 1970 and a glorious time to be in Paris with the man you love, thought Rina.

They went to a studio and had their photographs taken. She, in a gorgeous, pink, French chiffon sari, draped in the latest daringly low hipster fashion, exposing her shapely waist and the curve of her hips. He, in a beautifully tailored dark suit, handsomely debonair as always.

The photographer, adjusting his camera lens, exclaimed, 'C'est magnifique,' as Rina turned under his direction to glance up at the man she loved. Nimahl's eyes gazed tenderly into hers with the look that always made her breathless.

'These can be our pretend wedding pictures, baby,' he told her, when they went back to the studio to collect them. The photographer was so pleased with the prints he said he was going to display them in the window. And did. They went back a couple of days later and laughed with delight to see their "wedding pictures" displayed in a studio in Paris.

They were snuggled up in bed. It was their last night in the city of romance.

'When we get home I want you to see a gynaecologist and find out why you're not falling pregnant,' Nimahl said to Rina. 'I want you to have a baby.'

'It's going to be hard having a baby and not having you around,' she told him.

'I'm telling you again, darling. I will come to you. Please be patient. I promise you we will be together one day, and we will get married,' he declared passionately. 'Don't you want to have my baby?'

She leaned over him and covered his face with kisses, 'More than anything in the world I want to have your child. I dream of having a little girl.'

'A daughter just like you,' he murmured. 'What a dream!'

'I've even chosen a name. If I have a girl, I'm going to call her Michelle. It's such a soft, sweet name.'

'And she'll be a beauty like her mother.'

Nimahl took Rina back to London with him. He stayed with her for a night before returning to his wife. Rina had made contact with some old friends from Ceylon and she stayed with them. They were delighted to see her again and glad to learn that she was "happily married!"

The next day Rina rang her mother.

CHAPTER TWENTY

'He telephoned the day after you left, Rina. What could I do? I had to tell him the truth.' Anita was distressed.

'It's alright, Mum. Don't worry.'

'He was terribly upset ... Are you coming back, darling?'

'Yes I am, Mum.'

'Things will work out, Rina. Don't worry. It won't be long before we can all start a new life in Sydney. Just be patient for a little while longer.'

'Okay, Mum, I've got to go now. Please look after yourself.' Rina replaced the receiver and sighed.

According to her mother she had to be patient to go to Sydney, and according to Nimahl she had to be patient before he could come to her. *Patience — the only virtue left for me now,* she thought, with resignation.

When she returned to Ceylon, Rina spoke to Charles Nathan and started working again at Neyrgelex in Colombo.

Chandi, her former colleague, was still at the French company. Rina confided in her, glad to have someone she could talk things over with now that her cousin Stella wasn't around.

'Don't stop working,' Chandi advised in sisterly fashion. 'You must never give up your financial independence for any man, Rina. That'll keep you tied to him. The trouble with you is that you're too much of an idealist to keep this kind of relationship going. But for God's sake, whatever you do, don't have a baby now!'

CHAPTER TWENTY-ONE

1971 – March

Rina turned on the radio as she did every day on waking up, but no matter how much she fiddled with the dials she couldn't raise even a tiny crackle. The radio stations started their daily broadcasts at six in the morning. It was almost seven now and the airwaves were silent.

'Damn!' she said, thinking their suburb was experiencing a power failure. She got out of bed and flicked a switch at the wall. The overhead light came.

Puzzled, she switched it off and left the room.

She found Michael getting ready for school. 'Have you been able to get anything on the radio, son?' she asked her brother.

'No, it's dead. Is yours not working too?'

'It's not. I wonder why?'

She tried her sister's little transistor radio. That too was silent.

'What on earth's going on?' Rina asked, of no one in particular.

The whole household was awake now and wondering what was wrong with all the radios in the house.

Rina opened the windows in the living room and they heard raised voices outside. The neighbourhood seemed to be astir.

Rina and Michael rushed out to the garden to find people milling about on the street, expressing bewilderment and concern.

'Why can't we get anything on the radio?' was the complaint on everyone's lips.

Radio Ceylon, the island's only broadcasting entity, was off the air.

'Hey, Rina,' Michael shouted to his sister, 'why don't you try the world set?'

CHAPTER TWENTY-ONE

Rina flashed her brother a smile. 'Brilliant boy!' she said as they dashed back inside the house.

Rina got out her small portable radio. She turned it on to the shortwave band and extended the spindly aerial.

Michael called out to his mother and May that trouble was brewing. They gathered around the dining table, watching Rina fine-tune the dial as she tried to pick up a signal. Soon, over the static and crackle came a crisp English voice from the BBC in London, accompanied by a few excited exclamations from around the table. Getting sound from any radio station anywhere in the world was a relief.

Within a few moments, as the world news was being broadcast, they heard the distressing report. Overnight there had been an armed insurrection in Ceylon. Insurgents had launched well-planned and simultaneous attacks on police stations and on several other key government installations. The information, though somewhat sketchy, filled them with alarm.

Instructing May and Michael to remain indoors with their mother, Rina asked her two servants to accompany her to the main road.

A number of folk from the neighbourhood were already gathered at the top of the street. Rina spoke to a few of them. They too had learned of the uprising from the news desk of the BBC in London. And there they stood — a cluster of bewildered citizens watching the soldiers going to and fro in army vehicles.

A police jeep slowed down and an officer hailed the small group with a megaphone. He commanded them to return to their homes and stay indoors, announcing that a twenty-four hour curfew was in place.

In response to shouts of 'What's going on?' the police gave no reply.

In a land where there was no television, radio was a lifeline, and without the local broadcasts, people felt abysmally abandoned.

The next morning Radio Ceylon was back on air, informing the country's anxious listeners that a state of emergency had been declared in the nation, and that another twenty-four hour curfew was in force. News of the actual insurrection was brief.

It was March 1971, and the country's first civil uprising had already spread through half of the island. The nation's armed forces were engaged in serious combat with the insurgents who waged a well planned and relentless guerrilla war from their jungle bases.

Much later, people learned that the broadcasting station in Colombo had been infiltrated. Coded messages were regularly aired under the guise of false obituary notices. Names, funeral locations and times of burial gave vital clues to insurgents to band together to receive their instructions, in order to synchronise the fierce, nationwide attacks.

Once the twenty-four curfews were lifted, within the hour Rina heard the familiar drone of Nimahl's Citroen coming up the driveway.

She rushed out to greet him, embracing his tall frame as he stepped out of the car. Housebound for the two days of total curfews, he hadn't been able to call her.

'Are you okay?' he asked, looking somewhat worriedly at her.

'We're fine and quite safe here, darling,' she replied, linking her arm in his as they walked into the house. 'It's pretty private and cut-off in this cul-de-sac,' she added.

'I don't know about that, baby. I think you still need to be careful,' he cautioned.

She was disappointed when he said he couldn't stay.

'I've got a hundred and one things to do today,' he explained. 'But I've brought you all the groceries you'll need for the next couple of days. Now don't go out of the house and don't send the servants to the markets either ... Not for the next few days. We don't know what's likely to happen till this is quelled.'

Nimahl asked the servants to unload the car while he gave them instructions. 'Lock the front and back doors during the day and make sure all the windows are well secured at night.'

He was ready to leave. Rina stood near the car, as he got behind the wheel. He looked at her and their eyes held, both revealing the longing for comfort, denied for now. Rina leaned in through the window and gave him a lingering kiss.

He held her hand tightly and pressed it against his cheek. 'I love you, baby. Please take care of yourself.'

She waited in the garden till his car was out of sight. With her head bowed and praying silently for his safety, she returned to the house.

The nightly ten-hour curfews didn't affect the Roberts family much, except that Nimahl couldn't visit Rina during weekdays. But he rang her constantly from work.

CHAPTER TWENTY-ONE

Newspapers informed the shocked nation that the armed services and the Royal Ceylon Air Force were vigorously engaged in crushing the Che Guevara styled uprising. Former university graduates headed the movement, which had gained wide sympathy in rural communities down south. Many youth were ardently involved in the insurrection under the banner of a legitimate, socialist, political party.

Rumours circulated that the party's manifesto was similar to Pol Pot's in Cambodia: discarding of the nation's ancient history, dismantling its social structures, destroying institutions set up during the island's colonial regime, stripping away wealth and power from the country's reigning elite, and commencing a new communist era from year zero.

There were other rumours that added to the heightened tensions. One that particularly worried folk was the report that as the insurgents were disbanding, under the punitive government crackdown, many of them were seeking refuge in ordinary suburban homes, taking whole households hostage.

Parents were deeply concerned for their young sons. The police were vigilant and deadly in their search for suspected insurgents, often pulling young men out of buses and off the streets and dragging them into police stations for brutal questioning. Michael Roberts had to travel some distance by bus each day to get to his college, and Anita and Rina were paranoid about his safety.

In the living memory of Ceylon's peace-loving population, no one had witnessed such a large-scale and armed attempt to take over the nation and bring it under forced rule.

The island was ill prepared to counter the attack. Many countries offered military aid, including the Russians, whose MIG fighter planes, though not engaged in combat operations, performed aerial surveillance of the dense jungles where the rebels were holed up.

The ten-hour curfews were strictly enforced. No one could be on the roads after eight pm at night or before six in the mornings, unless there was a medical emergency.

One of the stories Rina heard was that of an old man who had gone to an artesian water-well, at the edge of a suburban road, around five-thirty one morning, seeking to avoid the six am rush for water. A passing convoy of soldiers stopped. Seeing that the man was well advanced in years they asked him to return to his house and wait until the curfew was over, before venturing out onto the street. As the soldiers drove off and disappeared round a bend in the road they heard the sound of gunshots. Swinging their jeep around they came back to find the old man lying on the ground beside the tarred road, the earth stained red under his frail body. A police convoy had come by just after the soldiers had warned the old man, and a nervous young policeman had shot him dead.

Other stories were more fearful and terrifying as the armed services fiercely stamped out the rebellion.

'The age of innocence is over,' Rina wept, as she wrote in her journal.

> I hear of bodies floating in rivers and rivers turned red with the blood of our young men. And the sounds of gunshots and firing squads are heard in a gentle land of palm trees and golden beaches ... a land of smiling, hospitable people, who sing songs of harvest in the rice fields ... a land where the morning fishermen harmonise their melodies with the wind and the sea as they drag their nets in from the burdened shore.
>
> This is the land of serendipity that once smiled peaceably on white-clad young girls carrying baskets of frangipani blossoms to the temple shrines. A land where processions of jewelled, caparisoned elephants and noble Kandyan dancers proudly grace the realm of kings under the Esala moon ... A carefree land, where Vel carts have paraded the roads without fear, and the pageantry of the Corpus Christi children strewing flowers have decorated our streets and gladdened our hearts ...
>
> But I see soldiers now,
> rifles and guns assault my eyes
> and overhead I hear the distant roar of fighter jets
> that dim the sun,
> and drown out the sound of mothers weeping,
> while young men carry weapons that kill and maim; body,
> soul and spirit — others' as well as their own.
> How could this be happening to us?
> I can hear the voice of outrage from the earth,
> for we are the land of the 'lotus-eaters',
> the 'Pearl of the Indian Ocean;'
> how could we have become murderers overnight?
> It's too frightening to consider what lies ahead
> for I fear this is only the beginning.
> Heaven help us!

CHAPTER TWENTY-TWO

1971 – June

Life returned to some degree of normalcy in Ceylon after the insurgency had been effectively crushed, but it was the harbinger of significant political and economic upheaval in the fractured nation.

The insurrection and subsequent unrest had made many people nervous and a steady exodus began. Doctors, surgeons, engineers, accountants and other professionals would eventually leave the country in droves. They went to England, USA, Canada, Europe, Australia or any other nation where their services were in demand. And a new slogan appeared in the press: "The Brain Drain."

As for the Burghers, they had been leaving Ceylon in trickles since the 1960s, challenged by the switching of the national language from English to Sinhala. Some had started migrating as early as the mid-fifties, mostly to England and Canada. But after Australia lifted its "white's only" immigration policy, they headed en-masse for the land down-under.

1971 proved a restless year for Rina. She was twenty-five and grappling with the knowledge that her life lacked any sense of direction. The feeling of an unnamed dread persisted, hanging over her like a blanketing dark cloud.

'It's because you're stuck in a rut, girl,' said her friend, Chandi. 'Why don't you go off for a holiday somewhere?'

'You know we're all migrating to Australia next year,' said Rina.

'I know. I'm going to miss you,' lamented Chandi.

'I'll miss you too, darling,' said Rina, reaching out a hand to her friend. They were lunching in one of Colombo's cafes.

'Why don't you take off to Sydney for a little break, Rina? With your sister there, you wouldn't have to go around looking for a place to stay,' Chandi suggested

'What do you think, Mum?' Rina asked her mother, when she got home. 'Shall I go to Sydney for a holiday? I can get a three-months' Visa.'

'Three months!' exclaimed Anita. 'That's a long time.'

'Can you manage here?' Rina asked quickly.

'Of course I can,' replied her mother reassuringly. 'But how are you going to manage without Nimahl for three months?'

'I guess I'll have to find out, won't I?'

Rina felt elated. She had seen a bit of Paris, London and Bangalore. Now she wondered what Sydney was like. The travel bug was biting!

Nimahl was supportive. 'It'll be good for you to see what it's like over there, baby, before you all make the decision to leave for good.'

Nimahl was also toying with the idea of joining Rina in Sydney after she had migrated with her family.

But no matter what ... it was a given that they would somehow find a way to be together.

And so it was settled. Rina would go to Sydney.

She busied herself getting a passport, an airline ticket and a three-month holiday Visa for Australia.

Two weeks before her departure, Rina had a call from her former parish priest. She had been surprised when she answered the ringing telephone that morning.

'It's Father Justin here,' said the caller.

'Hello Father, this is Rina.'

'How are you, my dear?'

'I'm fine.' *I wonder what he wants*, she was thinking.

'Rina, could you pay me a visit this evening? I have something important to discuss with you.'

'Sure. What time do you want me to come?'

'Seven o'clock would do fine,' said the priest.

In church parlance, Rina knew she was a "lapsed" Catholic.

Under the circumstances she was in, attending church would be a further transgression she felt. However she made token visits during Easter and Christmas, and always sat at the back of the church feeling

CHAPTER TWENTY-TWO

quite the outcast. She was disconnected from her faith and alienated from the devoutly religious upbringing she had received as a child. The separation didn't sit comfortably with Rina, adding to her burden of guilt.

She hadn't talked with a priest for many years, not since her last confession after her abortion at eighteen. Both events had left deep scars.

Rina glanced at her watch before she rang the bell at the church sacristy. She was on time. It was just after seven pm.

'Come in, come in, my dear,' said Father Justin.

Rina had known the old priest since she was twelve. He had come to St Lucia's church in Merinda in 1958, a year after her baby sister Cecily had died.

Father Justin led Rina to a chair in one of the small visitors rooms. A much larger meeting was going on in a hall nearby.

She had barely sat down when he fired his question.

'Rina, do you know Nimahl Singram?'

Father Justin had always been direct. She didn't mind that, though her heart lurched at the implications of the question.

'Yes,' she said, simply. 'Why do you ask, Father?'

'I had a visit from a couple of people yesterday,' he said, taking care not to mention any names. 'They're very concerned that Nimahl Singram is having an affair with you. He's a married man with three children, Rina! Did you know?'

'Yes, I do.'

'How long have you known him?'

'Four years — since 1967.'

He studied her face for a moment. 'I imagine this can't be easy for you.' The priest knew what had happened to the Roberts family.

'No, it's not, Father, and I also know I've stepped outside the boundaries of the church,' she said, eager to claim guilt. She dreaded another priestly accusation.

He ignored the moral issue, much to her surprise. 'And what does Mr Singram plan to do? You know his wife is well aware of this now.'

Rina's heart thudded. 'I knew she was bound to find out sooner or later. As to what he's going to do, I really don't know. He tells me he'll leave his wife and we'll get married some day, but I don't think that would ever happen. And besides, I don't know if I can live with that. I don't think I can handle the guilt for the rest of my life.'

'No, of course you wouldn't. Not after what happened to your mother. I imagine that weighs heavily on your mind.'

'More in my heart,' she said.

'I can't see you being happy with such an arrangement, Rina.'

'I'm not, Father. I assure you, I'm not.'

'A couple of months ago your mum told me you were all planning to migrate to Australia. Are you going too?'

'Yes, I am.'

'Any idea, when?'

He's probably going to report all this back to someone, she thought. 'Next year,' she answered as she got up to leave. The shock of Nimahl's wife finding out made her feel ill. Old memories of her mother's distress in Merinda were bearing down on her. 'I've got to go, Father ... I have to go home now.'

'You don't attend church anymore, do you Rina?'

She didn't answer, fearful of what would follow next.

'Don't give up on your faith,' said the priest, gently. 'God is a forgiving God.

She wasn't expecting clemency. The tears sprang, not unnoticed by the priest.

'Before you go, let me pray for you child — that God will grant you the courage to do what's right.'

'Yes, she knows,' said Nimahl, when he visited Rina that night. He looked miserable as she questioned him.

'Oh my God! I never wanted this to happen. I can't handle it.' Despite her own distress, Rina's heart was moved with pity for this man she loved so dearly. 'Don't you think it's time we ended this, darling? I know how hard it is for us, but let's finish it now and go our separate ways.'

He gave her a harrowing look. 'Don't think I haven't thought about it, Rina. I have. But I can't live without you.'

'I can't either, but we have to be strong. We must! It'll hurt, but we can do it. We should!'

They were both scarred by troubled childhoods. Though Nimahl hadn't gone through the material deprivations Rina had, his parents had

CHAPTER TWENTY-TWO

also separated when he was a young boy. There was a well-hidden angst within Nimahl, Rina knew.

Although the guilt each felt was a constant battle, they simply couldn't stay apart. Every good intention they had to separate and say goodbye had failed in the past.

It failed again.

'Keep an eye on Mum for me,' she pleaded, as she farewelled him at the airport.

'You know I will,' He told her quietly. 'Just come back, when the three months are up, baby. We'll plan what to do when you return.'

Rina found Sydney in July unbelievable. The winter sunshine seemed endless and she had never seen such luminously blue and cloudless skies.

She loved the relaxed and casual lifestyle that was a feature of the social fabric of Australia.

Finding a job as a secretary was easy. There were plenty of jobs around.

On the weekends she and her sister Esther talked for hours and romped around with Esther's little son.

It was a much needed and refreshing break for Rina.

'What are you planning to do?' Esther asked her sister one day as the two of them discussed Rina's relationship with Nimahl.

'I don't know, Esther. We both assume we'll be together for the rest of our lives. And yet the stress we're going through at the moment is taking its toll. We've been having a few fights lately. Most of the time I want to get away from the whole damn mess, but then my heart hankers after him.'

'I've extended my Visa for another three months, darling,' Rina informed a very disappointed Nimahl when he rang her towards the end of her holiday.

Within a week he was in Sydney. 'I thought I'd come and have a look around the place — check it out,' he told her.

'Why do you want to stay back for another three months?' he asked her, a few days after he had arrived.

'Nimahl, I dread the thought of returning to Colombo. Now that all this is out in the open we don't know what's likely to happen.'

207

'Nothing is going to happen, baby,' he assured her. 'I'm there for you.'

Nimahl Singram was a forceful man. He had an engaging but rather "patriarchal" character, and during the four years of his relationship with Rina he had slipped into the role of her caretaker.

Though Rina didn't realise it at the time, his direction gave her a sense of belonging and safety, something she had craved for and sorely missed since childhood. At times she chafed bitterly against the restrictions she was forced to endure, but in a strange way she was securely tethered to him.

They had a strong and passionate bond that defied sense or reason. Like the magnetic pull of the tide they were irresistibly drawn to each other, drifting precariously on unchartered waters, neither knowing where the wind was taking them.

Rina returned to Ceylon with Nimahl.

'Brought you some gifts from Sydney, come over for a visit,' Rina wrote in a postcard to Stella.

The following weekend the cousins met for the first time in two years. Rina had missed Stella and the long talks they used to have that sometimes lasted till the early hours of the morning, which they had again the first night Stella visited. They were both lying in Rina's bed, talking, until they heard the first birdcall.

'He must love you very much,' said a sobered and sleepy-eyed Stella, when she heard all that had happened over the previous two years — how Nimahl had gone to Paris and then to Sydney to fetch Rina back each time.

'I love him too, Stella, probably more, considering all the restraints I'm under. I wonder what he'd do if were in my shoes? He'd never be able to handle it, he'd be insanely jealous. God knows I've tried to walk away from him, but as soon as I see him my determination to say goodbye vanishes, and all I want to do is rush back into his arms. You know his wife knows about us now.'

Stella was shocked. 'Oh my God! Is it bad?'

'I don't know. He doesn't tell me what happens at home and I don't want to know either, but someone had visited Father Justin.' Rina grimaced. 'I suppose I'm being painted the scarlet harlot.'

'What are you going to do, Rina?' Stella sat upright. They both did.

CHAPTER TWENTY-TWO

'Honestly, Stella, I don't know what I'm going to do or what might happen from one day to the next.' Rina's voice was troubled. 'This whole thing could blow up and get very nasty. I'm dreading that. And of course he won't hear of us parting now.'

CHAPTER TWENTY-THREE

1972

'Have a look at this, Rina,' Anita said to her daughter, handing her a letter she had received in the post.

Rina read the letter in happy disbelief. Her father's solicitor had written regarding the proposed sale of their family home in Merinda. Since Ben's two sisters Irene and Elaine were now deceased, and Anita and her children were migrating to Australia, Ben was proposing the sale of their family home, said the letter, which went on to inform Anita that her signature was needed on behalf of the children who were under eighteen, and, as well, signatures from her children who were over that age were also required to permit the sale of their former home.

While her children were growing up, Anita had often told them that when their house in Merinda was being built in 1952, their father had applied to the courts for the withdrawal of some ancestral money that was held under a Fideicommisum Trust. The relevant will had been written by one of Ben Roberts' ancestors, a wealthy woman of Indian (Chetty) origin, named Joanna Maria Tissera, who had lived in the late 1700s. She had amassed a great fortune in landholdings and gems and the monies from her entire estate were lying in the courts since her demise.

Though each suceeding generation could draw interest from the funds, only the sixth generation after her could finally access her fortune in real terms, her will had stipulated. Ben's children were a part of that sixth generation.

Anita had also made it known to her children that when the courts had released the money to Ben during the building of their home, it

CHAPTER TWENTY-THREE

was under the strict provision that the sole beneficiaries of the property would be his children.

"My client, Benjamin Roberts, wishes to be relieved of his responsibilities from managing this property any further, Mrs Roberts," the lawyer had written. "When the house is sold, the proceeds will be equally divided among your six children.'

Rina, who had grown up quite embittered towards her father, said, 'At last we're getting some recompense from the man, Mum, it'll be nice to have a bit of money to take with us to Australia.'

Anita and her children happily trooped off to the lawyer's office to sign the papers authorising the sale of their family home.

Ben Roberts' lawyer, Upali, was a gregarious man. He raved on about the unusual will of Ben's ancestor. 'It's one of the most interesting wills ever written in this country,' he said. 'You'll be surprised to see the names of people you are all connected to down the line of six generations.'

None of Anita's children were interested in finding out.

Their old home in Merinda was sold within a month and fetched a handsome price.

Emma brought Anita the news. 'Dad's not going to give us any of the money, Mum,' she told her mother. 'I rang him this morning and he said his solicitor had advised him to keep the money for himself, seeing that we're all going to Australia. Obviously the lawyer has done the dirty on us — probably cut himself a good deal out of it.'

Emma and Rina were devastated.

'I'm not surprised,' Anita told her daughters, acceptingly. 'Your father doesn't realise what he's doing. He's still under the influence of that cursed charm.'

'Bullshit, Mum!' Rina roared, angrily. 'There's a limit to this charm business you've been mentioning for the last fifteen years. I don't believe in all that rubbish anymore. Dad knows exactly what he's doing. Why don't you accept the fact that he doesn't give a damn about us? He never has and he never will.'

It was a wicked plot and there was nothing Anita and her children could do. They were due to leave the country in a couple of months and didn't have the time, the knowledge or the resources to launch an appeal in the courts. The lawyer, who had obviously been in cahoots with Ben Roberts, played sweet ignorance of duplicity in the horrible betrayal when Rina confronted him in his office. She poured out a fiery outburst at him in front of his astonished clerk. She called him a liar, a cheat, and a swindler, and reminded him that he had deprived an innocent mother and her six children of the justice long due them.

'They say my father is charmed and that's the reason for his abominable behaviour,' she told the stunned lawyer, 'but you're not, Upali. You're in full possession of your faculties, and you've robbed us intentionally. The pickpockets that roam the streets of Colombo are more honourable than you. You ought to be ashamed to display these framed certificates on the wall. Why don't you throw them out in the dustbin,' she said, as she stormed out of his office in disgust.

Her anger burned for several days. Rina was bitterly unforgiving towards her father and frequently shot forth a volley of invective against him to anyone in her family who would listen, usually Anita and Nimahl, who did his best to placate her. He kept telling her that she needed to go and see her father and say goodbye to him before she left the country.

Rina was outraged. 'I don't want to ever see him again in my life, Nimahl,' she declared, stormily. 'Not only did he abandon us and reject us so heartlessly, he has cheated us out of our inheritance. If he's dying on the street, I'll pass him by without a second glance.'

'Sshh, baby,' said Nimahl, attempting to calm her. 'Don't say such things. No matter what he's done, he's still your father.'

'Still my father? Still my father?' she shouted. 'When was he ever my father?'

Within a few days Rina ended up with a severe bout of dangerously high fever and chest pains. Her mother kept a constant vigil by her bedside, placing an ice cap on her head to bring down her temperature that raged out of control. At times Rina was delirious.

It was a turbulent period for Nimahl as well. The British company he worked for was forcibly nationalised and his career was in tatters.

The government was now in a stampede to nationalise foreign-owned establishments, obviously shaken out of its complacency by the wide rural support of the armed uprising two years before.

British companies, corporations and tea plantations were taken over with unseemly haste, practically overnight, and hurriedly converted into government enterprises. The people at the top were dismissed or their jobs made redundant and they were forced to leave without any form

CHAPTER TWENTY-THREE

of compensation. It was an all out effort to discard every vestige of the country's colonial past.

But unfortunately in its haste to reclaim its nationalism the ruling parties paved the way for political instability. Nepotism, corruption and economic chaos followed in its wake. And anti-western and anti-capitalist slogans and invective suddenly became the catchcry of all politicians, whether in or out of government.

The writing was on the wall for the Burghers. Their exodus accelerated.

Besides the unrest in the country, Nimahl and Rina were under further pressure. Their secret life of five years was out in the open and they were faced with Rina's imminent departure to Australia.

Nimahl made a decision. 'I'm going to England, baby,' he told her. 'I'll start my own business there and I'm determined to make it a success. Nothing's going to stand in my way.' His arrangement was that he would send Rina an airticket from London as soon as he was settled in, so that she could join him from Sydney.

Rina could sense how much Nimahl was affected by the loss of his career, just as it had reached its zenith. It had wrought a significant change in him, perhaps opening old wounds that were hidden deep in his psyche. He seemed withdrawn and pre-occupied as they made plans to leave Ceylon, together, at the end of October 1972.

As time approached for the Roberts family to leave, despite not having fully recovered from her serious bout of fever, Rina rushed around frantically, organising passports, medicals, air tickets, various tax clearances, vaccinations and a myriad other things that had to be done for her family.

Nimahl was worried for her safety. And so she moved out of the house that belonged to him, and together with her family, rented a house a few suburbs away. Unfortunately, some of Nimahl's in-laws who lived in the same neighbourhood saw him visiting Rina almost daily now, and they stoned her house.

Nimahl was incensed. He fronted up at their doorstep in broad daylight and abused them verbally in such a threatening manner that it frightened them off.

Rina was counting down the days for their departure.

'Where is he, for heavens sake?' Rina was agitated. They didn't have a telephone in their new house, so she had sent her young brother Michael to the General Post Office in Fort at ten o'clock in the morning to despatch a telegram to Esther in Sydney. It was now six in the evening and Michael hadn't returned.

Young men were still being hauled away for questioning by the police, and Rina and her mother constantly worried about Michael. The insurgency, though largely quelled, was still thought to be smouldering underground. But of course Michael Roberts, with the typical invincibility of the young, felt he was in no danger.

Anita and Rina were discussing what could possibly have happened to him, when May innocently revealed that when Michael had left the house that morning he had taken with him the damaged grenade shell their old friend Mahen had given him as a souvenir, back in 1968.

Rina exploded. 'Oh my God,' she shouted. Her heart lurched with fear.

The General Post Office, where she had sent her brother to that morning, was right opposite the heavily guarded Governor-General's residence in Fort. Rina had visions of Michael being pulled in by the police for questioning.

She was pacing the floor, almost in a state of shock, trying to figure out how to locate her young brother, when one of Michael's friends walked in.

Responding to Rina's frantic questions, the young boy, Ravi, said he had seen Michael at a friend's house nearby, at around five in the evening.

'Could you go and get him for me, Ravi?' she asked the boy, feeling relieved, but still angry. 'And tell him to come home immediately.'

Michael returned, fuming and embarrassed by his sister's imperious summons. 'I'm not a baby for you to be so worried about me,' he told her, petulantly. 'I'm an adult now. I'm eighteen!'

'I wouldn't worry if you were a baby, Michael,' shouted his sister. 'You'd be in nappies crawling around the house where we can all keep an eye on you. But as an eighteen-year old adult,' she said, pointedly, 'you did a stupid thing this morning. Why the hell did you take that grenade shell to the post office?'

He answered her sheepishly. 'I wanted to give it to one of my friends as a parting souvenir.'

CHAPTER TWENTY-THREE

In a fit of pique, after she berated her young brother for being so foolhardy, Rina took ten milligrams of Valium and went to bed. And she locked herself in her room. Something she never did.

The incident with Michael's empty grenade shell turned out to be a blessing in disguise.

That very night the Roberts' house got burgled. Electrical goods, money and jewellery were stolen, even as May, Anita and Michael slept in their beds. There was going to be a bank strike in Colombo the next day and Rina had withdrawn all the money for their airfares, plus funds to purchase the allocated foreign exchange they were permitted to take out of the country. All that money was in Rina's bedroom, the only room in the house that had been locked from the inside that night.

Their last few weeks in Ceylon turned out to be a nervous, nail biting time for Rina and her family. They hardly slept a wink after the robbery.

Nimahl took Rina away to a coastal resort for a few days to settle her nerves.

A couple of days before they left the country, Rina read in the local press that their father's lawyer had been involved in a fatal car crash. He had died instantly.

On the 23rd of October 1972, Rina, her mother Anita, and her siblings Michael and May, prepared to leave the land of their birth on an early afternoon flight to Sydney, Australia.

Nimahl hired a van and took Rina and her family to the airport. He wanted to see Rina safely away first, before he boarded his flight to London, eight hours later.

Emma and her husband and children came along to say farewell, as did Rina's younger sister, Jean, and her husband and baby daughter. It was a time of tears, kisses, and hugs, a few photographs for souvenirs and sad goodbyes.

> *Then will I never see again*
> *sunrise on Adam's Peak,*
> *or lie beneath the cascade of a waterfall and dream,*
> *while listening to an urchin play a bamboo flute.*
> *will I never hear again Sinhala songs,*
> *are the lotus eating days forever gone.*

CHAPTER TWENTY-FOUR

1972 – 1974

'I was hoping you'd start a new life for yourself here, darling,' Anita told her daughter, a month after they had arrived in Australia.

'Mum, I can't think of a life without Nimahl. He's alone in London now and he needs me.' Nimahl had sent Rina an airticket so she could join him in London.

'You seem to be forgetting that he has a wife and three children.'

'I haven't forgotten.'

'And what's happening with his marriage?'

'I don't know. He doesn't talk about it and I don't want to probe.'

'Don't want to probe? For God's sake, Rina, have you lost your brains? You have every right to probe. Are you forgetting that this is your life that's going down the drain?' Anita was having a rare fit. 'I don't know where you're heading, child. You don't listen to reason. And now you're going to be so far from your family as well.'

'Mum, I'm only going on a twelve-month working Visa.' Rina pleaded, trying to allay her mother's fears. 'I'll be back this time next year.'

Anita was tearful as her daughter left for London. 'This'll be our first Christmas without you, darling.

'I'll miss you too, Mum, but I'll be back soon. Please try not to worry about me.' She knew her mother would, anyway.

As her flight took her half way around the globe, with each stopover and every country she crossed, Rina's heart was yearning for Nimahl. *Gone will be the many years of visits,* she thought. *We are going to be with*

CHAPTER TWENTY-FOUR

each other day and night, and night after night. At last we can have a life together! Her cup of joy was brimming over.

The welcome she received from Nimahl at Heathrow airport seemed subdued, and Rina's feelings of elation plummeted. They took a brief taxi ride to the little bed-sitter Nimahl had rented for seven pounds a week in Hounslow. It was only a furnished room in an Indian household, with use of the kitchen and bathroom. But for Rina, being with Nimahl even in a bed-sitter was bliss.

He took her to meet his sister who lived with her family in Middlesex. Rina was glad for the welcome she received from Sybil. The only friends she had in London had now migrated to Australia, and apart from Nimahl and his sister's family, Rina didn't know another living soul in England.

She was soon shopping in the Indian grocery stores around Hounslow, delighted to find she could get most of the familiar food and spices they were accustomed to back home. Rina was a good cook and Nimahl loved the Ceylonese food she prepared for him in the tiny kitchen she shared with several other lodgers.

But Rina felt very much a stranger under the cold, grey skies of England. And as the days went on she found it discomfiting to see Nimahl in such an alien setting. The special aura of his personality, which was powerful and charismatic in their tropical homeland, had somehow dimmed in this land bereft of sunshine, she thought.

He told her he had plans to start his own company, but in the meantime he was working in a biscuit factory until he could make the necessary arrangements. The fact that Nimahl, who belonged to the upper echelons of Colombo's class-conscious society, was now a "blue-collar" worker in a London factory was disconcerting to Rina.

London in November resplendently heralded the Christmas season. The girl who loved things that sparkled and shone was entranced by the festive decorations. Visiting the shops in Oxford Street seemed like a foray into Aladdin's cave. Rina had never seen so many shops and such a large variety of merchandise before.

As she went traipsing through the stores, she heard the familiar Christmas songs and old memories kept stealing into her mind — those wonderful days of her childhood in Merinda at this time of the year: the shopping, the making of the cake, setting up the Christmas tree with all the family, the fun and laughter, and her father's abundant love that had so enriched her life when she was a child.

Her constant recollections of the past awoke sentiments long dormant and a strange yearning for her father seized Rina. It surprised her, for she had dismissed every vestige of affection for him a long time ago. She didn't think she had any feelings left for him. But the memories and emotions persisted so strongly that after some deliberation she decided she would send her father a card. She had his address. Emma had given it to her before she left Ceylon.

Dear Daddy, she wrote, on a special Christmas card she bought, *you probably won't believe this, but I think of you often and wish things hadn't happened the way they did. I hope to see you soon when I come to Ceylon on a holiday. Love. Rina.*

She posted the card to him on the tenth of December.

Sleep eluded her that night. Rina sat up in bed, moved the curtains aside and peered out at the cold, but beautifully clear, midnight sky. She caught sight of a shooting star and immediately thought of the good old days back home, when her family would sit outdoors and look up at the dark skies, waiting to catch a glimpse of a falling star. That innocent life was aeons away. Now they were in different countries. Her once-beloved father, Emma and Jean were in Ceylon, her mother and the rest of her siblings were in Australia, and she was here in England. The icy cold from outside seemed to penetrate her heart. Rina closed the curtains and snuggled up to Nimahl, embracing his warm body as he stirred.

It was a strange dream she had, a week before Christmas. She described it to Nimahl the next morning.

In her dream she was in the garden of her old home in Merinda, when she noticed some young boys tying a string of black flags on the lamp-posts outside the house. This was the local custom to indicate where a funeral was being held. She ordered them to take the flags down. 'No one has died here,' she told them somewhat angrily. They seemed to mock her as they discarded the flags. After they had gone, Rina went inside the house, but on hearing a peculiar sound outside she came out to the garden again. The sound was overhead. She looked up and saw a single, large black flag tied to the façade of the house, right at its very summit. It was flapping wildly in the wind.

CHAPTER TWENTY-FOUR

'It's probably because you've been hearing me talk of my mother,' Nimahl offered, by way of explanation. His mother was terminally ill.

'I don't think so, darling. Why would I be dreaming of Merinda, if it's to do with your mum?' she reasoned.

Rina's first Christmas in England was subdued and unmemorable, compared to the spectacular Christmases she was used to back in Ceylon. She forced herself to be cheerful as she and Nimahl spent the day with his sister's family. She missed her own terribly.

The Indian household where Rina and Nimahl were lodging fairly bustled during the Christmas break. Everyone was home on holidays. But by the 28th of December they had all returned to work, including Nimahl.

Rina was alone in the house when the doorbell rang at about ten o'clock that morning. She hurried downstairs and opened the front door, thrilled to find the postman handing her a telegram for Miss Rina Roberts. *A job*, she thought. *How lovely!* She had been expecting to hear from the employment agency she had registered with in mid-December. The prospect of starting work in London excited her.

Standing outside in the cold little vestibule, while the postman waited, she read the telegram. 'Daddy died 25th. Cremated 26th.' Emma's name was at the bottom.

'Oh my God!' she shouted, 'Oh my God!'

'Are you all right, Miss?' the young postman asked, with concern.

'My daddy's dead ... He's dead!' she told him, thrusting the telegram into his hand.

The postman read it. 'I'm truly sorry, Miss.' Soberly, he handed the telegram back to her and walked away, hesitatingly.

'My daddy's dead!' She shut the front door.

Ashes! That's all he is ... Ashes! His tall frame and the face she once loved floated before her. Ashes! That was the only significant word her shocked brain was able to register.

She rushed into the lounge room and noticed the ashtray. That's all he is now — that's all he has become. She was trembling from head to foot.

She ran upstairs, grabbed her coat and purse and rushed out of the house, heading for the nearest phone booth. She rang Nimahl. 'Daddy's dead, Nimahl,' she sobbed. 'I've just got a telegram from Emma. He died. They cremated him — he's only ashes now.'

'Stay calm, baby, I'll be there in a minute.' The factory Nimahl worked in wasn't far from where they lived.

The dread in Rina's heart was palpable. She didn't return to the house, but paced up and down the street in the bitter, winter chill. The rows of terraced houses, the deserted road and the stark winter trees, silently witnessed her terror. She had raced out of the house without her gloves. Her fingers felt frozen now. Soon she saw Nimahl hurrying down the street towards her.

She ran to him and flung herself into his arms, sobbing, 'He never got my card, Nimahl! He never got my card!'

He held her close. 'Of course he did, baby.'

'No,' she wailed, 'I just know it. He didn't get my card. I know it in my heart. He doesn't know that I love him. He doesn't know that I love him,' she kept repeating the words.

Noticing her uncovered hands, Nimahl pulled off his padded gloves and got her to wear them. He held her arm and walked briskly with her towards their lodgings.

They entered the house and went straight to their room. Rina threw herself on the bed and wept bitterly.

The agony of losing her father so suddenly was a savage blow. She remembered how much Nimahl had tried to get her to reconcile with her father before she left Ceylon, but in unforgiving anger she had refused. Grief and remorse consumed her now.

Nimahl sat on the bed and held her till she quietened down.

He got up and packed a bag. 'You can't stay here alone, baby,' he said gently. 'I'm taking you to Sybil's.'

Within a few minutes they left their lodgings and walked up the road in silence. Rina was moving in a daze, overcome with grief. Nimahl had his arm around her and held her, comfortingly. He hailed a taxi and took her to his sister's house.

Benjamin Roberts had died of a heart attack on Christmas Day 1972 — two months after his family had left Ceylon. He was fifty-nine. He and Anita were never divorced.

Rina rang her mother from London. Together they wept. Anita mourned for the father of her six children. What gripped her the most about her husband's death, she told Rina, was the deprivation his children had suffered, not only by the tragedy that had befallen them,

CHAPTER TWENTY-FOUR

but because they had never discovered the wonderful personality and character of the man their mother had loved so dearly.

For Rina it was a tragic loss. She was stricken with guilt that she hadn't said goodbye to her father. Her pain was an open wound that bled daily, as she thought of his wasted life.

The Christmas songs were torture now. Inside her head she could hear her father's voice, singing the beloved tunes. She tried her best to shut down the memories that dragged her down, but this strategy that had worked well in the past, failed her now.

She couldn't talk about her grief to Nimahl. He had his own burdens. He had lost his mother too, and he was still coming to terms with the sudden changes in his life — leaving Ceylon, his wrecked career and the family he had left behind.

Rina felt they were hiding their feelings from each other. She knew she did. There didn't seem to be an avenue for her to talk to Nimahl about the deep things in her heart. He was becoming a preoccupied and sombre man.

In the new year of 1973, a few weeks after her father's death, Rina and Nimahl moved from their little bed-sitter in Hounslow. They rented a small flat for eighteen pounds a week in Turnpike Lane, one of London's northwest suburbs. Again, it was in an Indian household.

Rina went out to work temping for Brook Street Bureau and Nimahl joined a firm of commodity brokers.

Resuming his career in London energised Nimahl considerably. But in a few months, and to her utter dismay, Rina found that his job had swallowed him up alive.

Work became a driving force that overpowered Nimahl. Although she understood the need he had to rebuild his career, Rina was distressed to find that Nimahl had little interest in her or anything else anymore.

All she had longed for and thought she would have with him in England was disappearing like a mist, before it had even begun to take shape.

The rest of the year also vanished like a summer cloud for Rina.

In 1974 Nimahl bought his first house in London. And immediately he started his own trading company. A couple of his former colleagues from Ceylon, who had also moved to London, joined him.

Nimahl's business took off like a rocket. It thrived, due to his unceasing devotion to it. Their house in Wood Green became a second office, with three telephone lines and a telex machine. The rat-a-tat of the incoming telexes punching out the tape could be heard from their upstairs bedroom throughout the night.

The world of trading and brokering was mercurial and volatile, and Nimahl Singram was the very epitome of it. He was like quick silver. Adrenalin charged, voice raised, arms gesticulating, he thrived on the challenge of tracking the commodity trading markets ... taking risks and winning.

Rina and Nimahl both bore scars of innocence darkened in childhood, caused by their individual family traumas.

Rina's troubled past had formed her nature into one that was emotionally labile, highly-strung, and sensitive, while Nimahl's well hidden angst drove him to seek power, fame and fortune. The fast pace of the business world in London was the perfect foil for his ambitious and success-oriented personality.

Rina often felt he had embarked on a journey to prove he was someone special and powerful. It was a compelling need that drove him relentlessly. Their worlds were going in different paths, not close enough to even collide, she thought, sadly. She knew she was losing him to a more alluring mistress — fame, and her golden calf, fortune.

Living in London opened up another period of self-discovery for Rina. She loved the theatre, ballet and music, and tried to get Nimahl to share her love of the arts. After much pleading he made a couple of feeble attempts to accompany her to one or two events. To her chagrin, he slept through most of Rudolf Nureyev's performance in Swan Lake.

At the end of each year Rina had to return to Australia to reinforce the validity of her migrant status there, for she wasn't a citizen of Australia yet. And in order to gain some credence to her residency, she usually stayed a few weeks in Sydney before returning to London.

But these trips had a more significant purpose. Rina had to obtain a twelve-month working holiday Visa from Australia to permit her to come to the United Kingdom each year. There was no other legitimate way she could be with Nimahl in England.

Rina's sojournings backwards and forwards and Nimahl's preoccupation with his new company took a heavy toll on their relationship.

CHAPTER TWENTY-FOUR

'I don't know where I belong any more,' Rina confided in her sister, Emma, when she was back in Australia on one of her trips. 'I see all of you married and having babies, while I'm out there wandering about like a gypsy, not knowing how my future is going to turn out.'

'I suppose there's no point telling you to end this relationship with Nimahl and return to Australia for good, is there?' Emma had to ask.

'Oh I've thought about it.'

'And?'

Rina shrugged her shoulders. 'And nothing, Emma. There's nothing for me without him.'

'Rubbish!' said Emma. 'You're languishing at the moment, Rina. It must be dreadful for you being alone in England. I don't know how you can do this. I'm sure if you're back here with your family around you, you won't feel so depressed. And you need to get married, have children and settle down.'

'But I love Nimahl, Emma. How can I ever find someone to take his place?'

'Rina, it's not a matter of replacing him,' said her sister, with a tinge of impatience in her voice. 'You need a new life. In eight years, Nimahl has done nothing to fix anything with you. Can't you see that, you silly girl? Once you're back here, in time you'll get over him.'

'Will I, Emma?' Rina asked her sister unconvincingly. A future without Nimahl seemed inconceivable.

As Rina's emotional state deteriorated Nimahl became increasingly impatient with her. 'You're so inconsistent,' was his catchcry over her bouts of depression.

The accusation hurt. She buried her pain in the poems she wrote. But he never read them.

Rina's doctor had put her on barbiturates, but as she spiralled down into deeper depression he wanted her to see a psychiatrist regularly.

Dr Henley was impressed with Rina's poems. 'Your whole life's in here, Rina,' he told her during her first session with him. 'You hardly need to tell me anything.'

'The paper is the only thing that hears me,' she told the psychiatrist. 'He doesn't anymore.'

Over many consultations, Dr Henley explained to Rina what he considered to be the cause of her ongoing depression, which worsened each year. 'You do know what the reality is, Rina. You don't have much of a life with this man. Though you feel you cannot live without him, as far as I can see you'll never be happy with him. He is unable to give you what you want, and that's his time and attention. And you're grieving deeply for his love that you feel you've now lost. Besides all that you're unable to get over your guilt that he has a wife and three children. And the man doesn't even mention a divorce or talk of getting married to you. All round it's a pretty unsatisfactory life for any young woman, and you've been living this mess for eight years. I'm not surprised you've lost your equilibrium, you're bordering on despair.'

'Pretty hopeless then, is it?'

'Not quite, Rina. All you have to do is make a decision.'

But that was what Rina Roberts simply could not do.

In between her bouts of depression, Rina worked in London. She went to the theatre, the ballet, and saw numerous musicals, sometimes with friends, sometimes alone.

There was only one movie she and Nimahl attended together for the time they'd been in London — a James Bond film in the summer of '74. Rina could never forget it. There was an IRA bomb scare in the vicinity of the cinema, and in the middle of the screening a sudden loud announcement asked people to vacate the building immediately. It caused untold panic. Rushing down the stairs Rina twisted her ankle in the melee. It happened a few days before her planned pilgrimage to Lourdes.

She took the trip alone, journeying by rail from Victoria Station to Dover, crossing the English Channel to Calais and then taking a late-night bus trip to arrive in Paris the following morning. That evening she was on an overnight train to Lourdes.

With a swollen ankle, she hobbled through the narrow, crowded streets of Lourdes, buying souvenirs for her family, joining the throngs of pilgrims at the Marian grotto and Basilica, and retiring at night to a pensione run by nuns.

On her journey to and from the scenic Pyrenees, Rina had many hours to waste in Paris. With almost a sense of bereavement she recalled how wonderful it was back in 1970, just four years before, when she and Nimahl were together in the city of romance … when their love was strong and sure, and his sights were set on her, before the glittering sirens of power and wealth had lured him away. She even found the little studio where they had their pictures taken. Their "wedding" photograph was still in the window.

Back in London the two of them rarely went out together, except for a hastily grabbed meal at a local Indian Restaurant in Wood Green on the odd occasion.

Most of the time Rina did the groceries alone, she cleaned the house, did the laundry, ironed Nimahl's clothes and selected his matching shirt and tie every morning like a dutiful wife. She cooked their meals, shared a bed with him, gave him her body, heart and soul, and sank further into depression.

The sum constellation of Nimahl's life now was his business world and Rina was excluded from it, outward bound in the realms of another galaxy where the sun was in exile.

CHAPTER TWENTY-FIVE

1975

In the spring of 1975, as London's parks blossomed into glorious colour, Rina's thoughts turned to babies and the child she'd always craved for. She thought her life would have some meaning if she had a baby.

Her doctor referred her to a renowned gynaecologist and surgeon in Harley Street.

After an initial consultation and a subsequent laparoscopy the specialist gave her the results. 'They shouldn't have touched you at four and a half months,' said Professor Brudcnell, referring to the back-street abortion Rina had had when she was eighteen. 'Whatever they put inside you has burned out your Fallopian tubes. That's where the problem lies. Everything else is fine. But we're going to do a tubal reconstruction,' he told her, 'and I'm confident it'll be a success.'

Four months after her operation Rina was experiencing abdominal pain. As usual, Nimahl was too busy to pay attention to what was happening to her.

During those four months she frequently walked over to the adjoining suburb of Bounds Green, dragging her shopping trolley filled with wallpaper, paint, and other items needed to refurbish the house Nimahl had bought for his wife and children. They were coming over to live in England.

This was the arrangement Rina and Nimahl had made a few months before, when the gloomy political and economic situation in Ceylon kept worsening.

'Nimahl, I've been thinking,' she told him one day.

CHAPTER TWENTY-FIVE

'Dangerous thing to do, baby,' he joked. 'What about?'

'Why don't you bring Anoma and the children out here? You know you're constantly worried about them,' she said. But she too hated the fact that his wife and children were alone in Ceylon.

'What about us?' he asked.

'If they come, I think you should live with them. I'll manage here on my own.'

Throughout the eight years of her relationship with Nimahl, Rina was burdened with guilt. More than anything else in the world she wanted him to be with her. But the destruction of her parents' marriage and her own traumatic childhood had affected her deeply. And she knew that Nimahl couldn't tear away from his family easily, either. But while she was his, completely and utterly, he didn't really belong to her.

Nimahl never did understand that wound.

After their many discussions he made a trip back home to finalise the move. It was settled. His wife and three children would be joining him in England.

Rina advertised for a lodger. That was the other arrangement she and Nimahl had made so she wouldn't be entirely alone in the house at Wood Green.

Peggy Chang, a young Malaysian girl, together with her English boyfriend, Graham Whittaker, moved into one of the rooms downstairs. Peggy and Rina struck an easy friendship, and Graham's esoteric knowledge of the spiritual realm fascinated Rina.

Nimahl also arranged for his former secretary in Colombo, Rose Solomons, to join his thriving company in London.

Rose was going to be living with Rina and Nimahl until the scheduled, later arrival of her husband and two children.

Rina knew Rose. They had both lived in Merinda and had attended the same school.

Rina was glad for the company she now had in the house with Rose. Nimahl was jetting about all over the world and often she was alone for several days at a time.

While Rina busied herself getting the house in Bounds Green ready for the arrival of his wife and children, Nimahl was moving his business to new and better premises. Rina had helped with the relocation. She'd even carried a heavy typewriter during the move.

The next day her pains were severe. She rang Professor Brudenell and he wanted to see her immediately.

After examining her, he said, gravely. 'I'm sorry, but it looks like an ectopic pregnancy. We've got to operate. And quickly.'

He had her admitted immediately to Kings College Hospital in London. Rina was devastated.

The following morning she was alone in a little cubicle in the hospital, waiting for the anaesthetist.

Four months after her successful surgery, the baby she had always wanted was going to be removed from her body. And the man she loved — whose child she was carrying — wasn't even by her side.

A feeling of intense anguish swept over her as she drifted into unconsciousness.

Professor Brudenell's face was leaning towards Rina as she stirred awake after her operation. 'You're still pregnant,' he was saying.

'I don't understand,' she responded, groggily.

'You conceived twins,' he said. 'One was lodged in your left Fallopian tube, which we had to remove, but the other made it to your womb. We're hoping you'll be able to carry it full-term.'

It was a bright summer afternoon. Sunlight streaming into the hospital ward made it look like a light-filled atrium. The news the doctor gave Rina made the room shine even brighter.

'What are my chances, doctor?' she asked. A glorious feeling of elation swept over her.

'We're hoping,' he told her, with a smile. 'But we need to keep you under observation for a few days.'

Three days later Rina miscarried the other twin.

For days, she wouldn't eat.

Nurse Benton, a middle-aged, large Jamaican nurse felt pangs of pity for the girl who had lost her long-held hope of becoming a mother. The nurse would frequently sit beside Rina's bed, coaxing her to eat even a little bowl of jelly and ice cream.

Rina refused. All she had was water and cups of tea.

Her grief was immense.

Nimahl came to see her, but as usual he was impervious to everything outside his business. 'I've got to go to Canada for a couple of days, baby,' he told her on one of his visits. 'I'll be back before you're discharged from

CHAPTER TWENTY-FIVE

the hospital.' He'd hardly displayed any sense of remorse or sadness over her loss.

When Rina returned home, Nimahl hired an agency nurse to take care of her.

June Thomas would shake her head in disbelief when she arrived for her nursing duties in the mornings. Nimahl would be using three telephones simultaneously, shouting and gesticulating with great enthusiasm as he communicated with buyers and sellers all around the world.

'I don't know how you can stand all this commotion so early in the morning,' Nurse Thomas would say to a forlorn-looking Rina, as she lay in her upstairs bedroom.

One evening, while Rina was still convalescing, Nimahl recounted an incident from his recent trip to Canada. He pranced about in the bedroom, boasting about the pretty blonde who had eyed him on the trans-Atlantic flight. He seemed exhilarated that she had flirted with him quite openly. The Canadian woman had invited him to join her on a summer holiday in Europe, and he had told her, 'If I didn't have my girl friend in London, I'd take you up on your offer.'

Rina was outraged. She had been drinking a cup of tea and she flung the cold remnants of the cup at him.

Laughing, he left the room.

Her idol had feet of clay. The lofty pedestal she had placed him on when she was twenty had shattered into untraceable pieces.

But she still clung to the memory of the adoring and tender man she had fallen in love with.

Where was he, she wondered?
What had become of him?
Would he ever return to me? She lived in hope.

As soon as she was up and on her feet, Rina continued supervising the renovation of the house at Bounds Green. It was a big and costly exercise. The whole rear section of the ground floor had to be protected from rising damp. Central heating was being installed, the roof had to be fixed and then there was the final painting and carpeting.

Rina had to make several phone calls to organise a shortlist of contractors, and she had to pick the best price and the best workmen for the different jobs. She had no previous experience with such a task and in a country that wasn't home to her it was an onerous undertaking.

One Thursday evening Rina informed Nimahl that she needed more money to pay the last account for the painter and decorator.

He shouted at her. 'What the hell are you doing with all this money, Rina? I'm not plucking it from a damn tree, for God's sake.'

'It's not for me,' she yelled back. 'I'm trying to make that house as comfortable as possible for your wife and your children. You haven't even bothered to go and inspect it to see how much work has been done.'

'But there's a limit ... a limit!' he shouted.

They continued arguing.

The fight spilled over to the next morning.

'What are you spending all this money on, Rina?' he asked her angrily. 'I can't believe it's all gone on the house.'

The accusation was devastating. 'What are you insinuating, Nimahl?' she screamed.

'I want to know what you've done with this money. I want an account of all that you've spent — every single penny of it,' he said, as he stormed out of the house.

Shades of her father's bitter quarrels with her mother over money, she thought and shuddered at the painful memory.

She was shattered by his insinuations.

She ran upstairs, threw herself on the bed and wept over the hopelessness of it all. She was still struggling with depression, still grieving over the loss of her twins, with hardly a display of concern or care from him. Here she was making the house in Bounds Green as beautiful as she possibly could for his family, without any acknowledgement or thanks from him.

She had even gone shopping and bought warm coats for his wife and children, instructing him to take the coats to the airport so that they, coming in from the tropics, wouldn't be exposed to the chill of London's autumn weather. They were due to arrive in two weeks.

And besides all that each time he had travelled to Ceylon to see them, it was she who had done all the shopping for him, buying clothes, toys, gifts, chocolates and sweets — the very best for his family. She had done all that for him and this was how he was treating her, she thought, despairingly.

CHAPTER TWENTY-FIVE

At twenty-nine, like a brittle, frozen reed snapped by a harsh wind, Rina Roberts broke. Two decades of continuing heartbreak and disappointment tipped her over. The tenuous cord that had held her life together had snapped apart and she was split asunder. Now every closed door was open and everything inside was splattered out.

From her bedside cupboard she pulled out a photograph of her father, the only one of him she had, and threw herself down on the carpet in her bedroom. With her father's picture in her hands, she rolled on the floor, curled in a foetal position and yelling as if in mortal pain.

'I can't bear this pain, Daddy — do something!' She was hysterical. 'Why, why, why, did you do this to us? Why did you abandon me? Why did you reject me? If you had loved us, this wouldn't have happened to me. If you had looked after us, this wouldn't have happened to me. Why, Daddy ... Why?'

It was a Primal Scream.

She felt as if a roaring dam had broken and its raging waters engulfed her, sweeping her away into a place she had never known before. Every cell in her body screamed for relief.

She put the photograph down on the floor, bent over it, and with her closed fists kept pounding at her father's face, sobbing and screaming at her dead parent. 'Do something! I can't live this pain. Do something, Daddy! DO SOMETHING!'

In her tortured state she was confronting him as if he was in the room with her.

Suddenly she stood up, oddly calmed. She knew what she was going to do.

It was simple and obvious. SHE had to do something. Her father never did and never would. SHE had to end the pain.

She picked up the glass on her bedside table and walked unhurriedly down the hallway to the bathroom. She filled the glass with water and returned to her bedroom.

She took out her writing pad, sat on her bed and scribbled a few notes — to her mother, to her sister, May, and one to her brother asking him to take care of their mother.

She rang Nimahl.

He was apologetic.

'I'm very tired and I'm going to sleep for awhile, Nimahl,' she told him, her voice flat. 'Please don't ring me.'

'Okay,' he responded, 'and I'm sorry I shouted at you, baby. Forget what I said.'

The fact that he still called her baby was obsolete, she thought, without emotion. He might as well have called her table ... rug ... chair. She had become an inanimate object, something to use — no longer cherished. It doesn't matter anymore, she told herself, as she took out a pair of scissors and cut the telephone wire.

She emptied the contents of two plastic bottles onto her bed and threw the empty bottles to the floor. After she had swallowed a handful of pills with the glass of water, she walked calmly back to the bathroom and filled the glass again. Returning to her room, she swallowed the rest of the tablets and lay down on her bed, completely at peace.

No one will ring. No one will find me — they're all at work.

She sighed with relief. 'It's all over now,' she whispered. 'No more pain.' It was a blissfully comforting promise.

And the wounded child waited with hope.

She noticed she had forgotten to shut her bedroom door. She tried to get out of bed to close it, but couldn't.

It was through that half-opened door that Graham Whittaker entered a short while later and found Rina semi-conscious.

The last thing she remembered before she blacked out was the sound of the ambulance siren.

CHAPTER TWENTY-SIX

1975 – 1976

Anita Roberts was devastated to learn of her daughter's attempted suicide. Rose Solomons rang her frequently from London to keep her informed of Rina's condition.

Rina was now in the psychiatric ward of North Middlesex hospital, but Rose refrained from burdening Anita further with the news.

Nimahl's wife and children arrived in England while Rina was in hospital. She was sitting on her bed one afternoon when she saw Rose running towards her.

'My God, you won't believe what he's done!' Rose said, on reaching Rina.

'What?"

'He's brought Anoma and the children!'

'Where?'

'Here — they're already here. They're in the waiting room.'

'Oh my God!' Rina trembled from head to foot. She staggered down the corridor to the waiting room and saw her.

Rose led the children away.

Rina ran over to Nimahl's wife and fell at her feet. 'Please forgive me.' Her body shook with sobs. 'Please forgive me.'

The response came from a composed woman. 'I don't blame you,' she said. 'I blame Nimahl. You're just a young girl. If it hadn't been you it would have been someone else.'

One of the nurses rushed into the waiting room, picked Rina up off the floor and led her away.

O FATHER MINE

She saw Nimahl hovering in the corridor. She tried to go to him, but the nurse wouldn't let her. She looked at him and sobbed desperately, unable to stand.

Rina was taken back to her ward and sedated.

'Hello Rose,' said Anita as she answered another phone call from London, 'Is Rina back home now?'

'No, Aunty, she's still in the hospital.'

'Still? It's over two weeks now, Rose,' Anita's voice was edgy. 'When will she be going home?'

'Aunty, I'm really sorry to tell you this, but Rina isn't very well at the moment. She has a ... she's regressed. She's had a nervous breakdown.'

'Oh my God!' Anita sounded desperate. 'I felt something was wrong the other day. She made a collect call to Michael and he couldn't make any sense of what she was saying. She kept asked him to send her ten pounds. She was disoriented, he said, and she couldn't stop crying. She told him she had no money for cigarettes. How bad is she, Rose?'

'I've spoken with her psychiatrist today, Aunty, and I told him I was going to talk to you and that I needed a report on how Rina was faring. He says she's in a fragile emotional state, but he's convinced she'll come through okay.'

'Perhaps I should fly out to London to be with her. What do you think, Rose?' asked Anita.

'Aunty, I know this is hard for you, but please try not to worry too much. Rina is well looked after. There's nothing more you can do for her by coming over right now. It might even upset her. I know for a fact she wouldn't want you getting anxious over this.'

'I know, child, I know. She has always worried about my health. But in fact we're all concerned at the state she's in right now. Will you keep me informed, Rose?'

'I will, Aunty. I promise you I will. I'll ring you every week.'

As Rina recovered from her nervous breakdown, Dr Isenberg scheduled regular meetings with her.

At first she was reluctant to talk of her father, but as the psychiatrist gently prodded she told him about his sudden death.

While she gave him only sketchy details, she relived the whole painful episode.

CHAPTER TWENTY-SIX

'How did you feel about his death, Rina?' asked the doctor.

She spoke slowly and pensively. 'It didn't matter to me anymore that he had hurt us so badly and wronged us so much. When he died I was shattered that he never knew I loved him — in fact I didn't know I still loved him, until he died. And I had no way of letting him know. That was all that mattered to me. It still does.'

'And did you find out if he'd received your card?'

'No he didn't. And that made it worse! At least if he had received my card and read it he would have known that I did think of him and that I didn't hate him,' she said, still agonised over the tragedy. 'He had moved away from that address, and my card was lying at the post office. My sister Emma collected it later.'

She glanced up at the psychiatrist. 'I wrote a poem to my dad after he died. Would you like to read it?'

'Yes, I would.'

She opened the slim, red vinyl folio she had brought with her. It was full of typed pages. She pulled out the first page and handed it to the doctor.

He read, silently.

O FATHER MINE

Oh Father Mine!
Why did you relinquish your role of parent to your child?
Flesh of your flesh; blood of your blood
'twas you who gave me life,
and yet,
as whims of fancy do grip men,
when I was only ten, you chose to break the ties.
You turned me loose into this world —
floundering!
like shell-less mussel, discarded on the shore;
you took away the very roots of life,
all that and more;
a child was I,
uncomprehending then
the vast complexities of life that lay in store.

> *O Father Mine!*
> *Did you not see as years went by*
> *the silent begging in my eyes,*
> *though words I never spoke —*
> *for poignant, child-like hurt stood in the way,*
> *and pride, born of rejection made me dumb,*
> *although I hovered shamelessly*
> *for crumbs of love you threw my way,*
> *once in awhile.*
>
> *O Father Mine!*
> *Too late!*
> *for now you'll never see,*
> *to dust you have returned;*
> *and I — a small memento of your sad and brief sojourn —*
> *can see my life like raging waters*
> *that your stormy hand has churn'd;*
> *though now that stormy hand lies still'd,*
> *the waters never will.*

Dr Isenberg returned the page to Rina and gazed thoughtfully at her.

She kept staring at the floor.

'This is a beautiful poem, Rina,' said the doctor, gently, 'and it tells me a lot about you.' He briefly touched the red folder she had placed back on his desk. 'Are these all your poems?' he asked.

'Yes,' she said, raising her head to look at him. Picking up the folder she held it close to her chest. 'It's all I have.' Her face was expressionless.

'I'll see you again on Wednesday, at two o'clock,' said the doctor.

'In here?' she asked.

'In here,' he replied.

Rina returned to Ward 46.

She was discharged from the hospital, a month later. Rose Solomons took her home. Nimahl had gone to Europe on a business trip.

Rina smoked profusely now, a pack a day and sometimes more. A cloud of smoke billowed over her face as she and Rose sat together in her living room. 'I don't know what to do with my life, Rose,' she told her friend. Her eyes had a haunted look.

'Don't think of anything right now, girl. You've got to rest and recover your strength first,' said Rose, firmly. 'Why don't you go to Sydney for

CHAPTER TWENTY-SIX

a holiday? I think it'll do you a world of good to see your Mum and be around your family for a while.'

'I can't let them see me in such a pitiful state.'

'I'm sure you'll be fine in a few weeks,' said Rose, encouragingly.

'How's Anoma and the children?'

Rose baulked, visibly. 'They're okay Rina. You just concentrate on yourself.'

Rina had forgotten to collect her medication from the hospital before she left, and her first night at home was terrifying. She kept having fearful hallucinations. She woke Rose who tried to calm her down.

Peggy and Graham heard the disturbance and got up as well. They kept all the lights on in the house, while Rina sat in the lounge room, shaking, and in terror of the dreadful hallucinations. She knocked down a lamp in one episode as she tried to run from a malevolent figure she saw approaching her. In another she bolted for the front door to avoid a pack of wild dogs that were trying to attack her.

Peggy, a trained nurse, telephoned the hospital. The medical officer in the ward Rina had been in asked her to send someone over immediately to collect Rina's medication. He emphasised that she shouldn't be without the prescribed drugs until she consulted her own doctor. Peggy and Graham rushed over to the hospital and brought home the tablets.

Over the next few weeks Rina grappled with her emotional and mental state. Alone in the house all day, she drifted in a shadowy world of medication, alternating between periods of numbness and despair.

Often she would rush to the Catholic Church in Wood Green for morning mass. Father O'Reilly would see her crying in the pews. Sometimes she entered the church, windswept, without an umbrella and lightly drenched from the fine London drizzle. He talked to her whenever he could and rang her at home to find out how she was doing. When she couldn't go to church he brought the Chalice of Holy Communion over to her house.

Father O'Reilly didn't pontificate and didn't condemn. The priest had wisely discerned that Rina's faith was the only slender thread holding her life together.

Drinking endless cups of tea, smoking cigarettes, and listening to the Neil Diamond album "Jonathan Livingstone Seagull," over and over again, was how she passed the time. The music resonated in her soul.

She would wait for Nimahl to come home. The sound of his voice comforted her, although she knew she was now an expendable appendage in his life. He wanted her to snap out of it, whatever the 'it' was that had gripped her, not understanding that she couldn't.

In her cerise coloured, chenille dressing gown she would sit around or walk listlessly through the house all day. From time to time, she would stare out through the little dining room window, watching the birds circling in the warm air currents outside, their wings glinting like silver in the shy autumn sun. In one of her poems, she wrote:

> Who cares that I alone can see
> the silver doves that daily circle in the sky,
> are really flying a futile orb with me ...

She would sit in her living room and look around, noting the beautiful, ivory-coloured brocade curtains she had sewn to decorate the front bay-window. She had loved the rich, elegant material and had lovingly crafted her own curtains.

She remembered how excited she had been when she and Nimahl had moved into their house at Wood Green. *At last, we are in our own home together*, she thought.

With great energy she had decorated and furnished the house, all by herself.

She stripped off the old wallpaper, expertly hung new wallpaper, and painted and prettied up the house tirelessly. She got it carpeted and made new curtains for every room.

She shopped for furniture ... alone. She even bought a second-hand piano, which she rarely played.

But the house never did become a home, she reflected, sadly.

She knew she was lost, hopelessly lost, and so afraid that she would never find herself again.

So scared, so scared am I of all the endless morrows I must face.

Anita expressed concern when she heard her daughter's listless voice each time she phoned her from Sydney. She urged Rina to come back to Australia for a holiday.

'I will Mum, just give me a few more months and I'll be there,' Rina told her mother.

CHAPTER TWENTY-SIX

Nimahl was now shuttling between his two homes at Bounds Green and Wood Green, spending some days with his wife and children and some days with Rina.

Peggy, Graham and Rose still lived in the house with Rina, and their support was invaluable as she recovered.

Rina loved Rose. She was a powerhouse of energy. Her lively personality and constant words of encouragement were shafts of light through Rina's dark days.

'Rose,' said Rina one morning, as her health was improving, 'Could you come with me to Dulwich Hill next Saturday. I want to consult this famous palm reader and astrologer from Ceylon. He's in London at the moment and I'm not sure how long he's going to be here.' Rina had seen an advertisement about the astrologer's visit in a local spice shop, she told Rose.

'Sure,' said the energetic Rose, 'let's go. I might consult him too.'

It was a cool autumn day when the friends set out. The sun was hiding its warmth, but despite the bleak weather Rina enjoyed the excursion. She hadn't ventured far out of the house over the last couple of months, except going to church and doing her weekly shopping in the local High Street.

Rina and Rose travelled on the London Underground and walked the short distance to the address in Dulwich Hill.

Kingsley Jayatilleke greeted his young clients and drew two chairs out for them. Rina said she wanted to consult him first.

On a piece of paper, Kingsley took impressions of Rina's palms with indelible ink and laid them aside. Next he charted her horoscope.

Rose and Rina watched with fascination as he drew diagrams, consulted a few books and made various calculations on paper.

Kingsley studied the paper imprint of Rina's palms, intensely. Finally he put his spectacles down on the table before addressing her. 'I don't know how you're sitting here in front of me, Miss Roberts,' he told her. 'According to all my calculations you should be dead! All I can say is that divine providence has saved your life from a very recent calamity.'

Rina was stunned. So was Rose. They looked at each other in shock.

Kingsley went on to tell Rina that there was still a threatening black cloud hanging over her life.

Altogether he gave her pretty hopeless forecast.

Summing it up, he said, 'Men are disastrous for you, Miss Roberts. They'll bring you nothing but ruin in every way. I strongly advise you to keep away from them.'

Rina pulled a face, but Kingsley was adamant. He looked at her intently and declared again. 'Throughout your life, men will cause you trouble ... a great deal of trouble.'

After hearing Rina's forecast, Rose said, 'No thanks.'

She wasn't about to invite such gloomy predictions for herself, she told Rina as they left the building and walked back to the Underground station.

'How about that, Rose. Keep away from men — plural!' laughed Rina. 'I'm only twenty-nine,' she said to her friend. 'How am I supposed to do that? I can't even keep away from one man — singular, for now.' She broke into laughter.

'It's nice to hear you laughing again, Rina,' said Rose. 'I'm cheered by the sound.'

By the middle of December 1975 Rina had recovered sufficiently to return to Sydney for a holiday.

Being with her family was therapeutic.

All of the Roberts clan were now living in Australia. Rina joined her brother and his wife, and her sisters and their husbands at family gatherings, Christmas parties, and of course the New Year's Eve dance, which was a gala celebration among the many Burgher communities in Australia.

Rina felt rejuvenated.

The beautiful sunshine of Sydney's glorious summer enlivened her, but she felt rudderless without Nimahl.

They made plans to meet in Sri Lanka towards the end of January 1976, before she was due to return to London. The country's name had now been changed from Ceylon to Sri Lanka.

From the descending plane, as she caught a glimpse of the island's palm trees, Rina was overcome with emotion. It was her first trip back home since she had left Ceylon in 1972.

With great delight she met up with her cousin Stella, who was happily married now. And Rina caught up with her old friends and former work mates. Seeing her Aunty Vivien and her beloved family servant, Aslin,

CHAPTER TWENTY-SIX

again were special treats. They all clamoured over Rina, but the change in her appearance worried them. She looked gaunt and had lost the sparkle in her eyes, they said.

Rina joked about it. 'I'm missing you all, that's why.'

Only Stella learned of her trials in London.

Nimahl joined Rina a few days later. They holidayed with a couple of friends, travelling to places Rina had never seen before: the eastern harbour and famous hot springs in Trincomalee, the legendary rock fortress of Sigiriya and the ruins of ancient kingdoms in Anuradhapura and Polonnaruwa, before returning to the capital city down the north-western coastline.

Nimahl was going to be staying for a couple of weeks. He had rented a bungalow in central Colombo and he and Rina entertained a few friends.

Rina felt some of her old *joi de vivre* returning, and she pleaded with Nimahl for him to stay a bit longer.

'I'm really sorry, baby, but I can't. I've got urgent business to attend to in London.'

He surprised her by arranging for them to be married according to Muslim law in Sri Lanka, which allowed a man to have more than one wife, concurrently.

'It was farcical, Stella,' Rina confided in her cousin afterwards. Nimahl had already returned to London, and Rina was due back in a fortnight.

'Where did you have to go for the marriage?' asked a curious Stella.

'Nowhere, it was done in the house,' said Rina. She stood up and made a sweeping motion with both hands.

'Here's how the wedding took place,' she mockingly announced to an amused Stella. 'The bride wore a pair of faded blue jeans and a white T-shirt, the bridegroom donned a large hanky on his head before a Muslim cleric, two friends were the witnesses to the marriage and they all sat solemnly around a dining table. Some invocations were made, the pair recited some vows, the cleric made a pronouncement, and hey presto — Rina Marie Roberts became Mrs Nimahl Singram. The second,' she added as an afterthought. Her voice was stormy. 'It was a desecration of marriage.'

'But is it valid?' asked Stella.

'Probably only in Sri Lanka ... I suppose Nimahl felt he had to keep his promise that he'd marry me someday. Now that he's living with his wife and children in England I guess this was the only way he could. But it was a dreadful sham, Stella. I wish I hadn't done it.'

'Dear God,' said Stella. 'I don't know how you're coping with all this, Rina. I would have gone mad a long time ago.'

'Perhaps I will one of these days, dear cousin. Then they can put me away in an asylum and that will be the end of Rina Roberts ... Singram.'

'Rina darling, don't say such things,' said Stella, in a pained voice.

Stella and her husband took Rina to the airport for her flight back to England.

Leaving her beloved homeland again was a wrench. Rina clung to her cousin. 'Don't ever leave here, Stella,' she whispered, tearfully. 'Nothing can compare with this feeling of being in your own country — nothing.'

CHAPTER TWENTY-SEVEN

1976 – 1977

It was March when Rina returned to London. The rest of 1976 rushed past like a speeding train.

Nimahl resumed living with her now and only visited his family a couple of times during the week and on weekends. He didn't mention what had transpired between him and his wife, and as usual Rina didn't probe.

In April, Rose Solomons' husband and children arrived from Sri Lanka and they rented a house a few suburbs away from where Rina lived. Rina's boarders Peggy and Graham moved out too. Now only Nimahl and Rina lived in the house at Wood Green.

In June, Nimahl took Rina to Holland for a brief trip. While he was attending to business in Amsterdam, she humoured herself, shopping and sightseeing … alone.

In mid-July, Rina was sliding downhill again. She had another severe bout of depression and her doctor put her in a private hospital.

Rose came to see her every day. Nimahl was conspicuous by his absence.

Rina had an awful episode in the hospital when they tried a new drug on her. Her brain fairly exploded as if it was on fire. She held her head in both hands and screamed in agony while the antidote they gave her took its time to work.

This time it was a much older psychiatrist who was assigned to her.

One evening he was sitting in a lounge chair at the foot of her bed, looking like a pleasant, cuddly grandad.

Rina couldn't stop talking. She found herself telling him all about her childhood in Merinda, about her baby sister Cecily — her death and funeral — and thinking to herself, *this is the first time I'm talking about this.* She knew she was unusually voluble.

'You've given me something to make me talk, haven't you?' she asked the doctor.

He smiled at her almost affectionately. 'Yes, Rina. We need you to talk. You've bottled up a lot of stuff from your childhood.'

She rambled on till evening turned to night and the clamour in the hospital ceased. And when her chatter slowed down, she fell asleep like a child.

The psychiatrist drew the covers over her, switched off the light and left the room.

In late September Rina went to Lourdes again for three days, finding comfort in being with other pilgrims … all on a journey of hope.

In late November Nimahl took her with him to Singapore. He had opened a branch office there and was going to check on its operations.

Rina was with him in the office the day two policemen walked in with a security guard.

Just then a call came through from Rose in London.

'Call me later Rose I can't talk to you now. I'm having a problem here,' she heard Nimahl say.

'Pardon?' He was shouting to Rose. 'Call me back, call me back.'

He was ordered to cease all trading activity and leave the office with his staff, immediately. The police sealed the door and a guard was stationed outside.

Rina was perplexed. She and Nimahl returned to their apartment, which was on the twenty-sixth floor of the same building. The office was on the twentieth floor. Nimahl asked three of his staff — two young men and a girl named Betty — to join them in their apartment.

'What's gone wrong, Nimahl?' Rina asked him.

'It's too complicated, baby,' he said, impatiently. 'I've no time to explain it to you now, I've got to look for a barrister in Singapore … while I'm away don't open the door to anyone.'

He got ready to leave the apartment and asked Betty and the two young men to stay with Rina until he got back.

Soon there were taps on the door. Rina didn't respond.

CHAPTER TWENTY-SEVEN

An hour later there were more taps. Male voices called out. 'This is the police. Open up!' They threatened to break the lock and enter.

As soon as Rina opened the door, four policemen burst into the apartment.

'Where's Mr Singram?' demanded one of the uniformed policeman.

'He's not here,' answered Rina.

'Are you Singaporean?'

'No.'

'Can we see your passport?'

She took it out of her bag and handed it over. It was a Sri Lankan passport issued to Rina Roberts.

'Are you a relative of Mr Singram?'

'Yes,' she said, thinking *what difference does it make how I answer.* While the police were grilling Betty and the two young men, Rina slipped away to the bedroom. She remembered Nimahl had left his briefcase on their bed. *I'd better hide that,* she thought, instinctively.

She locked the door and pulled down her suitcase from the top of the wardrobe.

The police were soon banging on her bedroom door. 'Open this door,' they demanded.

'Just a minute,' shouted Rina. She hid Nimahl's briefcase among her clothes and returned the suitcase to the top of the wardrobe before opening the door.

All four policemen barged in and rushed out to the balcony. 'Are you hiding him?'

'Hide him where?' she asked sarcastically. The room was functional and small, and the balcony a mere strip.

After they'd gone, Betty seemed nervous 'Rina, we don't know if they really were policemen or what,' she said. 'We have our doubts after we heard one of them say in Chinese, "Grab the wife. Let's take her," but when they saw from your passport that you didn't have Mr Singram's name, "She's not the wife," they said.'

True, thought Rina, unless you counted a mock Muslim marriage. 'Are Muslim marriages valid in Singapore?' she asked.

'Oh, yes,' they answered in unison, looking puzzled when she laughed, mirthlessly.

When Nimahl returned and learned what had happened, he was worried. 'I've got to get you out of here,' he told Rina.

Again she asked, 'Nimahl what's gone wrong?'

The young men and Betty echoed Rina's anxious query.

'I've got a problem with one of our shareholders,' he said. 'I'll explain it to you all later.'

He made some phone calls and booked Rina on an evening flight back to London.

'I'll be following on a later flight tonight,' he told her, as he took her to the airport in a cab.

As they farewelled each other, he said, 'I've arranged for one of the chaps in the office to pick you up from Heathrow.'

Rina looked at him with concern.

'Don't worry, baby. I'll explain it to you when I get home. We're having the same trouble in the UK office. That's what Rose was ringing me about this morning.'

When Nimahl got back to London, Rina learned that one of the firm's shareholders, a wealthy but dubious Asian businessman was mounting an ownership challenge to takeover Nimahl's thriving company. There had been a significant dispute between the pair and the action was launched to disrupt Nimahl's lucrative trading both in Singapore and England.

From the very next day, Rina's home in London became a circus. Lawyers, office staff, Nimahl hollering, and the sound of the telex machine and ringing telephones inundated every space, physical and auditory. And it continued for several days.

Rina accompanied Nimahl to the office. Although an embargo was put on his trading, in London and in Singapore, the administrative side of the business still operated. Everyone was concerned over the imposed restrictions as every day without trading brought significant losses.

The battle was going to be played out in the law courts, but Nimahl was convinced the dispute would be resolved in his favour and that he would soon be trading again.

The festive season was upon them and Nimahl organised a Christmas party for his staff at a lovely Italian restaurant in the heart of London.

After weeks of tension and turmoil everyone looked forward to unwinding at the party. Rina wore a beautiful white chiffon gown, and her long dark hair was elegantly styled in an upswept coiffure. A few wispy curls framed her face.

CHAPTER TWENTY-SEVEN

'You look a picture of elegance,' said Rose, as she greeted her friend with a kiss.

Nimahl and Rina headed towards either end of the long table that had been reserved for their party.

Afterwards Rina remembered that Nimahl had moved first to take his position at one end of the table. As she took her place at the opposite end, she noticed, fleetingly, that one of the young female clerks in his office, who had quite a crush on him, was seated immediately to his right. Later Rina wondered if that was pre-arranged.

After a few rounds of drinks and bantering conversation around the table, Rina was stunned to see Nimahl leading the young girl to the dance floor. Cheek-to-cheek and locked in a fond embrace, he danced with her throughout the evening.

The expertly masked Rina also danced the night away.

Once, just once, he came up to her as she was seated at the table. 'Can I have this dance with you, for old time's sake?' he asked his Muslim wife.

She entered his embrace like a stranger, knowing beyond the shadow of a doubt, that this would be the last time he would ever hold her in his arms.

After they finished up at the restaurant, the party of sixteen, including the young girl, went back to Rina's home for more coffee and to listen to music.

It was well past midnight when they all dispersed. Nimahl offered to drop the girl home and didn't get back till four in the morning.

It was the needed catalyst. Now I can make that decision, Dr. Henley, thought Rina, as she lay awake, fuming. The vacillating is over. You'll be proud of me! *Up with this I will not put,* she said to herself in bitter irony, recalling Churchill's famous words. She waited up to note what time he returned before she took fifteen milligrams of Valium. She could hear him moving about downstairs, and by the time he came to bed she was drifting off to sleep.

It was almost ten o'clock when Rina awoke the next morning. Christmas Eve. She put on her dressing gown and came downstairs looking for Nimahl. He was in the living room.

She erupted like a volcano. With one swipe of her hand Rina swept everything off the top of the piano. Lamps, figurines and ornaments crashed to smithereens on the floor as she shouted a furious tirade. 'You've ruined my life, Nimahl! You don't give a damn about anything or anyone but yourself and your bloody company. You don't care about the sacrifices I've made to be with you these last ten years. I gave you my whole life, and you took it and dashed it to pieces.' She was on a rampage and looked the part. She tried to strike at him but he rushed into the adjoining room and locked the door from the inside. Rina drove her left fist hard through the glass. With one stroke it shattered. She put her hand through the jagged hole and turned the key in the lock. Entering the room, she picked up a sturdy vase from a table and moved swiftly towards Nimahl.

They had a guest in the house. He was hovering about nervously. Nimahl shouted to him. 'Joe, Joe, please — get her away from me!'

Joe rushed in and grabbed Rina from behind while Nimahl tried to wrest the vase away from her. She threw it against a wall. The vase shattered to pieces.

'You promised me the world,' she screamed, 'but all you gave me was heartbreak and this shit. You didn't care that I lost my babies. You've forgotten all that we shared and went through together in Ceylon. You only care about money and power now. It's gone to your bloody head.'

She broke down, sobbing. Rushing to the telephone, Rina dialled her friend. 'Rose, please come and get me. I can't go on, Rose. I can't! Please come and get me.'

Her left hand and arm were cut and bleeding, and her blue velour dressing gown was splattered with blood. She ran upstairs and sat on her bed, trying to calm her raging emotions.

She could hear Nimahl shouting downstairs.

With trembling hands Rina slipped her two bottles of barbiturates and Valium into the pockets of her dressing gown. Grabbing her red folio of poems and her handbag, Rina hurried downstairs as Rose and Derek arrived. They took in the scene ... knew it was bad.

Derek examined Rina's bleeding arm as he led her out to the street. Rose followed.

Nimahl was yelling and threatening to call the police.

'I'll grab some clothes for you,' said Rose, rushing back into the house. She returned to the car with a small bag of clothes and a towel, which she wrapped around Rina's hand and arm.

CHAPTER TWENTY-SEVEN

Rose sat in the back seat with Rina, comforting her as she wept.

The next day Nimahl came around to Rose's house.

Rina was seated at the dining table with her arm and hand in bandages. Rose had dressed her surface wounds when she refused to go the hospital.

Nimahl greeted Rina. 'Merry Christmas, baby,' he said, as if nothing had happened.

She ignored him.

He went to the kitchen and returned with a knife. Handing it to her he said, 'Here's a knife! You wanted to kill me yesterday, kill me then.' He had an amused look on his face, attempting to humour her.

The look she gave him was one of utter contempt. 'Kill your bloody self,' she said, her anger still potent. 'I never want to see you again, Nimahl Singram. Never, ever! Go away from me and leave me alone. It's over between us.'

'You can't leave me, baby. I won't let you,' he said, as he left.

Rose looked troubled. 'What are you going to do, Rina?' she asked, after Nimahl had gone.

'I'm going to take a flat for myself,' said Rina, firmly. 'I don't like placing you in this awkward position, Rose, you're working for him. I'll find some place to rent until I leave for Sydney. I'll have to ring Mum and ask her to arrange an airticket for me.'

After the Christmas break, Rina found a little furnished apartment in Willesden Green that was available for the short term. She paid the bond and collected the key, feeling more in control of her life than she'd been in a long time. Rina gave Rose her new phone number and address. She was going to move in the next day.

'I've got to collect some of my stuff from the house,' she told Rose the following morning. It was Saturday, and they were having coffee in Rose's kitchen.

'And how the hell are you going to do that?' asked Rose.

'I've got an idea, Rose. I hope it'll work.' Rina could feel her former tenacity returning.

She went to the Catholic Church in Wood Green, looking for Father O'Reilly.

'He's out today,' said Father Jim, a tall, Jamaican priest. 'Can I help?'

Rina told him that Father O'Reilly knew her story. Briefly she explained what had happened and asked for his assistance. Could he accompany her to the house, so she could collect some of her personal belongings?

The priest agreed and they took a taxi to Millett Grove.

Nimahl answered the door and was taken aback to see Rina with a priest.

'Nimahl, this is Father Jim from St Mary's,' Rina said, in a matter-of-fact voice as she made the introductions.

'Please come in,' said Nimahl, the consummate host, leading the way into the lounge. 'I tell you Father, this girl … ' he closed the lounge room door.

Perfect, thought Rina as she shot upstairs.

She packed a small case with a few clothes and some personal items — all she could carry in her hands — and telephoned for a taxi.

She watched from the upstairs window. As soon as the cab approached, Rina tiptoed down the stairs with all her stuff, opened the door as quietly as she could and rushed out to the street.

'Willesden Green,' she said to the driver, 'and make it quick.'

'Running away?' he asked, jokingly.

'I am,' she replied in deadly earnest.

She realised she didn't have the keys to her new apartment. Remembering that she had taken them out of her handbag in Rose's kitchen that morning, she directed the driver to Rose's house first and got him to beep the horn. Rose appeared at the door, dashed back inside and came flying out with the keys. She had noticed them lying on the kitchen table after Rina had left, she said.

Sitting in the taxi, Rina told her friend what she had done. 'I feel bad about the priest, Rose, but that was my best shot.'

'You do well under pressure, Rina,' said Rose, admiringly.

'I've had a lot of practice in Merinda,' said Rina, with a sad little smile. 'I'll ring you later in the day.'

They said goodbye and Rina gave the driver directions to her new address. When they arrived at the apartment block, the cab driver offered to take her case upstairs. She thanked him as he carried her suitcase to the second floor and into her little flat.

As soon as the driver left, Rina threw herself on the couch to unwind. Her old survival mechanism had sprung into action and she had shut down emotionally.

CHAPTER TWENTY-SEVEN

She tried to figure out a plan. At least she had an overcoat, her boots and some winter work clothes … she could do a few weeks' temp work in London, so she'd have some money to take with her to Sydney. All she had left was forty pounds in her handbag.

She jumped when the phone rang.

It was Rose. 'You won't guess what's happened'

'What?'

'That shit of a taxi driver went back to Nimahl's place and told him, "Give me fifty pounds and I'll take you to your wife." Rina, Nimahl's on his way over to your apartment. He stopped here first. He's pretty mad and raved on that you brought a black man to the house dressed up as a priest! He thinks it was all a ruse.'

'The man's crazy,' declared Rina, and hung up.

She was furious. Bastard, bastard, bastard, she said of the taxi driver, kicking the wall in her rage.

She looked out of the window and saw the taxi returning. Peering through the curtains she watched Nimahl disembark and walk up to the entrance with the driver at his heels.

The building was a small security block with only twelve apartments. Rina heard all twelve buzzers sound. Some kind soul gave them entry.

Of course the taxi driver knew she was on the second floor, and which apartment was hers.

Nimahl was soon banging on her door. 'Baby, please open the door. I know you're in there. Please open the door. I've come to take you home.'

She didn't respond.

'Please, baby, let me in. I want to talk to you. You've got to come home. Please!'

After a few minutes of persistent banging and pleading, Rina opened the door. The taxi driver was standing behind Nimahl.

'You bastard,' she shouted at the cab driver. 'What right did you have to do this, meddling in something that's none of your business? I'm going to report you.'

'I have a wife too, Ma'am. I was only trying to help your husband.'

'Husband?' she shrieked. 'He's not my husband! He has a wife and it's not me, and he has three children too and they're not mine.'

'Go, go, go!' said Nimahl, to the taxi driver. 'Wait outside for me.'

The man hurried down the stairs.

'It's finished, Nimahl,' said Rina, panting with anger. 'It's finished. I'm never coming back to you.'

'You can't leave me, baby. Please come home. I love you.'

'No, Nimahl, you never did. I was an obsession for you. Find a new one — seems like you have already.' She slammed the door in his face.

Later in the day Rina telephoned her mother.

'Mum, can you send me an airticket back to Sydney? I'm coming home ... I've left Nimahl.'

'Yes, Mum ... it's true. I have. Honestly I have.'

'No ... it's all over between us.'

'Mum, please believe me. It's true. I'm coming home. It's all over!'

The words sounded unreal even to her.

Rina decided she would go back to Sydney immediately, without working in London. She couldn't face another encounter with Nimahl.

Over the next several days, until the day of her flight, Rina mulled over it all dispassionately. Parting from Nimahl had been unthinkable once. But where was the tender-hearted and adorable man she had fallen in love with when she was twenty, she wondered, almost in a daze.

He had reduced her to a mere bystander as he forged ahead in London, inebriated by the power and wealth that had extinguished the more appealing and endearing parts of his nature.

And who am I in all of this, she asked herself? I'm only the girl with whom he began his life in London, in a seven-pound a week bed-sitter in Hounslow, in the winter of 1972 ... That's all I am.

As her plane ascended into the skies above Heathrow airport Rina said to herself. *This is Merinda all over again.*

She likened it to the day she had left her father's home when she was thirteen, leaving all her treasures, her books, her trinkets and her once beloved father.

Now again, her beautiful clothes, her trinkets, her books, her home and the great and shattered love of her life were all left behind in London.

Rina arrived in Sydney, destitute, with only a small suitcase of her belongings.

She endured days of agony. Anita Roberts nursed her daughter as she came off her medications cold turkey. Rina suffered high temperatures, chills, the shakes, vomiting and headaches, but she was determined to get off them; determined to live again and come out from under the black cloud of depression and dependence on barbiturates and Valium.

Nimahl tried to get her back. The wife of one of his directors sent Rina a letter, pleading for her to return, 'None of us can believe that you've really left him and that you're never coming back.'

Rina returned every letter Nimahl wrote her. She put each one (unopened) in another envelope, addressed it to him and mailed it back. She wanted him to see that she hadn't even bothered to open any of his letters. Such was her potent anger.

She needed that rage. It fuelled her survival.

Two months later, in March 1977, in clothes borrowed from her brother's wife — for she only had a few winter clothes from England — Rina started a new job and a new life in Sydney.

Ten years to the date when it had all begun in Ceylon, back in March 1967, it ended.

And she made an oath. 'Never again will I allow myself to become such a pitiful object, so help me, God. Never will I return to this man, and never again, dear God, will I get hooked on any kind of prescription drugs.'

It wasn't long before one of Nimahl's influential relatives in Sri Lanka wrote to Rina and made arrangements for Nimahl's Muslim divorce from her. She wrote out a voluntary disclaimer, saying she wanted nothing from him, and she received not a penny.

She sealed the door firmly between her and Nimahl Singram, vowing that it would remain shut forever. She didn't let anyone in her family talk about him. No one could even mention his name.

It's all over, she told them. It's finally over.

> *And tomorrow with my mask in place, I'll step outside and*
> *live — a harlequin's lost hope*
> *the world still spins*
> *Kaleidoscope!*

CHAPTER TWENTY-EIGHT

1999 – January

Twenty-two years later ...

Rina's home in Sydney was filled with members of the Roberts family, gathered to celebrate Anita Robert's eighty-third birthday. Her birthdays were joyful occasions. Nothing pleased the old dame more than having her loved ones around. This day in particular was precious to her children. Their mother's health was in serious decline, and another birthday was a milestone!

'Where's the birthday girl?' shouted Michael as he entered his sister's house.

'I'm here, darling,' a feeble voice answered from the sunroom at the back of the house. Anita's eyes lit up when she saw her only son. He was the apple of her eye, and her family and friends knew it well.

As usual, at such gatherings, each of Anita's children arrived with a dish they had prepared and there was a lavish spread of food in the kitchen. Whenever the Roberts family were together there would be music and singing and the retelling of old anecdotes from "back home." It was a familiar bonding ritual. But they always kept it light. Anita and her children delighted in recalling only the funny episodes that took place in their home — and there were many.

Anita also loved reminiscing about her parents, the days of her youth and the handed-down stories from the era of Ceylon's old colonial days.

Her children would wink at each other and prompt their mother for the familiar lines or well-known phrases she meticulously

CHAPTER TWENTY-EIGHT

remembered, and repeated, whenever a story was told, particularly those of her grandfather, who was a Chief Inspector of Police during the British administration of the island. His exploits were fascinating and Anita's memory was remarkable.

It was a rousing and fun-filled evening.

The dinner was a feast and afterwards Anita blew out the few candles on her cake as everyone gathered around to sing "Happy Birthday." They gushed over the delicious chocolate cake May had made for her mother.

May, the baby of the family was now a gourmet cook, and her chocolate cakes were legendary.

The celebrations ended with plenty of hugs and goodnight kisses for the birthday girl. She was a very tired but happy old lady, as Rina tucked her into bed.

By eleven pm everyone had left except Michael, who had fallen asleep in one of the lounge-room chairs. His wife Evadnie was seated at the dining table, chatting to Rina.

She didn't know how it all began but Rina found herself talking to her sister-in-law about Nimahl Singram. How she still thought of him and how she had never gotten over their ill-fated love affair.

Evadnie was astounded. 'I can't believe what I'm hearing, Rina,' she said. 'In all of these years you've never mentioned his name once. I didn't think you even remembered him anymore'

Hesitatingly, Rina revealed to Evadnie that she had never dealt with the pain of her parting from Nimahl in 1977. It was a survival mechanism, she explained. One she had learned while young — shutting down and closing off to things that wounded her. But now, suddenly, twenty-two years later it had erupted almost violently, the pain, the love, the anguish.

'It's only now I seem to be going through the heartache that I blocked out when I left him. I can't get him out of my mind, Evadnie. I can't understand it. The memories are torturing me.'

Rina confessed to her sister-in-law that over the last twenty-two years as painful feelings about Nimahl emerged from time to time, she'd written poems to him, her only outlet, and then she'd quickly close the doors again.

'Could I read a couple of your poems?' Evadnie asked.

O FATHER MINE

'Of course! You can read the lot if you like,' said Rina, relieved that at last she was able to share her secret with someone, and particularly with Evadnie; she was a gentle and caring woman.

Rina walked over to her bookshelf and brought out her red vinyl folder. The same one she'd had in England, only now it contained new poems. She handed it to her sister-in-law.

Evadnie opened the folder and read aloud, but softly.

LOVE'S ASH HEAP

From darkened turrets of the watchtower ramparts
an edifice of war has suddenly appeared;
walls and gates to shut out enemies,
while overhead, the skies are cold steel-grey.

Gone are the arbours
filled with fragrant jasmine, sandalwood and myrrh;
no swaying love seat 'neath a canopy of stars
where two eager lovers, tenderly embraced;
the fragile casing of their golden chrysalis,
 crushed beneath such hasty chariot wheels.

> *The watchtower posts look out*
> *for warriors with arrows slung from spoken words*
> *that wound far deadlier than sword.*

One lonely lover stands on distant shores
and sees the tide turn slowly red,
lapping round her bare and tired feet;
she is a pilgrim from another land
of bright horizons, soaring dreams ...
but now she gazes at the sea,
the endless, heavy sea of hopes long dead;
in tattered dread
she slowly sinks into the ash-heap of her burned-out soul
and weeps,
so long and silent through the night.

Evadnie eyes glistened as she looked across the table. 'I'm so sorry we didn't know. You've carried this burden alone.' She turned over a page and read, further.

CHAPTER TWENTY-EIGHT

NIMAHL

Nimahl!
the very mention of your name sounds strange and sweet
I'm so afraid to say it, lest I weep.
I've searched for you in many places, many faces,
pretended many times that someone else was you.
Out on the streets my eyes search out
a tall and handsome stranger,
always looking for someone who looks a bit like you.

In dreams I see you in a busy, city lane,
rushing past and never seeing me
as I wildly call your name ...
I race across the traffic
just to hold you once again,
running faster till I reach you,
triumphant hope regained!

Then darkness ...
shutters close
the dream has ended,
and your memory,
my mocking ghost

Now the room is coldly silent,
witnessing my pain
as I curl into my pillow,
weep,
and softly call your name.
Nimahl!
love of all my lifetimes,
will I see your face again?

'Oh darling, why? Why did you hide this from us?' asked Evadnie.

'I can't trouble anyone else with my pain, Evadnie,' said Rina. Her identity was deeply etched in her soul: caregiver and nurturer — the oak tree in the family.

Evadnie continued reading. She put the red folder down at last and sighed. 'It's amazing you know, your mum's perceptions of you are "spot on." After your last marriage ended, she said to me one day, "Rina may marry a hundred times, Evadnie, but all she's doing is looking for someone to replace Nimahl and she never will. Though he hurt her badly, deep in her heart she's still wedded to him. She's my daughter all right." That's what she said.'

Rina sighed. 'How well she knows me. But it is true, Evadnie. I was only twenty when I met Nimahl and I was an impressionable young girl. He loomed large on the canvas of my life and I've never been able to blot him out. God knows I've tried.'

'But darling, he doesn't even know this is how you've felt about him all these years,' said Evadnie, pointing to the book of poems. 'The way you left London in '77, with all that mess. There was no closure and that's why this is hurting you so much now. You should get in touch with him, Rina,' she urged.

'I don't know,' said Rina.

'Why not? You shared ten years of your life with this man, it wasn't a small dating episode. You lived with him as husband and wife for five years in London, and before that you had five years with him in Ceylon. And you even had that Muslim marriage with him, didn't you?'

'I surely did,' said Rina ruefully, recalling the sham marriage she and Nimahl had entered into in 1976, while he was still married to his first wife.

'Is there any way you can find him?' asked Evadnie. 'Do you know where he is?'

'I know he's married again and living in England.'

'Find him, girl,' prompted Evadnie. 'Get in touch with him and close this chapter of your life. It's been a festering wound and you need to deal with it. Dear God, I don't know how you've kept it hidden for so long. Please, darling, promise me you'll get in touch with him.'

Rina sighed. 'I guess I'll have to Evadnie, if I'm to get on with my life. After all with or without a piece of paper signed by a Muslim cleric, he was my husband once.'

'You're absolutely right!' declared Evadnie, fervently. 'If those five years you spent with him in England happened today you would have been his defacto wife, with all the legal rights and privileges of any married woman in any court of law. So you have every right to get in touch with him again. That's how I see it. And anyone who has half a brain would agree.'

CHAPTER TWENTY-EIGHT

After a few weeks of hesitation Rina decided to send Nimahl a message. She had some contacts in England.

A month later Anita Roberts had suffered a thrombosis in her right leg and had undergone surgery. Rina had just got home from visiting her mother in the hospital one evening when the phone rang. She moved to the lounge, sat down and picked it up. 'Hello?' she said.

A male voice spoke. 'You wanted me to ring you.'

She thought it was the handyman she had contacted to get some paving done in her backyard. 'Who is it?'

'You should know,' said the voice, rather brusquely. 'You sent me a message across the seas saying you wanted me to ring you.'

'Oh my God!' she exclaimed. 'Nimahl?'

'Yes, it's me.'

Sobs rocketed ... gushed forth in a torrent. She had no control. 'I can't speak,' she uttered between sobs. 'I'm sorry. I'm in shock. Can you call me back in ten minutes?'

He rang her back in three.

She struggled to compose herself, struggled to keep her voice steady. 'I'm sorry, I just couldn't talk to you before. It was quite a shock.'

'Are you okay?' he asked. She could hear the raw emotion — she knew every nuance of his voice.

'Yes, I'm all right, and thank you for ringing me, I really appreciate it. Mum's in hospital and I've just got home from visiting her.'

'I'm sorry to hear that, Rina. Is it serious?'

'She's had several bouts of heart failure over the last few months, Nimahl, but this time she threw a clot in her leg and needed an operation. Thank God it was successful.'

'How's the rest of the family?'

'They're all okay,' she said.

There was a pregnant pause.

'It's been a long time, hasn't it?' she ventured.

'Yes, it has.'

The voice was so familiar and so beloved. 'It's lovely to hear your voice again, Nimahl. It still sounds the same.'

'I'll tell you a story,' he started, rather oddly. He always made odd beginnings, she thought. 'Once upon a time there was a beautiful princess ... '

She began to cry, soundlessly. He still remembered how she had loved fairy tales as a child.

'She was very beautiful,' he continued, 'and she was struggling to look after her family. I loved her very much and I did my best to take care of her, but … '

'Nimahl, please … don't. Don't say anymore,' she interrupted him, brokenly. 'If it's any consolation to you, I have suffered. I've suffered terribly over the last twenty-two years and I … '

'No, Rina,' he interrupted her gruffly. 'That's no consolation to me. I can't bear to think that you've suffered.'

'I have, Nimahl, terribly,' she said, and changed the subject, desperately needing to be buoyant. She was drowning. 'What is it you remember most about me?'

'Your laughter,' he said promptly. 'I always loved the sound of your laughter.' He took his cue from her. 'And what do you remember about me?'

'Your smile and your eyes — they are unforgettable.'

'Are you working now, baby?' The term of endearment slipped in, almost unnoticed.

Her throat ached. 'No, not at the moment. I'm taking care of Mum. I've got to go now, Nimahl.'

'I'll ring you tomorrow,' he said, gently.

His voice was still the deep, alluring voice that had always entranced her. Hearing it again awakened memories that were buried deep.

Dinner went unmade.

Rina retired to bed with a cup of tea, glad that her mother was in hospital; relieved that Anita Roberts couldn't hear her daughter's wracking sobs throughout the night.

He rang her again the next day, and the next and the next. They were like old friends. The gap of twenty-two years was pencil-slim.

'I'm going to Egypt on business,' he informed her a few days later. 'I'll call you from there.'

He was on a cruise along the River Nile when he telephoned her next. 'You would love this, Rina, it's beautiful.' He described the scenery so vividly, Rina felt she was Cleopatra going down the River Nile on a barge.

'It does sound lovely, Nimahl. I've never thought of visiting Egypt before. Perhaps I might one day.'

CHAPTER TWENTY-EIGHT

'Angela!' she thought she heard him say.

'What was that?' she asked.

He laughed.

'*Enshallah*! He spelled it out. They say it a lot here in Egypt. It's an Arabic saying for "God willing." It's a nice phrase for you to remember ... *Enshallah!*'

Arabic words, she thought, and smiled. Quite fitting for his former Muslim wife!

They chatted like old friends, both avoiding any reference to his second marriage. He had eventually married the young girl with whom he had "danced all night" at the staff Christmas party in 1976, and they had two children.

'I'm planning to go to Sri Lanka in May, Nimahl,' she told him the next time he rang her from England. 'Will you meet me there? I'd love to see you face to face and bring closure to what happened between us. You know the way we parted was so traumatic for me ... I really need to do this now.'

'Not in Sri Lanka, Rina. I'll meet you in Singapore.'

A few weeks later Rina left Sydney for a long overdue journey back to her homeland. A deep yearning to see the land of her birth once again gripped her. She hadn't visited it in sixteen years.

Stella met her at the airport.

Rina and her cousin had always shared a special bond and were still as close as sisters.

They were thrilled to see each other.

Stella and her husband lived in one of Colombo's outer metropolitan suburbs. They had been in the same house for twenty-seven years and were married for that length of time. Rina was happy that her cousin had enjoyed such stability. But Stella was grieved over her cousin's ill-fated life.

Nimahl rang Rina in Sri Lanka and told her he had made reservations for himself at the Sentosa Island holiday resort. She made her own bookings from Colombo.

And so it was that on the 26th of May 1999, Rina Roberts boarded a flight to Singapore, to meet the husband from whom she had parted company in London, in January 1977.

CHAPTER TWENTY-NINE

1999 – May

He arrived on schedule around noon the next day. Phoning her from his room he said he'd be over to see her soon.

'I've left the door unlocked, Nimahl. Just walk in,' she told him.

Rina stood near the windows, some distance away from the entry to her room. When she heard the door being opened she wanted to bolt.

As soon as he entered, she felt as if her heart had plummeted right out of her body.

This was a stranger walking towards her!

His once dynamic vitality had vanished.

Gone were the twinkling, mischievous eyes that had captivated her. The fire, the sparkle and passion they once held had been totally extinguished.

How can this be my beloved Nimahl? Her numbed mind asked the question, astounded at the change the years had wrought. Somehow she felt this aberration was not due to age. It was an unnatural invasion, like a defenceless shoreline plundered by a savage sea. He seemed like an effigy of the vibrant man she once knew

She searched his face for some sign of resemblance, some link to the past. It wasn't there until he spoke.

'Hello, baby,' he greeted her, awkwardly. The deep alluring voice still had the power to make her catch her breath. Affirming her look of amazement he said, 'Yes, I know ... I've changed.'

They gave each other a quick embrace.

'I would never have recognised you had I met you on the street, Nimahl. I can't believe it's really you.'

CHAPTER TWENTY-NINE

She noticed his once wavy and full head of hair was now silver white, cropped short and spiky.

He didn't remark on her appearance. She knew she had changed too, but only in weight. Her old friends never failed to tell her that her face was still attractive. And her dark hair, tinted now with amber highlights, still cascaded down to her shoulders.

They were wary, hesitant and nervous. He sat on one of the chairs in her room and avoided her gaze.

And behind what she was seeing now, Rina was remembering ... the once beloved face, the chiselled nose, eyes that had burned her soul with looks of love, and their life together in a world that was paradise.

Fort, Colombo, 1967! His first visit to the little French office where she worked. Seeing him in the lifts and how he would edge close to her, pretending to look down at his shoes until she could feel his breath on her back. A few minutes later he would ring her, romancing her delightfully, saying he could still smell her perfume and that thoughts of her seriously disturbed his work. And she would laugh — the bubbly laughter he said he adored.

She visualised the many country roads they travelled on back home. How they lost their way in a rubber estate the first time he took her away for a weekend. She pictured again the bathing wells they had both loved, the waterfalls, the mountains, the many places they had visited both in their homeland and overseas: Paris, Sydney, Singapore, San Francisco, Holland and Bangalore. Yes Bangalore ... she still had the opulent blue silk robe he had bought her.

And flashbacks of Ceylon, her beloved Ceylon ... *Blue Haven*, their beautiful home in Nawala, their dog Bruno and the games they used to play with the big German Shepherd.

The intimacy, the passion, and the love they once shared were now in the room like unsummoned ghosts.

Bittersweet memories of the way they were engulfed Rina completely, threatening to drown her.

As they chatted amiably, the years receded faster than a swiftly ebbing tide, leaving ripples of pain in Rina's heart. She thought of the daughter, *Michelle*, they had always longed for and she could never have. They had a picture of a little girl on the wall of their living room in London. He would look at it and say, with confidence, 'That's what our daughter is going to look like.'

As she sat before him now, Rina Roberts was expertly masked. Nimahl knew nothing of the turmoil inside her. There were moments when she wanted to die, to never see the light of another dawn without him.

That evening they had dinner together at the Resort. Both seemed unwilling to share anything personal. They returned to their separate rooms.

The next day they took the shuttle bus to downtown Singapore. To anyone that might have observed them they looked like a long-married couple having a retirement holiday on Sentosa Island.

The familiarity between them didn't need rehearsing. It was like slipping into a well-worn glove.

They lunched and shopped, then returned to the resort and back to their rooms.

They were together again at dinner. Whenever she caught sight of him gazing at her, he would turn away and look at his meal or at other diners.

She was friendly and light-hearted.

He seemed ill at ease and restless. He watched her easy camaraderie with people she had never met before and made comment on how gregarious she was.

Over the next couple of days they visited each other's rooms and talked in a rather abstract fashion.

He told her more about his childhood.

She spoke of the jobs she'd had in Sydney, and gave him news of her mother and the rest of her family.

He wanted to know about her marriages and what had happened.

She gave him the barest details of the three disastrous marriages she had made over the last twenty-two years.

They talked about old friends they both knew.

Through it all they seemed like polite strangers discussing a book or a movie.

He had asked her to bring her old photographs. They were sitting on her bed the next morning, pouring over the pictures he had taken of her: in Bangalore, Ceylon, Paris, England, Holland, San Francisco, and Sydney — her ten-year history with him, captured on film. It was he who had taken every single photograph of her during her twenties.

CHAPTER TWENTY-NINE

While they were reminiscing the cleaning lady came in. Edging close to the bed, she peered at the photos. Rina smiled at the woman. Over the last few days she had established a friendly rapport with her.

Nimahl placed a hand on Rina's shoulder and said to the woman, 'This is my old girlfriend and these are her pictures — when she was young.'

'Oh!' said the old Cantonese woman. She looked at several photographs and picked one up: Rina, in a beautifully draped magenta sari, her dark hair cascading down to her shoulders. 'Look ... she's beautiful! Why you no marry her?' queried the woman, frowning. She placed the photograph back on the bed and picked up another.

'I know, I know, but what can you do, la,' said Nimahl, adapting to the lilting speech of the Singaporeans. 'That's fate!'

'Fate? No fate, sir,' said the old woman, standing akimbo, looking comical in her unconcealed displeasure. 'This lady is your lady! You should have married her,' she declared again, shaking her head.

Rina chuckled as she put away her pictures. Linking her arm with Nimahl's they exited the room. They were taking the shuttle bus downtown again.

The following day he broke the embargo.

It was mid-morning and they were sharing some fruit in her room.

'How could you have left me like that, Rina?'

For an instant, a tiny instant, her anger flared. 'Nimahl! How can you ask me such a question? It was because of what you did. Have you forgotten what happened at the company dance? How you danced with her all night? How you came up to me and said, "Can I have this dance with you for old time's sake?" How we all went back to our house and how you took her home and didn't return till four in the morning? Have you forgotten the fight the next day, and the madness and turmoil before that. How much like strangers we had become in England. Have you forgotten all that, Nimahl?'

She had waited twenty-two years to lay the charges, having paid the cruel sentence herself for his misdeeds — the solitary confinement of her heart in chains, with no hope of freedom.

'But you know I loved you,' he said lamely, acquitting himself of guilt. 'Why didn't you put up a fight for me? You should have stayed. You should have considered me ... I loved you.'

'Once, Nimahl. You loved me once! During the five years we were in Ceylon, I know you loved me very much. But after we went to England you had no time for me. All that mattered to you was the company and your trading. It was an addiction. Like gambling. You cared for nothing else.'

He was silenced by her verdict, unable to meet her accusing eyes.

'You know I've written many poems for you over the last twenty-two years, Nimahl. Would you like to read them?'

'Yes, I would.'

She handed him her red folio.

After he had read them all he went out to the balcony and stood gazing at the bleak shore.

The sun was obscured that morning, as if in sympathy with their loss.

Nimahl returned to the room. 'I didn't know. Didn't know you were pining for me all these years.' He seemed shocked.

'I did, Nimahl. How could I forget you? I don't think you realised how much I loved you. You filled my heart, my soul, my body — every little part of me. I longed to see you again, longed to tell you how much I was hurting, although I never replied any of your letters at the time. I was too devastated to even read them. I was stubborn and angry and afraid I'd come rushing back to you. That's why I closed the door between us. There was no point in going back to you, I told myself. You had no time for me.' She trailed off as her mind drifted back to those dreadful years in London.

'It was a hard time in my life, Rina,' he countered. 'You left me at a very hard time in my life, when the court case and all that shit was going on.' His voice was rough with emotion.

'It was worse for me,' she argued, passionately. 'The whole damn five years in England were worse for me. My father died, I was alone, I had no family around me and I lost you to your business long before what happened that night.'

They both fell silent.

'Listen, darling,' Rina pleaded, desperately seeking peace. 'This meeting is to close off the past and to say goodbye, decently and in order ... without any ill-will. Surely we owe each other that much after all we've been through.'

CHAPTER TWENTY-NINE

He picked up the red folder, and again he poured over two decades of her hidden laments.

He closed the file and sighed. 'Well, baby,' he said, very gently. 'I can see how much you've been hurting and I'm shocked. I'm truly stunned. I had no idea you felt this way after we parted. And all that you've said is true. When I look back now I realise how young you were when you came to England. You had left your country and your family, you knew no one in London, your father had just died, and you were a very sensitive and somewhat immature young girl. It must have been hard for you. I didn't realise it at the time and I'm truly sorry I neglected you.'

Three doves long lost in a storm flew into the room for Rina: confession, vindication and justification. 'But I'm glad you see it now, darling,' she said. 'You did neglect me — horribly, so much so that I wanted to die, especially after my ectopic pregnancy.'

He looked at her rather wistfully. 'Yes ... Perhaps if you had *Michelle* it would have anchored you.'

'You were my anchor, darling. Didn't you know you were my anchor?' Her voice throbbed. 'And when you drifted away from me, I was lost. I was a fractured girl at twenty when I fell in love with you, but I was ripped apart by what you did to me ten years later.'

Silence again. And aching memories.

Rina broke from her reverie. 'I think neither of us really understood that the kind of love we shared was something beautiful and rare. Extremely rare! After twenty-two years, I know that now. A love like ours only comes once in a century. We were both careless and found unworthy to keep it, and so that precious gift was taken out of our hands ... That's what I believe.'

'That's sad, Rina, the way you put it. But it's true. We did have a very special love. Nobody will ever understand it. Nobody knew what we felt for each other, and no one will ever know the extent of it except the two of us. No-one, no-one!' he shook his head and went out to the balcony again.

Rina knew it was time to say goodbye.

Nimahl turned to look at her as she joined him out on the balcony.

She pulled the shutters down over her heart and said to him. 'I wish you all the best in your marriage, Nimahl, I really mean it. I always pray for you and your family — for all of your family.'

'Thank you, baby, I appreciate that.'

'I'd like to go back to Colombo now,' she told him, as they walked back into the room. 'This is all I came for. I wanted to speak to you and make my peace with you. Now that we've cleared the air ... now that we've spoken again after twenty-two years, we can say goodbye with no hard feelings.'

After he left her room Rina telephoned the airlines and managed to get a flight back to Colombo that very evening.

Nimahl took her to the airport in a taxi.

Rina knew this was their last farewell. She was brave as they embraced. Her body trembled and he held her tightly for a few seconds. She kissed him on the cheek. For the four days they were together they hadn't so much as shared a single lover's kiss, a room, or a bed.

Her conscience was clear.

As she left him at Changi airport, the thought of never seeing him again was a knife-twist in Rina's heart.

She wheeled her light luggage into the terminal building. She didn't look back.

The passengers on the Singapore Airlines flight to Colombo were sparse. Rina pushed back the armrests and stretched out across a whole row of seats. She smothered herself with the airline blankets and pillows, while the roar of the jet engines drowned out the sound of her weeping.

A bright moon was hanging low in the sky when her plane touched down in Colombo. It was two am.

As Rina walked into the terminal building the Muzak system was playing a poignant Sinhala song, made famous by Rukmani Devi, the island's favourite songbird in ages past.

Her crystal-sweet voice delivered the heartbreaking, opening line. *Mal bara himi thiriye, Koi badde meh yanneh. While the flowers are still burdened with the dew, where are you going to?* The unspoken sentiments of the line were equally searing. *Your heart must be troubled that you've risen so early, to journey before the dawn.*

Rina came outside the terminal building and looked for Tony, a friend who was going to be meeting her. He was well known to Nimahl.

But Tony wasn't there and she couldn't ring him, she didn't have his phone number. She went back inside the terminal building to call

CHAPTER TWENTY-NINE

Nimahl in Singapore. It was he who had made the arrangements for Tony to meet her.

'Tony isn't here, Nimahl. Are you sure he knew what flight I'd be on,' she asked him, when the Hotel Operator put her through to his room.

'Of course, Rina. And I told him to make sure he was at the airport by two, the latest.'

'It's after two-thirty now and he isn't here … I think I'll catch a cab to the hotel.'

'Hotel? Aren't you going to Stella's?'

'I don't like to wake them up at this hour. I've decided to go to the Mount Lavinia Hotel, just for the night,' she told him.

'Good idea, baby.'

'Good-bye, Nimahl. God bless you.'

Goodbye my heart, goodbye.

'Take care, Rina.'

'You too. who knows we may meet again someday.'

Somewhere, my love.

'*Enshallah.*' He uttered it softly.

But she knew she would never hear that beloved voice again. She walked away from the phone booth and out to one of the waiting taxis.

Sitting in the back seat, as the car sped through the night-lit streets Rina counted the many times she had been in cabs, leaving her heart behind somewhere … buried in dreams that had died.

In a little less than an hour the taxi brought her to the grand entrance of the beautifully lit Mount Lavinia Hotel.

She booked herself in for the night and was shown to her room — a double suite with a balcony, overlooking the rocks and the pounding surf below.

As soon as the bellboy left, Rina threw herself down on the bed.

There was no need for restraint. She had the rare and privileged freedom to cry unheard. No one would hear her above the sound of the roaring surf.

The doors she had closed for twenty-two years were flung wide open and there was no anodyne that she could take.

She walked out to the balcony.

The thunderous crashing of the breakers was like an orchestra, punctuating her torment.

She stared desperately at the high and tumultuous moonlit surf, oddly comforted by the wild surging of the waves, as if they too were lifted up and dashed on monstrous rocks that ripped and tore.

Clasping her arms and doubled over as if in mortal pain, she sank to the floor, while her body, soul and spirit expressed a deep and primal pain for the second time in her life.

But this time she had no barbiturates or Valium.

> *How could we have ended such an endless love?*
> *How did our love fall through such careless hands?*
> *Like autumn leaves my dreams died on the forest floor*
> *Tonight, my soul is like a darkened winter tree*
> *Without your love there is no source to nourish me.*

CHAPTER THIRTY

1999 – June

Stella dropped the garden hose and rushed to the gate. 'Oh my God, Rina, what's happened? You look a wreck.' Stella couldn't hide her dismay.

Rina knew she looked ghastly. 'I'll tell you in a minute.' She paid the taxi driver and came through to the garden.

Stella closed the pair of metal gates and ran back to turn off the garden tap.

Once inside the house, Rina clung to the girl that had been like a sister to her since the days of their youth.

After a few minutes Stella pulled herself together. They were sitting on the couch in the living room. 'Please, darling, forget him,' Stella pleaded. 'No man is worth this agony you're going through, Rina. No one!'

'How do we tell our hearts to stop loving, Stella. Tell me! Is there something I can take to blot him out?'

'But now that you've met him again, I'm sure you'll be able to put it all behind you,' said Stella.

She went away and returned with a damp face towel. Gently wiping her cousin's tear-stained face, she said. 'Your heart is bigger than the ocean, Rina, and when you love and give, you hold nothing back. But he's the fool in all of this,' she said sharply. 'He's lost out as well. All the money in the world can't replace the kind of love you had for each other. It was so special … we all saw it. He probably knows that now.'

'I really can't understand what happened to the two of you, Rina — you were both so madly in love.' Stella almost groaned. 'I remember those days in Nawala, when you used to get dressed up in those gorgeous saris and go out with him to the movies. The two of you looked so wonderful together … it was pure magic. Oh Rina, this is what I call a tragedy.'

'Don't I know it, Stella. Don't I know it,' said Rina.

'And all this sort of thing is so commonplace now. Unfortunately Nimahl never had the courage to do something when he should have.' Stella was brooding. 'No one makes a big deal of marriages breaking up anymore, Rina. People divorce, they remarry — even here in Sri Lanka, it goes on all the time. And no one's exempt … look at the Royal Family.'

After she had spent a few quiet days with Stella and her husband, one of the first things Rina did was search for her old servant, Aslin. She had her address, and had often written to Aslin from Sydney through the years.

The hired car took her down many dirt tracks in Homagama, a semi-rural district lying south of Colombo. Though she had difficulty finding the right road, Aslin's house was easy enough to locate. The number was painted large and white on a grey and weathered, wood-fronted hut.

Rina got out of the car. A few of the village folk looked at her enquiringly. She was wearing a colourful Batik caftan, sunglasses protected her eyes from the noonday glare and she had a large straw hat on her head. Workmen building a house nearby downed their tools and stared at her as she approached the half open door of the little cottage.

Her heart leapt as she caught sight of Aslin. Sixteen years had passed since she had last set eyes on her old servant.

'Aslin!' Rina shouted from the garden

The frail woman approached the door and looked at Rina hurrying across the little garden. 'Who is it?'

'Aslin, it's me! Rina-baby.' Though she was a grown woman, she was still *Rina-baby* to Aslin.

'Holy mother!' exclaimed Aslin in Sinhalese, rushing out to the garden.

They embraced each other.

Aslin clung to Rina. 'Look! She has come from Australia, and she has come searching for me. My holy mother! This is the child I nurtured! This is the child I raised and she hasn't forgotten me.' It was a loud wailing.

CHAPTER THIRTY

Neighbours soon gathered around in the manner of rural folk. Rina stood for a few minutes, receiving the head nodding, encouraging expressions and smiles from the small crowd as Aslin launched off into a brief history of the Roberts family, carefully avoiding any mention of the tragedy. She was full of praise for Benjamin Roberts, his wife Anita, and their six children.

Aslin and Rina farewelled the neighbours and went inside the hut.

Rina was grieved to find Aslin's son Danny, ill, and confined to bed.

'A charm,' explained Aslin. 'We've tried everything to get it broken, but it hasn't worked, and no medicine has cured him either.'

Danny's wife Kusuma hurried about, getting a meal ready. 'You must have some lunch with us, Missie,' she said.

'Of course, of course! She will!' Aslin spoke for her former charge. Rina kept hugging the elderly woman. She stayed and shared their humble lunch, served with an abundance of love.

They reminisced about the good old days. Aslin eagerly questioned Rina about Anita and the rest of the Roberts children. Rina had bought a pile of photographs from Sydney. Aslin poured over them. Her faded eyes filled with tears as she looked at the pictures, over and over again.

Rina left, promising to return. And she did, several times during her holiday.

Next, she visited her former office, Neyrgelex. The company was now located in a large bungalow in one of Colombo's central suburbs. Rina caught up with her old workmates and her former boss, Charles Nathan.

Charles took her out to dinner to the Mount Lavinia Hotel. They sat with their pre-dinner drinks on the sprawling open verandah at the rear of the picturesque hotel. A trio of talented musicians entertained guests, while the soothing sounds of the ocean and sea breezes drifted in across the grounds of the hotel.

Charles knew of Rina's old heartache. They talked about it and she told him of her recent sojourn to meet Nimahl in Singapore.

'What's sad about this whole affair is that you gave him your youth, Rina,' said Charles. 'You were only twenty at the time and very beautiful too, as I remember.' He smiled ruefully. 'A few guys in our building were smitten with you. Did you know?'

273

Rina laughed. 'Oh yes. I had a few messages sent to me.'

'I can still recall those days ... You were fresh-faced and lovely,' Charles reminisced, flatteringly. 'But you gave this man your whole life and he never truly appreciated it. I find that staggering.'

'I know, sir.' It was an old title, but an affectionate one now, without subservience. 'I could have done a lot better, couldn't I?'

Charles gestured with a wave of his arms 'Of course, Rina! Besides being good-looking, you were smart and talented.' He fell silent for a moment. 'And did he give you anything for the ten years you shared with him?'

'I got nothing from him, Charles. Not a penny. And that's how I wanted it. Everything in Nimahl's world was measured in terms of money in the end. He had forgotten what I'd gone through to be with him for those ten years. None of it mattered anymore. And contrary to what his family and friends thought, I truly loved the man, Charles. I would have been happy living in a rural hut somewhere with him, bathing in village streams, growing potatoes and living off the land ... as long as he was with me,' she said, with passion in her voice.

'Rina, Rina!' Charles shook his head. 'You've always been a magnanimous dreamer and I can see that you still are. You're a true artist, girl. You don't look at the world through the lens of money, do you?'

'The girl has never done so and never will.' Rina waved an arm in a grand gesture. '*She counts her treasures so intangibly, like sunsets, weeping willows, sixties songs and Eucalyptus trees.* That's a line from one of my poems. I'll be publishing them one of these days,' she told him with a grin.

'Beautiful. And I'd love to read them someday,' said Charles. 'But look at you, Rina. You're a winner! You're not bitter about anything that's happened to you. You're still charming. And your smile is as appealing as it was the first day you walked into our office back in '66. Now money can't buy any of that,' he declared firmly.

Rina's laughter rang out. 'Flatter me, sir,' she said, cheered by his encouragement. 'I'm badly in need of comfort.'

She travelled to the places of her past.

Visiting the house she had lived in when she first met Nimahl, she was dismayed to find it had been torn down. She stood where the gate

CHAPTER THIRTY

used to be, remembering the night he had turned up in his shining black Jag, surprising and delighting her. She was only twenty then.

'Excuse me, sir,' she said to the man who was watering his garden in the adjoining property. 'I'm sorry to trouble you, but can you tell me what happened to the big house that used to be here.' She pointed to the large derelict plot of land. The remnants of the former dwelling were still visible.

'The new owners pulled it down, Miss,' said the man. 'It seems they're going to put up a new bungalow,' he told her.

'How long have you lived here?' she asked.

'We came here in 1970.'

'The Gomes's used to live in that big house — an old lady and her daughter,' said Rina.

'That's right,' said the man. 'But the old lady died ... I think it was in 1973. And after that only her daughter lived there with the servant. But she too passed away some years ago. Now their relatives have sold the property.' Observing her attire, the man asked, 'Are you from overseas?'

In a colourful batik sarong and white camisole, and with a hat on her head, Rina wasn't dressed like one of the local women.

'Yes,' she answered. 'I'm in Australia now, but back in 1967 my family and I used to live in the annexe of the Gomes's.'

'Oh I see,' said the man, nodding his head. 'It must be sad for you then, seeing how it's all destroyed.'

'Actually it's quite symbolic,' she told him, cryptically. 'But thanks for your help.'

And there was a garden Rina had to visit.

She found the once narrow path leading to the property in East Merinda much wider now.

With some difficulty she identified the main house. Several new cottages had sprung up around it. She tapped on the door and was delighted to recognise the woman who approached her, the daughter of the former owners.

Rina addressed her in Sinhalese. 'I'm not sure if you can remember me, but my name is Rina Roberts. Our family used to live in the little annexe that was at the side of your house, a long, long time ago, in 1964. I was wondering if I could see it again. And I'm sorry but I can't remember your name.'

'My name is Priyanthi.' The woman nodded as recognition dawned. 'Yes, I do remember you all. Your mum, Mrs Roberts and the children. Which one are you — the eldest?'

'Yes,' said Rina. (Emma hadn't lived with them at the time.)

'Come with me, I'll show you around,' offered Priyanthi. As they walked around the property, she told Rina, 'We've renovated the old annexe. It's a little house now.'

Rina stood looking at the unfamiliar cottage, remembering the former lopsided little annexe. She pointed to an area of the garden. 'There used to be a large Tamarind tree here.'

'Yes there was,' said Priyanthi, 'but we pulled it down a few years ago.'

Symbolic again, thought Rina. She looked around, remembering how the tree was diagonally aligned with the well nearby.

In a few moments she was able to locate the exact spot where the Tamarind tree once stood, the tree beside which she had buried her aborted baby, back in 1964.

Thirty-five years fell away like a cloak as she remembered that tragic night.

She had gone through months of spiritual healing in Sydney earlier in the year, when she bravely began her journey of healing. Her counsellors had taken her through prayers for her dead son, and they conducted a naming ceremony for the infant in proxy. She had christened him Jacob.

Standing in the sunlight, with her eyes closed, she asked for forgiveness again, from her baby and from God, grateful for the sunglasses that hid her tears.

'Thank you for showing me around, Priyanthi.' Rina chatted with the woman for a few more minutes.

'Are you all living overseas now?' Priyanthi asked.

'Yes, we're all in Australia. And I haven't been to Sri Lanka since 1983,' said Rina.

'Oh! That's a long time ... Are you're enjoying your holiday?'

'Yes I am, Priyanthi. I am.'

Together with Stella, Rina next visited the house in Nawala, which Nimahl had bought for her to live in back in 1969. She had left the house in 1972 after their affair had come out into the open.

CHAPTER THIRTY

The front gates were locked as it used to be in days long ago. Rina walked a familiar path to the rear of the house and tapped on the back door. A servant soon appeared. In answer to Rina's request to speak to the lady of the house, the woman informed her that the family were out of Colombo for a few days.

Again, Rina gave a brief explanation, saying she was from overseas and that she used to live at this address many years ago. Could she take a few pictures of the outside of the house and the garden?

'Take as many as you like,' said the smiling servant. Rina thanked her and walked around to the front of the house.

In twenty-seven years the garden hadn't altered much. She felt absurdly pleased.

'The Jambu tree is still here,' noted Stella.

They walked over to the fruit tree, clasped the trunk and shook it vigorously, laughing as they recalled how they used to jolt the tree in similar fashion, to force the ripest fruits to fall off the boughs.

They were young girls again, swooping down to pick the glistening, red Jambus, and relishing its crisp, sweet taste.

'Look, Stella,' said Rina, pointing to the low-lying remnants of a decorative brick wall, now covered in moss. 'Can you remember Aslin's son, Danny, built this for my collection of orchids?'

'What beautiful orchids they were, and what a lovely home this used to be.' Stella sighed.

'I'm going around to the other side,' announced Rina.

She stood staring at the closed window of her old bedroom, looking through a tunnel of time. She could see it all: the black polished floors, the corner of her room where she had placed her dressing table, the lilac and cream walls, the large bed.

Once again she could hear the whirring of the ceiling fan, and could imagine herself with him under the voluminous mosquito net ... nights when the world had ceased to exist.

How fiercely and tenderly they had loved.

She had to tear herself away from the window.

Walking through the garden for the last time, she vividly imagined her beautiful Bruno bounding through the property, hearing his bark of welcome at the sound of Nimahl's car driving up the gravel path.

Again, her sunglasses helped.

But there was one place she couldn't visit – her old family home in Merinda. She wasn't ready to open those doors. Perhaps on her next trip, she told herself.

Rina spent the remainder of her holiday travelling around with her old friend, Chandi. They visited the glorious southern beaches of Sri Lanka, and travelled to historic Kandy and other places Rina had always loved.

Her first sighting of the rice fields on the road to Kandy left her gasping. She asked the driver to stop the car.

She got out and walked over to the grass verge.

Standing in silence — almost paying homage — she gazed at the sunlit rice fields blowing gently in the morning breeze. She watched and waited for the air currents to move, rippling the slender shoots in a continuous wave. *Like a jubilant, welcoming dance,* she thought. It filled her with joy.

The rice fields deeply signified to her who she was and who she would always be — a true daughter of this land, one who loved it dearly. At dawn the next morning, Rina wrote her ode to the rice fields.

> *O morning wind,*
> *take me to the rice fields once again,*
> *let me drift on cotton clouds beneath the sky,*
> *and gaze upon the beauty of those sunlit fringes —*
> *green silk tassels*
> *tying me to this land I dearly love.*
>
> *O gentle wind,*
> *I'm pliant too,*
> *the years have made me bend with you,*
> *surely you must know the longings of my heart,*
> *the secret whisp'rings of my soul —*
> *I'm yearning to return on Zephyr's wings,*
> *back to my Island home,*
> *the rice fields,*
> *and the love I lost so long ago.*

CHAPTER THIRTY-ONE

2000 ...

The beginning of winter 2000 in Sydney saw the city gearing up for the Olympics. Anita Roberts was looking forward to watching the gymnastic events on television. But her family held their collective breath and wondered if she would make it to September.

Once again Rina had stopped working to care for her mother. The two of them lived together and had done so for many years.

They often spoke about the past; the good times, the bad, and how they had come through it all. Though wasted and frail at eighty-four, Anita's voice was strong and her memory never failed her.

She was lying in bed one evening and Rina was in a chair by her side. 'Do you remember that dream I interpreted for you in Ceylon, a long time ago?' she said to her daughter.

'Which one, sweetie? I had so many strange dreams back then.'

'This was the one about the overgrown brambles at Merinda.'

'Ah yes! The trinket roses!' said Rina, with a smile.

'That's right! And do you remember what I said? I told you that in spite of all the burdens you may have to carry in life, you would still be like those roses, blossoming under the thorns that bruised you so badly. And wasn't I right? Here you are today after all that life has thrown at you, and you bear no malice in your heart. You make music, you write poetry, and you still sing songs with a smile on your face. Your mother's very proud of you, child.'

Rina leaned forward to kiss her mother. 'We're alike, mother dear, and you know what? I'm going to write about it all one day — about your "Troubles" and mine.'

'Write it when I'm gone, darling.'

Anita had always referred to the break-up of her marriage as her "Troubles." Never once did she malign her husband. Never once did she speak of his infidelity or abandonment, which had ravaged her life.

'You know, Mum, we've both had similar tragedies with the men we loved. You always clung to your good memories of Dad and that's how you remembered him. It's been the same for me with Nimahl. The man I met and knew in Ceylon — he was the love of my life. I never think about those dreadful years in England. It's those sweet days in Ceylon that I can never forget.'

'And that's why my heart has always ached for you, Rina. I know what you've suffered. At least I had my children for comfort. You had nothing.' She placed her hands over her daughter's head. 'But God will surely bless you for all that you've done for me, and your family, darling. We would have been lost without you.'

'We would have been lost without Him, Mum. He's brought us all through an incredible journey. I've put my whole life in His hands now.'

'Stay in them, darling. Only those hands can carry you through the rest of your life.'

On a cold winter morning in July 2000, before the chanticleers were heard, Anita Rose Roberts slipped away to a brighter dawn.

Her life was a testimony of courage, dignity and graciousness. She was like a richly-coloured tapestry; a mangle of knots beneath, but facing the world with a rare beauty that touched the hearts and lives of those who knew her.

Every Christmas, every Mother's Day, and on the anniversary of her birthday and death, Anita's children visit the resting place where she is buried. But Michael Roberts — the apple of his mother's eye — makes a monthly pilgrimage to her grave. Kneeling on his haunches, he lovingly cleans the marble tombstone, clips the edges of the grass, and waters the length and breadth of the burial plot, 'to keep the grass always green.' He bows his head and prays, then looks up at the sky. 'This is all I can do for you now, doll, till I see you up there.'

They had taken to calling her doll. Towards the end she had grown rather doll-like, fragile and little, but her love for her six children remained strong and towering.

CHAPTER THIRTY-ONE

For Rina, at last the ghosts were leaving — slowly. With backward glances of reluctance they departed. She commanded them to go as she took control of her life.

Releasing Nimahl Singram from the throne of her heart made her feel as if she had no air left to breathe, Rina told her counsellors. It was a kind of death. But afterwards, and, surprisingly, she found she could live again.

And finally she stopped dreaming of the house in Merinda — the door-less second floor and the dark, shuttered rooms. Release came the night she dreamed she was standing on a little hill behind her childhood home, when she happened to look up. And there it was at the rear of the second floor — a shining, golden door, sparkling in the sunlight.

It was a mystical moment for Rina and it became her continuous epiphany, stripping away the layers of darkness and desolation that had confined her for decades.

Now she could move towards the sky. She would get out of that cage and fly, and nothing would imprison her again

EPILOGUE

'A bruised reed He does not break'
Isaiah 42:3a

St Philips church in Sydney's west is an impressive stone building, with stained glass windows and a high, sloping roof. Inside, the lofty cathedral-styled timber ceilings afford the church musicians and singers perfect acoustics.

The congregation listens to the middle-aged woman who sings and plays the keyboard some Sundays. The sounds reverberate beautifully under the domed ceiling.

Occasionally, she sings her own compositions. The lyrics allude to her story, which no one really knows. Their lavish compliments embarrass her. They love her voice, they tell her, and they acknowledge her gifting.

Her talents have been honed and finely tuned through decades of walking a path others have too — the journey of life, with its joys and sorrows, its tragedies and triumphs. Hers was arduous. Often she stumbled through the maze, wearing blindfolds, and fleeing the many nettled gardens she encountered; sometimes leaping headlong into muddy marshes. But in the end she discovered a golden door, and entering through it, found peace at last.

Now the barren deserts of her life are being transformed into gardens that flourish. The raging river that threatened to drown her once is a low-flowing stream. It passes over stones that are smoothed, its fury spent.

And so the songbird sings a new song.

O FATHER MINE

O Father Mine, Who art in Heaven
You are the only Dad I've ever really known
O Father Mine, Who art in Heaven
You'll always be the Oak Tree that I lean on
And I'm the bruised reed You never broke.

Through many dark and stormy nights
When I just couldn't see the light
You kept me safe beneath the shadow of Your wings.
You raised me from a tomb of pain
And brought me forth to live again
When every hope was gone
You gently led me to Your door.

O Father Mine, Who art in Heaven
Your love for me is now the sweetest thing I've known.
O Father Mine, Who art in Heaven
You're the Shepherd I will always cling to
And I'm the lost and wounded lamb that You brought home.

Rina's
Journey in Photographs

*Ceylon, 1962
Dewey eyed at sixteen.
No inkling then of the
heartache to come.*

*Four years later, a sad-eyed
girl. Leaving all the tragedy
and heartache behind in her
hometown, Merinda.
Ceylon, 1966.*

*August 1967 — In Bangalore, India.
Rina's idyllic holiday with Nimahl
at the start of their romance.*

The chrysalis has emerged. Rina at twenty-three.
She has found the love of her life!
Ceylon, 1969.

Nimahl takes Rina to Kandy, and this photo of her at the famous Botanical Gardens in Peradeniya. Ceylon, 1969.

Rina on holiday in Sydney, 1971.

Happier times in London: Rina's twenty-seventh birthday. Roses from Nimahl and cards from her family in Sydney. London, 1973.

Out to a gala event with friends. London, 1974.

Off to the Ballet with Nimahl – London 1975 But not really together anymore...

*Fragile. Recovering from her Ectopic Pregnancy and the heartbreaking loss of twins.
London, August 1975*

*A study in sadness.
Recuperating in Sri Lanka after her
attempted suicide and nervous breakdown.
Colombo, 1976*

Her dream has died.
Rina arrives in Sydney — a bruised reed.
Australia, 1977

Two years later:
The memory of him still lingers under the shadow of her smile.
Rina in Sydney, 1979.

Making a bad marriage in Sydney, 1983. It was over in a year.

Merely existing now! Sydney, 1996.

From Left to Right: Michael Roberts, Anita and Rina at a wedding in Sydney, 1997. Family ties are strong and comforting.

Sri Lanka, June 1999. At the entrance to the beautiful Mount Lavinia Hotel, after her meeting with Nimahl in Singapore. Seeking freedom from the shackles of her past — the healing begins.

*Visiting the land of her birth with Tsunami Relief in March 2005.
Rina (on the left) with cousin Vyvette, at Kandana, Sri Lanka.
A new woman has emerged, restored, and undefeated by her past!*

POSTSCRIPT
March 2005 – Sri Lanka

I knew I would visit it one day. Forty years have gone by since I left my childhood home, and here I am now ready to face those demons.

The old house is no more. A new dwelling has replaced it.

An enclosed metal fence is the new street-level boundary. I tap on the iron door where the old gate once stood. The peephole creaks open and I am face to face with the present owner.

I speak a few words and she opens the heavy, metal door.

She has heard of us, she says, through one of her husband's relatives, Celine.

I remembered Celine. She and my eldest sister were classmates and Celine had visited our home during the former days of glory.

As I enter the garden, a violent gust of anguish shakes me.

My cousin Vyvette's daughter, Vayomie, is with me. 'Don't cry, Aunty,' she says softly.

In a dreamlike state I step into the house — the new two-storied house. But I was back in the old. Back as a child in Merinda, seeing again:

the blue door

the gate and our daily pantomime with the red shoe-flowers

the front room that was our prison

the piano, and my father's living quarters behind the dining table …

A pendulum swings in my heart and I hear again the raging voice. And I remember the fear, the unending fear …

I walk towards the place where the old kitchen once stood.

'The well is still here,' the new lady of the house informs me.

I hold my breath and walk out the back door.

And there it was. The old well! My tears could have filled it as the memories reeled back and forth like a malfunctioning movie.

The lady was sympathetic. 'Stay for a cup of tea,' she invited.

I thanked her, but declined. The ghosts were all around me — like distant echoes faded through time. My beloved mother, and Hahminay, her old ally who had lived next door; Dad, his sisters Irene and Elaine, and our old faithful servants, Aslin and Mary ... I could still see them here, but they were all long gone.

I stood in the centre of the house and looked around, marvelling at how it had been transformed into something new and beautiful, erasing the painful scars the old house bore. I was glad.

It was time to leave. I had a vanload of goods from Australia to deliver to Tsunami victims down south. This journey from Sydney was a mission of hope.

I thanked the new hostess of my old family home. She was a gracious lady ... as gentle as the dove that nested there before

The sun was a bright orb in the sky as we drove through Merinda.

We drove past my old church. There it was, towering in the sky, still impressive and grand.

Soon we reached my old school, and happy memories of my young and carefree days filled my mind.

We passed the Mount Lavinia cemetery where Cecily was buried.

I had gone past it all I realised. It was all behind me now.

As we drove further south, the road looked clean and welcoming. The debris from the Tsunami had been cleared.

On my right, the boundless sea was a brilliant turquoise and emerald green. The white crest of the waves rolled onto the shore in an unhurried motion, ebbing and flowing peaceably.

My heart was at rest.

And the sun was still shining.

Erin Kelaart is a gifted writer, poet and singer. Of mixed European progeny, she was born in post-colonial Ceylon in 1946 when her homeland, now called Sri Lanka, was struggling to establish its independence after four centuries of foreign domination by Portuguese, Dutch and British colonialists. With her mother and siblings, Erin migrated to Australia in 1972, but shortly after arriving in Sydney she moved to London to join her partner. Returning to Australia in 1977, she has lived and worked in Sydney for the last thirty years.

A writer with a lyrical gift, Erin has poured out her soul in jottings and poetry since she was a teenager, but the many hurdles she encountered in her life hampered her from doing anything constructive with her creative talents. After the death of her mother, Anne Kelaart, portrayed as Anita Rose Roberts in *O Father Mine,* Erin took a two-year sabbatical to write about the tragedy that traumatised her family and robbed her of a loving father.

More books are in the pipeline for this author who has a vast repertoire of anecdotes handed down from her late mother, a born storyteller. 'I want to recapture the forgotten past of *Old Ceylon* in all of its glory and folly,' says Erin. 'And my era too — the fifties and fabulous sixties — which I believe was the sweetest the land has ever known, when the sight of guns and the sounds of battle were only heard in cinemas.' Halcyon days remembered in lamentations by the island's former inhabitants now in exile. Erin Kelaart is one of them.

Erin's turbulent life has zigzagged precariously, buffeted by a lifelong battle with depression. *So scared, so scared am I of all the endless morrows I must face,* she wrote in a poem when a young girl, but today at the age of sixty (seen here), Erin Kelaart like her mother before her, has overcome considerable adversity. Tempered by the hardships she has endured Erin is now passionate about helping disadvantaged women and children. She has personally supported victims of domestic violence, nurtured children of drug addicts, rallied to the cause of Tsunami relief in Sri Lanka in 2005 and continues to heed the plight of the needy. A committed Christian, she currently assists a small group of African refugees in her local church in Sydney, Australia.

Erin's next publication will be her collection of poems, *Child of Dust.*

See author website: www.erinkelaart.com for more information
email: ofathermine@yahoo.com.au